BARTHOLOMEW

BARTHOLOMEW

Apostle and Visionary

JOHN CHRYSSAVGIS

W PUBLISHING GROUP

AN IMPRINT OF THOMAS NELSON

Bartholomew
© 2016 Greek Orthodox Archdiocese of America

Published in Nashville, Tennessee, by W Publishing Group, an imprint of Thomas Nelson.

Thomas Nelson titles may be purchased in bulk for educational, business, fund-raising, or sales promotional use. For information, please e-mail SpecialMarkets@ThomasNelson.com.

Unless otherwise noted, Scripture quotations are taken from the New King James Version®. © 1982 by Thomas Nelson. Used by permission. All rights reserved.

Scripture quotations marked NAB are taken from the *New American Bible, revised edition.* © 2010, 1991, 1986, 1970 Confraternity of Christian Doctrine, Washington, DC. Used by permission of the copyright owner. All rights reserved. No part of the *New American Bible* may be reproduced in any form without permission in writing from the copyright owner.

The translation of the reflection by Pope Emeritus Benedict XVI is by Prof. William Madges of St. Joseph's University in Philadelphia, PA.

All photographs used with permission. The *New York Times* front-page photograph from January 8, 2006, © 2006. All rights reserved. Used by permission and protected by the Copyright Laws of the United States. The printing, copying, redistribution, or retransmission of this content without express written permission is prohibited. The photograph with Pope Francis and Presidents Peres and Abbas at the Vatican (2014) from Vatican Pool/Getty Images News/Getty Images. The photograph of the Phanar, by Levent Karaoğlu, reproduced from John Chryssavgis, *The Ecumenical Patriarchate Today: Sacred Greek Orthodox Sites of Istanbul* (Istanbul, 2014). The aerial photograph of Halki from the Archive of Halki Theological School, courtesy of His Eminence Metropolitan Elpidophoros of Bursa. Early photographs of Ecumenical Patriarch Bartholomew from the Archives of the Ecumenical Patriarchate. Other photographs of His All-Holiness courtesy of Nikolaos Manginas, Archon Dimitrios Panagos, John Mindala, and Andonios Archondonis.

Library of Congress Control Number: 2016908435

ISBN 978-0-7180-8689-3

Printed in the United States of America

16 17 18 19 20 RRD 6 5 4 3 2 1

To His All-Holiness
Ecumenical Patriarch Bartholomew

*for his exceptional legacy
of extraordinary mission and vision*

CONTENTS

CONTENTS

FOREWORD

IT IS WITH SENTIMENTS OF HEARTFELT CLOSENESS THAT I JOIN all those who celebrate, with joy and jubilation, the twenty-fifth anniversary this year of the election of His All-Holiness Bartholomew I as ecumenical patriarch.

My first meeting with my beloved brother Bartholomew took place on the very day of the inauguration of my papal ministry, when he honored me with his presence in Rome. I felt that I was meeting a man who "walks by faith" (cf. 2 Corinthians 5:7), who in his person and his manner expresses all the profound human and spiritual experience of the Orthodox tradition. On that occasion we embraced each other with sincere affection and mutual understanding. Our successive meetings in Jerusalem, Rome, and Constantinople have not only strengthened our spiritual affinity, but above all have deepened our shared consciousness of the common pastoral responsibility we have at this point in history, before the urgent challenges that Christians and the entire human family face today. In particular I hold dear to my heart the splendid memory of the warm and fraternal welcome extended to me by Patriarch Bartholomew during my visit to the Phanar for the Feast of the Apostle Andrew, patron saint of the Ecumenical Patriarchate, on November 30, 2014.

The Church of Rome and the Church of Constantinople are united by a profound and long-standing bond, which not even centuries of silence and misunderstanding have been able to sever. This bond is exemplified by the relationship between those to whom tradition attributes the foundation of our respective Churches, namely, the holy apostles Peter and Andrew, two brothers in the flesh, but above all, two disciples of the Lord Jesus, who together believed in him, followed him, and ultimately shared his destiny on the cross, in the one and same hope of serving the coming of his kingdom. Our predecessors, the illustrious Athenagoras I and Blessed Paul VI, have left us the sacred task of tracing our way back along the path that paved the separation of our Churches, healing the sources of our mutual alienation, and moving toward the re-establishment of full communion in faith and love, mindful of our legitimate differences, just as it was in the first millennium. Today we, brothers in the faith and in the hope that does not fail, are profoundly united in our desire that Christians of East and West may feel themselves part of the one and only Church, so that they may proclaim to the whole world that "the grace of God has appeared, saving all and training us to reject godless ways and worldly desires and to live temperately, justly, and devoutly in this age, as we await the blessed hope, the appearance of the glory of the great God and of our savior Jesus Christ" (Titus 2:11–13 NAB).

In the two joint declarations we signed in Jerusalem and at

the Phanar, we affirmed decisively and determinedly our shared commitment, drawn from our faithfulness to the Gospel, to build a world that is more just and more respectful of every person's fundamental dignity and freedoms, the most important of which is religious freedom. We are also fundamentally joined in our shared commitment to raising further the awareness of individuals and wider society regarding the issue of the safeguarding of creation, the cosmic scenario in which God's infinite mercy—offered, rejected, and restored—is manifested and glorified in every moment. I am deeply grateful for the leadership of the ecumenical patriarch in this field and for his reflections on this issue, from which I have learned and continue to learn so much.

I have found a profound spiritual sensitivity in Patriarch Bartholomew toward the painful condition of humanity today, so profoundly wounded by unspeakable violence, injustice, and discrimination. We are both greatly disturbed by the grave sin against God, which seems to increase day by day, that is the globalization of indifference toward the defacement of the image of God in man. It is our conviction that we are called to work toward the construction of a new civilization of love and solidarity. We are both aware that the voices of our brothers and sisters, now to the point of extreme distress, compel us to proceed more rapidly along the path of reconciliation and communion between Catholics and Orthodox, precisely so that they may be able to proclaim credibly the Gospel of Peace that comes from Christ.

For these many reasons I am very happy that the twenty-fifth anniversary of the election of my friend and brother Bartholomew as patriarch of the ancient and glorious See of Constantinople is being celebrated by so many who give thanks to the Lord for his life and ministry. I consider it to be both a grace and a privilege to walk together with Patriarch Bartholomew in the hope of serving our one Lord Jesus Christ, counting not upon our meager strengths, but on the faithfulness of God, and sustained by the intercession of the saintly brothers, the apostles Andrew and Peter.

It is in this certainty and with an unfailing remembrance in prayer that I express to His All-Holiness Patriarch Bartholomew my heartfelt and fraternal good wishes for a long life in the love and consolation of the Triune and One God.

—POPE FRANCIS
VATICAN, 4 APRIL 2016

PROLOGUE

THIS WAS VINTAGE BARTHOLOMEW! A VICTORY AGAINST ALL odds and against all expectations, possibly including his own. He had just convinced a diverse group of church prelates—each of them steeped in his own religious tradition, absorbed in his own national interests, consumed by his own internal troubles, and seemingly accountable to almost none but God—to rise above their disagreements and even divisions in order to convene what would arguably prove to be one of the most significant events in the history of the Orthodox Church and, undoubtedly, the most momentous in more than a century, perhaps a millennium.

On a late Wednesday night, January 27, 2016, Ecumenical Patriarch Bartholomew, the spiritual leader of more than 300 million Orthodox Christians worldwide and "first among equals" in a confederation of fourteen independent Orthodox churches globally, had just finished chairing an extraordinary session of religious leaders. The sole purpose for calling this meeting was to decide on whether finally to proceed toward a Holy and Great Council that would assemble delegations—some 300 bishops and advisors—from every Orthodox church in the world. Almost two years earlier the same prelates had already decided to convene such a council in Istanbul at the Church of Haghia Irene, where the Second Ecumenical Council had been held in 381; but recent geopolitical tensions between Russia and Turkey required moving the location outside Turkey. This possible move, coupled with additional long-standing internal church politics, now necessitated a sense of sensitivity and flexibility—even an unmerited generosity and graciousness—on the part of Bartholomew, who knew very well that a variety of calculated ruses, either to delay or boycott this historical event on the scepter—read: pretext or guise—of consensus by all, could derail the council altogether.

The Holy and Great Council had been on the table for discussion since at least the early 1960s, with preliminary meetings on the island of Rhodes in Greece and subsequently regular conferences at the Orthodox Center of the Ecumenical Patriarchate in Chambésy, Geneva, in Switzerland. Nonetheless, proposals for such a council had been discussed as early as the 1920s with meetings in Istanbul, formerly Constantinople, and the 1930s, with a meeting on the exclusive republic of monasteries in northern Greece, known as Mount Athos. It is during those early years of the interwar period that the Holy and Great Council was conceived. But preparations had been under way—delayed and postponed, undermined, and obstructed—for decades, indeed almost a century.

It was never going to be easy to convene the Great Council, and the patriarch knew it. He confided: "I was apprehensive; anxious, in fact. Not for myself, but for the church. Why should it take so much effort to convince people to do what they are supposed to do, to prevail on them that meeting together in council is what we *should* be doing as bishops? It is how the church regularly functioned and normally flourished for centuries."

The truth is, I'd never seen him more resolved—collected and composed, even calm—than during that January 27 meeting. All of his aptitude and adeptness had been fine-tuned over many years for calling and leading a council that would contain elements not seen since the Seventh Ecumenical Council in AD 787. In many ways he had prepared all his life for such a moment.

INTRODUCTION

The official title is ecumenical patriarch, but
for me, Bartholomew is sufficient.
—Ecumenical Patriarch Bartholomew,
60 Minutes interview, 2009

Just Call Me Bartholomew

He is patriarch—the ecumenical patriarch—bearing a title that dates to the sixth century and leading a church that has thrived and survived in the same city of Constantinople since the dawn of Christianity.

It was in this region that the first universal Christian creed was composed; it was here that the books of the New Testament were approved; it was in this city that the greatest and longest experiment in church-state relations was tested over an entire millennium; and it was here that the framework of Christianity was established.

But when Ecumenical Patriarch Bartholomew emerges to greet you from behind his desk, the kindness of his blue eyes and softness of his smile are disarming.

As patriarch, he wears a long, thinning beard—completely white in recent years, much like the ancient prophets. His hair, too, is now white, though it was once bright auburn, "almost caramel," he adds—what today we would call strawberry blond.

He has a striking refinement, both physical and moral. He is of medium height and slight weight, with a clear face and fine features.

In his presence you are surprisingly comfortable rather than awkward. In fact, he goes out of his way to make you feel relaxed: ordering water with a teaspoon of vanilla—immediately explaining how you should drink it—and offering you gifts, constantly showering you with gifts as if he has been awaiting your visit for days.

He transitions smoothly into conversation, telling you about his day and asking about yours. When you have an audience with him, it is just that: a time that he gives exclusively to you, a time when he listens. He takes notice and he takes time. He is generous with his time; in fact, you would think he has nothing else to do, no one else to see. He never hurries his guests; he waits for them to initiate departure. On occasion I have been in his office and prayed intensely for his visitors to stand; yet as I looked at the patriarch, he would seem undisturbed.

But of course he *is* busy. His office is a window to the world, the heartbeat of global Orthodox Christianity and its fourteen autocephalous (self-ruling) churches. He also holds immediate jurisdiction over the apostolic church of Crete, dozens of dioceses in Greece, the Autonomous (self-administered) Churches of Finland and Estonia, and numerous archdioceses in the United States of America, Australasia, and Great Britain, and across western Europe.

Moreover, it is at his initiative that the Autocephalous Church of Albania was resurrected, the Autonomous Church of Estonia was reactivated, and the Autonomous Church of the Czech Lands and Slovakia was raised to the status of autocephaly. It is during his tenure that a schism within the Patriarchate of Bulgaria was reconciled, a canonical infraction by the Patriarchate of Jerusalem was rectified, and an impasse in the Church of the Czech Lands and Slovakia was resolved. And over the past twenty-five years, he has established new metropolitan dioceses in Italy, Toronto, Buenos Aires, Mexico, Hong Kong, Spain, Korea, and Singapore, as well as in North America, in Chicago, Boston, Denver, Atlanta, Detroit, Pittsburgh, San Francisco, and New Jersey. Most recently, he called for and helped plan a historic Holy and Great Council—which has not convened for centuries—in Crete in the summer of 2016.

Let's just agree: he is a busy man!

Still, he is compellingly patient. In his office he even has an icon of Saint Hypomonē, an early Christian martyr, whose name means "patience." He is gracious. He is generous. And he is always grateful. He is polite. He is respectful. And he honors the fact that you have come to visit "the queen city" and "great church of Christ."

There was an early fifth-century monastery called "the sleepless ones"—or *akoimetoi*—in Constantinople; the monks were pledged to perpetual prayer and praise, performing successive shifts of uninterrupted hourly offices. While the *akoimetoi* are scarcely mentioned in second-millennium sources, an echo of their unceasing presence and service appears to reverberate in the life of the patriarch.

His schedule is filled to the brim. He will try to see everyone if possible: groups of students, visiting bishops, local authorities, and global politicians. In his office he seats you beneath an ancient icon of Saint Andrew the apostle, founder of the Church of

Constantinople—a symbol and reminder that Bartholomew is the direct successor of him. Otherwise, groups of visitors will assemble in the "hall of the throne," as the formal audience room is known. Everyone wants to pay his or her respects or kiss his hand, and he has something to give everyone: a signed copy of an icon, a small cross, or a booklet.

When in his office, there are seemingly interminable visits by secretarial staff bringing drafts for approval, letters for signature, revisions, and requests. The patriarch wants to respond to every letter, every communication. He considers it his pastoral obligation.

Even at lunch there are always guests who are invited to the dining hall: local ranking clergy, lay dignitaries, passing pilgrims. They all are invited to stay for coffee afterward; some of them return to his office to resume an unfinished audience or for the patriarch to send along a gift to someone.

This will go on until the evening vespers at four thirty, followed by more audiences, endless consultations, and literally mounds of correspondence.

After dinner, usually around eight o'clock in the evening, the younger clergy of the court will close the day with a compline service in the private patriarchal chapel. Then the patriarch will retire once more to his office—for an hour or two to work alone without interruption for the first time in the entire day—or else attend an evening function.

He works hard; he works endlessly and tirelessly. He is in the patriarchal church for matins, the morning service at eight. And the lights in his office will still be on at midnight, though he sends his attendant home. "He has a wife and children waiting at home; it's very different for us," the patriarch retorts.

He loves children and enjoys being with them. He will go out of his way to play with them, amusing them with his staff and producing sweets, knotted prayer ropes, or small change from his pockets. During one general audience in the hall of the throne, a little girl suddenly climbed up into the patriarchal chair before the patriarch had arrived in the room. As the staff tried to coax her down, the patriarch walked in and said, "Let her be. She belongs there." Bartholomew's love of children goes beyond simple amusement. "Christ told us that we will acquire the heavenly kingdom by becoming like children, so there must be a piece of paradise in them," he says.

He identifies with the person before his eyes—becoming a child with children, an adult with adults, a scholar with academics, a deacon with deacons, a priest with priests, and a patriarch with patriarchs. I can't help but think of the way Saint Paul envisioned his ministry in the early church:

> For though I am free from all men, I have made myself a servant to all, that I might win the more; and to the Jews I became as a Jew, that I might win Jews; to those who are under the law, as under the law, that I might win those who are under the law; to those who are without law, as without law (not being without law toward God, but under law toward Christ), that I might win those who are without law; to the weak I became as weak, that I might win the weak. I have become all things to all men, that I might by all means save some. Now this I do for the gospel's sake, that I may be partaker of it with you. (1 Corinthians 9:19–23)

He has an exceedingly acute sense of responsibility for Orthodox Christianity in the world of today and tomorrow. The unwieldiness and divisions of the church weigh heavy on his heart. He aches for the division of the Christian church, and he stresses over the disputes within it. He knows that the church is called to respect the entire truth about the entire human being within the entire created cosmos. These, he affirms, are the criteria for evaluating life and Christian conduct in the world.

The Priming of a Patriarch

What Bartholomew managed to achieve—namely, finally setting a date (June 16–26, 2016) and venue (the Orthodox Academy of Crete in Kolymbari) for the Holy and Great Council—was entirely unprecedented in the history of the Orthodox Church. It would mark the first-ever gathering of delegates from the fourteen autocephalous Orthodox churches, including the ancient Patriarchates of Constantinople, Alexandria, Antioch, and Jerusalem; the modern Patriarchates of Moscow, Serbia, Romania, and Bulgaria; the historical Churches of Georgia and Cyprus; and the more recent Churches of Greece, Poland, Albania, and the Czech Lands and Slovakia.

Never before had anyone undertaken such an extensive initiative in the Orthodox Church. In the first millennium of the Christian era, there were only five church centers, known as the *pentarchy*, all of them located exclusively around the Mediterranean; moreover, there was a secular emperor, revered and feared by all, whose concern for the Pax Romana necessitated rigidly monitoring the unity and orthodoxy of the imperial churches.

However, no longer is there such an authority, and Bartholomew's role is to coordinate and facilitate the same unity and orthodoxy, albeit by personal conviction and charismatic persuasion. The primacy of the ecumenical patriarch is unlike the papacy; its prestige derives from poverty and its authority from humility. His leadership does not lie in power but rather in sacrifice, in serving and coordinating all of his brother bishops in a synod where he serves as "first among equals." It is a strength that is defined in and through service.

Bartholomew became early acquainted with the system of councils. He was a young doctoral student in Rome from 1963 to 1966 at the time when the Second Vatican Council was in full swing, assembling thousands of participants and dozens of observers. Pope John XXIII completely shocked the world when he announced the convocation of Vatican II in January 1959; and the council, which commenced in October 1962 and concluded in December 1965, was also the first to convene in more than one hundred years. The future patriarch would be formally invited to attend some of the open sessions of the council, just as he would regularly be invited, along with other students, to lunch with Pope Paul VI.

Indeed, in his own ministry as priest and bishop, Bartholomew would later personally participate in many preparatory meetings for the Orthodox Holy and Great Council during the 1970s and 1980s, both as a member and later as the head of the delegation from the Ecumenical Patriarchate that convened and chaired such assemblies. Yet this was far more than a matter of education and experience.

He had spent years studying canon law, the formal rules and regulations governing church authority and administration. This, too, would shape his mind for the sorts of challenges he would face in his ministry. He had also spent years watching as his religious hero, the renowned Ecumenical Patriarch Athenagoras, had opened the Orthodox Church to a dialogue of love with the Roman Catholic Church when Athenagoras and Pope Paul VI met in Jerusalem in 1964 and later when the two same leaders lifted the 1054 mutual anathemas in 1965. Finally, he had spent an entire lifetime at the feet of his spiritual guide, Metropolitan Meliton of Chalcedon, who played a pivotal role in shaping the Church of Constantinople from the 1960s through the 1980s.

One might easily argue that all of Patriarch Bartholomew's previous studies and achievements had led him to the moment of the January 2016 meeting, when he faced a possible adversarial reception of a dream to convene the Holy and Great Council. This was a vocation and vision from the moment of his ordination to the position of deacon, the first rung of the priesthood.

THE ENTHRONEMENT OF A PATRIARCH

In brief, this was why he became patriarch. This was what he was groomed for; it was what he had long prepared for, and it was surely providence that provided him with one of the longest tenures as ecumenical patriarch in Orthodox history. This was quite apparent from the day of his enthronement as the 269th successor to

Saint Andrew, who was the first of the fisherman apostles called by Jesus of Nazareth and who is still respected as the founder of the Church of Constantinople. On November 2, 1991, the day on which Bartholomew was installed as archbishop of Constantinople and ecumenical patriarch, he clearly laid out the agenda of his legendary tenure.

Already from that very first address, as he stood on the throne, the young, fifty-one-year-old patriarch outlined with broad but deliberate strokes the dimensions of his service and leadership in the Orthodox Church: vigilance in theology and liturgy, advancement of Orthodox unity and cooperation, reinforcement of ecumenical engagement with other Christian confessions, intensification of interfaith dialogue and religious tolerance, as well as awareness about environmental protection and climate change.

Addressing the entire church in all corners of the world, his enthronement speech captured and encapsulated the profound and far-reaching vision of a newly elected prince of the church, casting the net of his hopes and dreams far and wide:

> Already, conscious of our unworthiness and humbleness, looking ahead to the insupportable cross which we have borne, we seek refuge in the mercy of the Lord, and we invoke his grace in order that his "strength is made perfect in [our] weakness" [2 Corinthians 12:9]. Indeed, the tremendous concerns, which the archbishop of New Rome assumes, and the various temptations and adverse influences with which he must struggle, demand that he be experienced in the task of piloting this great ship.

That is an accurate self-definition and sure description of how he was favorably predisposed and fully equipped to assume what, in the same address, he called "the sacred responsibilities of piloting the spiritual vessel known as the Church of Constantinople."

Bartholomew was, from the day of his election, already "experienced in the task of piloting this great ship." From the tender age of seventeen, during his final year of high school, the seeds of competence and vision of excellence were already discernible in his heart and in his handwriting. In an essay submitted that same year on the question "How do you contemplate your future?" the future patriarch recorded:

Everyone is born with an inner destiny. . . . I envision my future full of struggle and mission. Those of us who are called to become interpreters of the noblest ideology, the philosophy of the Nazarene, have greater obligations ahead of us. I foresee the words "struggle" and "sacrifice" in my life. . . . That is my task as a clergyman in the future. A modern clergyman should not reject science and its conclusions; instead, the clergyman should integrate science and religion. Wherever the clergyman serves, he should develop social, humanitarian, and ethical programs. That is my goal for the future. . . . Finally, the clergyman must have a cross, a martyrdom before his eyes, never surrendering to the temptations of the Sirens—namely, love of self and love of this world. These are the things I contemplate with regard to my future, my destiny, which is to serve my sweet Jesus and the church as his body.

The basic contours and configurations of his ministry had already been carved out and sealed from an early age in that journal:

+ the commandments of Jesus Christ, especially in relation to the unity of his disciples;
+ the suffering of martyrdom and sacrifice, especially through his providential ministry in Constantinople;
+ interaction with scientists and theologians, especially with his groundbreaking environmental programs; and
+ an emphasis on social justice and ethics, especially in championing human rights and religious freedom.

THE APOSTOLIC VISION OF A PATRIARCH

Bartholomew was ordained to be an apostle and a visionary. In this biography, I will endeavor to demonstrate how, as the "first among equals" of Orthodox bishops worldwide, he has been able to assume a leadership role on social and global matters from his sacred see (patriarchal throne) in Constantinople: bridge building among diverse faiths in a volatile world, facilitating dialogues with non-Orthodox churches and communions, fostering discourse and cooperation among the Orthodox churches themselves, as well as raising worldwide awareness of the connection between religion and the environment.

I hope to reveal how an ancient Christian faith, dating its existence to the earliest apostolic period and with a tradition spanning twenty centuries, has been able to address a contemporary world through Bartholomew's visionary leadership of 300 million Orthodox Christians throughout the world. How is it that a religious leader with apostolic origins, at the helm of an institution that is spiritual and not political, can speak *in* and *to* the world from a sacred perspective that is nonetheless neither *of* nor *from* the world?

There are some insights that may prove helpful to the reader in appreciating the mind-set or worldview of the patriarch. What, for example, will become immediately apparent is that Patriarch Bartholomew shows an absolute consistency in his commitment to an understanding of Christian identity that is central to the Eastern Orthodox tradition—namely, that to be a Christian is not primarily to adhere to a set of principles or be affiliated with an organization; it is to be taken into a comprehensive new reality. As he remarked in 1997 to an audience at Georgetown University, "being a Christian is not an act of cataloguing a person as a member of a group but the true rebirth of this person into the world of grace." Christian faith is about the alternatives of life and death rather than of abstract good and evil. To be a Christian is ultimately to participate and enter into dialogue, not simply to give mental assent or emotional loyalty.

Moreover, as much of his life and teaching makes plain, faithfulness to the church has to be distinguished from loyalty to national or cultural identities. Even while ever tempted to do otherwise, Orthodox Christianity is not and must not become the prisoner of local or ethnic identity; not that such identities are evil, but all of them are to be integrated within the wider—ecumenical or catholic—identity of the church in order to serve one another and the good of the whole

Christian community. Orthodox Christians are to celebrate the heritage of their past—of their history and of their culture—but they are also to look at it with a critical eye for what needs repentance. And as the patriarch explained in another moving address delivered in 1997 at St. Peter's Basilica, this acknowledgment of failure and repentance in history is something people must learn to *share*—not something they should exploit to reproach one another.

The patriarch takes for granted the importance of communion (*koinonia*), which Orthodoxy has shared with the rest of the world in recent decades. However, Bartholomew adds to this theme of communion the concept of sacrifice (*martyria*) and service (*diakonia*). Communion entails humility, a refusal of the isolation and security that result from authority and power. This is what enables him to emphasize the importance of "opening up to the heart, opening up to the other, and opening up to the whole world," as he observed in 2009 during a lecture at Fordham University. In this light the patriarch does not avoid difficult—sensitive and even controversial—questions, the often frustrating practicalities and painful realities of living in a divided world; instead, he locates all of them in the context of a spiritual worldview that is unambiguously grounded in the transforming effect of divine grace.

I believe that the Christian world is fortunate to have in the historic office of the Ecumenical Patriarchate an apostolic and visionary leader with the prudence and distinction of Patriarch Bartholomew. People everywhere may well give thanks for the witness of His All-Holiness to the great teachings of Eastern Christianity, as well as for his unfailing ecumenical charity and courtesy.

It is my honor and privilege to compile these biographical pages of a man who has guided the Christian East with dedication and conviction for the last twenty-five years. The contents of this book trace the sentiments of the patriarch himself, who summarized his own ministry in a brief statement on Easter 2016:

> This year, the Lord has rendered us worthy of completing twenty-five years as Archbishop of Constantinople and Ecumenical Patriarch. His blessing is great, while our inexpressible gratitude to him is equally great.
>
> Throughout this long period, we have endeavored to preserve the integrity and vibrancy of the precious legacy inherited from our fathers in order, together with our brothers and colleagues, to provide a dynamic witness for the first-throne Church of Constantinople in a manner that connects with contemporary reality.
>
> Thus we have cultivated inter-Christian and interreligious dialogue, developed a concern for respecting and protecting the natural environment, while laboring especially for Pan-Orthodox unity and cooperation by repeatedly convening assemblies of the Orthodox primates and particularly promoting the Holy and Great Council of the Orthodox Church that, with God's grace, will take place in Crete this coming June 2016.
>
> For all these and many more, again and again we offer glory to the holy God of our fathers, to whom we entrust the Ecumenical Patriarchate, the long-suffering Greek community in Constantinople, the entire Orthodox Church and whole world, along with the salvation of our souls.
>
> Glory be to God for all things!

The closing words come from his fourth-century predecessor, Saint John Chrysostom; they were also the first and last words of Bartholomew's enthronement address in November 1991.

The year 2016 marked twenty-five years since his election as patriarch and fifty-five years since his ordination as deacon. The conventional acclamation in the Orthodox ordination rite is *"Axios!"* "He is worthy!"

REFLECTION

JOSEPH R. BIDEN JR.
Vice President of the United States

SINCE BECOMING VICE PRESIDENT, I'VE HAD THE OPPORTUNITY TO spend time with His All-Holiness on several occasions—twice visiting the patriarchate in Istanbul, and once at my home in Washington. Each time, His All-Holiness sat and spoke with me about theology and the values we share across cultures and religions.

I was immediately taken by his warmth and spirituality. It envelops you. He radiates grace and conviction. But what impressed me most is the way His All-Holiness embodies our Christian faith—thoroughly and completely. To put it simply, he is one of the most Christlike men I have ever met.

His conviction is what makes him one of the world's most respected moral leaders. Throughout his twenty-five years as ecumenical patriarch, he has been a clarion voice in the struggle to protect basic human rights and bridge divides between people of faith—sponsoring conferences and interfaith dialogue to foster peace and tolerance among Christians, Muslims, and Jews.

His All-Holiness made history when he attended the installation of Pope Francis as the bishop of Rome. I was there at the Vatican that day—it's something I'll never forget. And the two great leaders have since made an apostolic pilgrimage together to Jerusalem, deepening the comity of faith between the Roman Catholic and Greek Orthodox communities after centuries of silence.

During that visit, His All-Holiness said, "The path towards peace is difficult. Not because shared values are hard to identify, or appropriate responses to injustice are elusive, but because the way of peace requires much from each of us."

In other words, it's not enough to proclaim our beliefs—we have to live them. We have to act. And that's what His All-Holiness has always done. He reaches out and seeks consensus. He defends freedom of religion not just for the Greek Orthodox Church but for people everywhere. He promotes peace.

So I was not at all surprised when my good friend, former Israeli president Shimon Peres, told me several years ago that both he and Palestinian President Abbas had asked His All-Holiness to pray for them. I did the same.

CHAPTER 1

A Delicate Mosaic

Bridge Builder in a Volatile World

Violence in the name of religion is violence against all religion.
—Ecumenical Patriarch Bartholomew, at the
Conference on Peace and Tolerance

Istanbul, the City of Constantine

Reflecting on Yesterday

Christians in Istanbul—much like members of other religious communities, such as their Muslim and Jewish brothers and sisters—are privileged to reside in a colorful city that once served as the capital of the Eastern Roman (Byzantine) Empire for more than one thousand years and of the Ottoman Empire for almost half a millennium. This historical and imperial city has been variously designated through the ages as Byzantium, Constantinople, New Rome, Royal City, and Istanbul. To this day, Greeks wistfully refer to Constantinople, named for Saint Constantine the Great

Emperor, as "the City"—with no further explanation. Its geographically strategic position—straddling two continents, Europe and Asia, bridging the Black and Mediterranean Seas—was recurrently desired and plundered. With one's first step into the city, this rich antiquity is as instantly apparent as similar legacies in such great cities as Rome and London.

It is here that the literary works of classical civilization and Roman law were preserved for the Western Renaissance. Plato and Aristotle would have remained inaccessible to us without Arabic translations of the High Middle Ages. Justinian I (527–565) pioneered reform and codification of Latin jurisprudence, while Leo III (717–741) influenced later Slavic legal institutions. It was the Byzantine East that Christianized the Slavic north and protected the European south from invasions by the Goths and Visigoths. And the silent presence of Byzantium is still more far-reaching. From the forks we use to dine, to the hospitals we depend on for healing, and to the academic universities where we pursue knowledge, the legacy of Byzantium has proved of lasting and profound influence. Byzantium was also the longest experiment in church-state relations, lasting from 325 to 1453, and Byzantine laws forbade the use of torture in legal proceedings—a more progressive policy than some modern societies, perhaps even our own.

Much like Rome, Istanbul sprawls across seven hills (*heptálofos*) and is famous for its striking cultural monuments and heritage, its religious character and diversity, art and imperial ceremonies, education and literature, music and folklore, and culinary and natural charm. With roots in the Byzantine civilization, this cosmopolitan ethos lies directly on one of the great fault lines of faith in today's world: the confluence of Islam and Orthodox Christianity. Even today, this colossal city—with a population in excess of fourteen million, and over 99 percent Muslim—boasts an astounding expansion and appeal, with its contemporary skyscrapers, albeit often lacking aesthetic beauty or balance because of mandatory antiseismic construction. Any observer familiar with the old city is immediately impressed by the obvious development and transformation.

Yet this is also the bloodstained cradle of the Phanar (Greek for "lighthouse," referring to the old lighthouse quarter of Istanbul)—a term coterminous with the headquarters of the Ecumenical Patriarchate of the Orthodox Church, since the residence and offices of the ecumenical patriarch are located there. This city is home to innumerable religious sites, elegant mansions, and the Crossroads (*Stavrodrómi*) commercial district and cultural gems, including renowned cemeteries and remarkable museums. The fourth-century walls of Constantine (surviving ramparts of a magnificent civilization), the fourth-century Church of Haghia Irene (where the Christian creed was formulated), the sixth-century Church of Haghia Sophia (an architectural wonder with structural elements emulated in the Blue Mosque), the sixth-century Studion Monastery (where religious life was reformed), and the extraordinarily vivid frescoes and mosaics of exceptionally unique iconography at the fourteenth-century Chora Monastery are but a few of the city's manifold treasures.

Indeed, for the Rum (Roman) Orthodox—a title used for centuries to describe Greek Christians living in Muslim states—Istanbul holds unique significance. Beyond the fact that they are natives and not immigrants, for two thousand years, this city has been the foremost seat of Orthodox Christianity and famous see of the Ecumenical Patriarchate, though its current leader, Bartholomew, is an individual of global eminence.

The Sober Reality

Reflecting on Today

In Istanbul, today, Orthodox Christians live alongside a host of other minorities and the contemporary ruling class, the Islamic leaders of Turkey, each with its own specific and turbulent history. Seasons of prosperity and fortune have frequently been succeeded by periods of decline and misfortune. Such circumstances were invariably instrumental in the shrinking of the Christian population, with an increasing shortage of clergy and closure of schools. On the other hand, it should be emphasized that new agencies have appeared, and the cultural initiatives of different organizations have risen dramatically, including various associations, foundations, and societies previously far more active when the Greek population flourished. At one time Rum Christians comprised the commercial and financial ruling class. Today they constitute a tiny remnant— barely four thousand people—that Patriarch Athenagoras liked to describe as "limited yet limitless."

Patriarch Bartholomew reminisces: "We are a small Christian drop in a vast Muslim ocean. Yet God's grace has deigned for us to survive." He remembers his parents describing the expropriation of properties and fields at Imvros in the 1960s: "I felt like Job in the Old Testament: I would hear the news of how much we had lost."

Within a period of just a few months, they lost everything—their homes and farmsteads, their monasteries and chapels. "What was most destructive," the patriarch bemoans, "was the forcible closure of schools. The Greeks would be unable to educate their children; that was the worst blow." Greeks were forced to emigrate within weeks; Bartholomew's family moved to Istanbul. Most of them refused—on principle, out of dignity—to accept any compensation: a square meter for the price of an egg! New Turkish residents—entire villages and communities—were transplanted; Greek real estate was converted into Turkish estates. Greek residents emigrated—some to the City, many to Greece, most farther abroad.

It was very different when Bartholomew was growing up in Imvros. The entire village was Greek and Christian; in fact, the island itself was almost entirely Greek and Christian. There was only one mosque, and that was in the capital, Panaghía. The only Turks that the islanders would relate to were civil servants and policemen. Bartholomew's first contact with a Turk was in the person of his Turkish language instructor at school, where he also first learned about the history and customs of the country. The patriarch still recalls the young Turkish teacher, who used to refer to Bartholomew (then Demetrios) as *"le petit"* (the little one), for his diminutive stature. Even at Halki, there was little association with anyone other than Greeks and Christians.

The patriarch's first substantial contact with other Turks or Muslims came during the two years of his military service (1961–1963), when he served first as warrant officer ("one stripe," he tells me) and then as second lieutenant ("one star," he remarks) in the fortieth infantry regiment. But his Turkish colleagues loved and trusted him: his assignment was to arrange the monthly salaries—keep records, go to the bank, withdraw money, and distribute wages. "When someone needed an advance on his pay, I would help out and give them money up front. So they liked me."

In contrast, prominent intellectuals have poignantly described the difficult situation and demeaning treatment Bartholomew has often experienced in Turkey: how he waited four years for a passport to be issued after his essential election as bishop—at barely thirty years of age—in order to assume his pivotal position within the patriarchate; how he has suffered harassment in a hostile environment, although internationally he is respected as the spiritual leader of three hundred million Orthodox Christians; the way extremists have threatened the patriarch with insults and assaults; how he has been cursed and derided, and has seen the patriarchate's windows shattered by rocks; how his effigy has been burned by fanatics outside the walls of the enclave and live grenades have been thrown into the courtyard of the Phanar—even maiming clergy and staff; and the way he has been jeered, his life verifiably threatened. Others of these intellectuals have noted the way petty bureaucrats have taken pleasure in summoning Bartholomew to their offices for questioning about irrelevant issues or obliged him to testify in small claims courts on trivial real estate matters; how his efforts or petitions for basic repairs to the few facilities of the patriarchal offices are often blocked or delayed without reason; how rumors are spread about whatever he says and does when traveling abroad; and the way that the sacred relics of Saints Gregory the Theologian and John Chrysostom gifted by Pope John Paul II to the Ecumenical Patriarchate were delayed for a prolonged period at Istanbul Atatürk Airport—so long that the faithful gathered at the Patriarchal Church of St. George for hours were obliged to leave after hours of anticipation; or—finally and most heartbreakingly—the endless promises, albeit fruitless promises, about reopening the Theological School of Halki, discussing its fate behind closed doors and frequently without the knowledge or participation of the patriarch.

THE PATRIARCHAL THEOLOGICAL SCHOOL OF HALKI

The patriarchate's international Theological School of Halki (on the Princes' Islands' Heybeliada) was significantly diminished in the 1950s and forcefully closed in 1971. The closure breaches Article 40 of the Treaty of Lausanne and Article 9 of the European Convention on Human Rights. Formerly, Halki served as the foremost and formative seminary of the (especially, but not only) Greek-speaking Orthodox world. Bartholomew laments:

> Whenever I travel to Halki—and I am there very often over the last twenty-five years for retreat and relaxation in order to withdraw from the daily drudgery of the Phanar—it pains me to see the classrooms and corridors empty. My heart feels constricted. This was a place buzzing with life. It's a sin and a shame—a crime actually. Forty years of forced closure, of imposed silence.

During its 127 years of operation (from 1844 to 1971), almost one thousand students graduated from the school, of which 330 became bishops; twelve rose to the ecumenical patriarchal throne; two were elected patriarchs of Alexandria; three became patriarchs of Antioch; one became exarch of the Bulgarians; four were ordained archbishops of Athens; one became archbishop of Albania; and 318 were ordained priests. Graduates have also included numerous Orthodox Christians from around the world—from Arabic- and Slavic-speaking regions—thereby sealing the school's international character. Even lay graduates acquired quasi-clerical status when they received the degree of master of Orthodox theology.

It is the patriarch's dream and prayer to reopen this nineteenth-century theological school. He persistently underlines the 1923 Treaty of Lausanne and Turkey's obligation both to recognize the legal status of the patriarchate as being ecumenical in scope and nature, as well as to respect its right to educate its clergy and leaders. In Turkey the Ecumenical Patriarchate is simply and solely recognized as a regular institution, while Turkish law from 1936 to this day places all Orthodox Christian property under the General Directorate of Foundations, which has the authority to dismiss foundations and seize property. Moreover, a 1974 ruling of the Turkish Supreme Court forbids the purchase or sale of property by minority groups. "But I am patient," Bartholomew notes with composure. "I want this so much."

In the United States the archons (the Order of Saint Andrew) have long supported and defended the religious freedom and rights of the Ecumenical Patriarchate to reopen the theological seminary at Halki by lobbying the Congress of the United States, meeting with the highest European and Turkish officials, and organizing international conferences on religious freedom to keep alive the memory of this vital school that was illegally and irrationally forced to close, as well as to advance the overall spiritual mission of the Ecumenical Patriarchate. As a result of the archons' efforts, Halki has received widespread attention—President Bill Clinton visited the seminary in 1999, urging the then Turkish president Süleyman Demirel to permit its reopening; in 1998, both houses of the US Congress passed resolutions that supported the reopening of Halki; the European Union has included the issue as part of its negotiations over Turkish accession; and in a speech before the Turkish parliament in 2009, President Barack Obama reaffirmed the importance of reopening the school:

> Freedom of religion and expression lead to a strong and vibrant civil society that only strengthens the state, which is why steps like reopening the Halki seminary will send such an important signal inside Turkey and beyond. An enduring commitment to the rule of law is the only way to achieve the security that comes from justice for all.

The cause also received global attention on the widely viewed American television program *60 Minutes* when host Bob Simon interviewed the patriarch in 2009, asking him how he felt about this ill-treatment and injustice. Bartholomew boldly replied, "We don't feel that we enjoy our full rights as Turkish citizens. . . . Still, we prefer to stay here . . . in our Jerusalem, even [if we feel] crucified sometimes." Probed further as to whether he feels crucified, the world gasped as Bartholomew firmly uttered with all sincerity and integrity: "Yes. I do." Turkish authorities were quick to deny any alleged mistreatment, dismissing the patriarch's remarks as "an undesired slip of the tongue."

Yet the reopening of Halki is much more than a matter of legal application or political reaction. It is also much more than emotional connection or historical vindication. Above all, it is the moral obligation of a democratic republic to its lawful and law-abiding citizens—and especially one of its most prominent and prestigious institutions—from whom Turkey only stands to benefit and profit.

An Ecumenical Patriarch for an Ecumenical Patriarchate

And in another denigrating turn of events, even as Prime Minister Recep Tayyip Erdogan promised the return of more properties to minority groups, the street that runs before the Ecumenical Patriarchate was recently renamed after a deceased controversial Turkish politician in northern Greece. Turkish authorities continue to belittle Bartholomew by referring to him as a local religious leader. They stubbornly refuse to label him by his office as "ecumenical patriarch," a phrase adopted in the sixth century to denote his wider pastoral and supranational ministry within the federation of independent Orthodox churches, which medieval historian Dimitri Obolensky referred to as the "Byzantine commonwealth."

Leading journalists in Turkey support the patriarch's claim and use of the title; universities have begun publicly recognizing him and awarding him honorary doctorates as "ecumenical patriarch"—the first academic institution in Turkey boldly to set right this wrong was Boğaziçi University in Istanbul in 2013. After all, since when does a state determine the identity of a religious or civil institution? Moreover, for centuries the Ottoman Empire had no problem with the "ecumenical" status of the patriarchate—could the Turkish Republic possibly be less tolerant?

THE REALITY OF HOPE

Still, in the last years, whether in its ambition for accession to the European Union, or in an effort to realize the democratic ideal pledged by Kemal Atatürk, the first president and founder of its democracy, Turkey has endeavored to forge new ground in its relationship to minorities by striving to create an atmosphere of equal, social, and human rights. The clearest evidence of this spirit today is in the regulation of clerical affairs of the patriarchate and the restoration of rightful ownership of properties belonging to minorities, including—but not only—the Greek community. However, this by no means implies a parallel decline in nationalism, racism, or even religious fanaticism, which Bartholomew has repeatedly denounced as the worst form of intolerance and bigotry.

In addition, in a landmark ruling of November 2010, Turkish judges complied with the 2008 decision of the European Court of Human Rights to return the remarkable nineteenth-century wooden structure of the Rum Orphanage on the island of Prinkipos (Büyükada) to its rightful owner, the Ecumenical Patriarchate. Legal counsel for the Phanar welcomed this as an important development demonstrating respect for law, democracy, and minorities. It was the first time in decades that the patriarchate's legal status was acknowledged in Istanbul. I was in the patriarch's office on November 29—the eve of the feast day of the Church of Constantinople—when he proudly held and read the first property title ever to be in the hands of an ecumenical patriarch. He had fought long and hard for his church's rights. And he never once submitted to the appeal of financial compensation in exchange for property; he sought only the return of a property that had been illegally confiscated. Bartholomew wants to use the building of the orphanage to establish a legacy in the areas that he has cared and worked for: interreligious tolerance and ecological awareness. He plans to build an interfaith center for the environment.

Constant policy swings and uncertainty have neither daunted Bartholomew nor diminished his compassion and support for the Turkish people, or his determination to serve as a mediator between Turkey and Europe. There is no resentment, no revenge, and no revulsion. Bartholomew knows that dwelling on the past can distort the present and poison the future. True peacemakers of history—such as Dr. Martin Luther King Jr. and Nelson Mandela—struggled to reduce conflict among others and demonstrated compassion toward their persecutors. Frequently called a "bridge builder," the patriarch has therefore supported international efforts to strengthen Turkey's economy and democracy, often inviting severe criticism from Greek chauvinists. He is a fervent advocate of Turkey's efforts to join the European Union, traveling throughout Europe to champion its admission.

He patiently respects the Islamic Call to Prayer (*adhan*) five times a day from loudspeakers on mosque minarets throughout the city and directly outside—literally only feet from—his compound. I recall the celebration of the Feast of Epiphany, on January 6, 2011, with the traditional casting of the cross into the waters of the Golden Horn. On this particular day, the Call to Prayer by the local muezzin interrupted—perhaps deliberately muffled—the Byzantine chant of the Christian ceremony. Without a moment's hesitation, the patriarch calmly invited the congregation to pause and wait until the Muslim prayer concluded, whereupon the Orthodox service continued.

Martyrdom is not merely exceptional but, in fact, essential in the life of the Christian church. Yet this tension between religion and state may actually be proving to be creative for the Orthodox Church in Turkey. In some ways, as the patriarch emphasizes, the categories of power are not Christian categories. And the function of the state, as Russian philosopher Vladimir Solovyev noted, is not to transform society into paradise, but to prevent it from becoming hell. This is why there can be no other way than cooperation and solidarity, tolerance and love, peace and justice. Religions are called to coexist harmoniously, reconciling fault lines that appear to divide them.

This is why, in many ways, Bartholomew is uniquely positioned and prepared to build bridges of tolerance and dialogue. His reconciliatory disposition and charitable nature have already brought about transformations that would have been inconceivable only a few years ago. Thus, he has persuaded government agencies, cultural authorities, and municipal officials throughout Turkey to grant permission for historic monasteries and churches to be opened either periodically or regularly for worship by Orthodox Christians.

This has opened up annual pilgrimages of hundreds, even thousands, of faithful from all over the world to the New Testament cities of Myra and Pergamon, the spectacular cave formations in Cappadocia, the ancient monastery of Panaghía Soumela in Pontus, and most recently, the region of Smyrna—a source of painful nostalgia, for tens of thousands of Greeks and Armenians were massacred there in the early twentieth century. On January 6, 2016, the Feast of Epiphany, the waters were blessed for the first time in ninety-four years on the shores of Smyrna. The patriarch told me: "When the cross was thrown into the waters, those diving to retrieve the cross weren't just doing it for good luck; they were stirring the sea so that our ancestors lying deep below would know what was happening."

Today, when he travels to such places throughout Turkey, Bartholomew is warmly received by local authorities, who sometimes even compete for the quality of hospitality extended to the patriarch. Mayors welcome him with town bands and parades, and people bashfully approach for "selfies" with the patriarch, whose conventional reply to everyone are the words of Kemal Atatürk: "*Yurtta sulh cihanda sulh.*" ("Peace to our nation; peace to the world.")

What he does, counts; and he uses it to help. He has successfully intervened in at least some cases—whether by communicating directly with political leaders or by commissioning senior bishops: for the release of Bulgarian Orthodox nurses from Muammar Gaddafi's Libya, for a young American citizen imprisoned in Iran, and for a Jewish American jailed in Cuba.

At other times his interventions relate to questions of moral protest at cultural or religious insensitivity, such as the time when he addressed a courageous, albeit courteous, letter to the Turkish minister of culture, Mustafa İstemihan Talay, to protest a millennial New Year's Eve party planned inside the former ancient Church of Haghia Irene. To his credit, the minister promptly canceled the event out of respect for religious freedom.

Strategic Location, Strategic Occasions

"We are on the frontier between Europe and Asia, Christianity and Islam, East and West," the patriarch tells me.

When Constantine the Great moved his imperial capital from the banks of the Tiber to the Bosphorus in 330, he surely appreciated the geographical advantages to be gained. The City of Constantine—Constantinople—would stand at the crossroads of trade routes north and south, east and west. Whoever occupied the straits controlled sea traffic between the Mediterranean and Black Seas. Militarily, economically, and politically, this was a location of prime strategic value.

Patriarch Bartholomew, however, perceives another and arguably greater potential in the placement of his ancient see, whose location he believes of prime strategic value in terms of *bridge building*. The modern city of Istanbul remains a critical crossroads between civilizations. Europe and Asia meet in her streets; Mediterranean and Middle Eastern cultures mingle in her bazaars. Above all, the whole panoply of the world's religious traditions thrives in and around an ancient city with a prominent presence of the three great monotheistic faiths: Judaism, Christianity, and

Islam. As the Orthodox primate of this uniquely situated city, Bartholomew views his patriarchal throne as having a unique responsibility and role in every direction to bridge gaps in religious tolerance and understanding.

He believes that—beyond interfaith consultations and ecumenical dialogues—cultural openness and religious tolerance derive from the common air that we all breathe and from the people with whom we associate, converse, and debate on a daily basis. For Bartholomew, in all corners of the planet, religion has always constituted—and must continue to constitute—the basis of civilization. He believes that religion should not divide along fault lines, but instead unite on the fundamental issues of human rights and social justice. Underlining the compatibility of Orthodoxy and religious freedom, he preaches while paraphrasing the Bosphorus Declaration from a conference in 1994 that violence in the name of religion is violence against religion. "On this planet created by God for us all, there is room for all of us," were his words uttered as he laid flowers at the site of St. Nicholas Greek Orthodox Church in New York City beside the ruins of the World Trade Center in March 2002. On official visits, his entourage will consistently include a Muslim associate.

To this end, Bartholomew has also maintained a regular program of international, interreligious programs and dialogues. Given that Orthodox Christians have a 550-year history of coexistence with Muslims, his bridge building has taken him to groundbreaking events and exchanges in Israel, Egypt, Libya, Syria, Jordan, Bahrain, Qatar, Kazakhstan, Iran, Azerbaijan—beyond the venues of global cooperation, such as the United Nations in Switzerland

and the United States, as well as the European Union and European Commission in Belgium. This has earned him greater credibility and led him to create more bridges between Christianity and Islam than any other Christian leader.

He has reached out to heal situations of tension in regions of conflict, such as the former Yugoslavia and the Balkans generally, but also the Holy Land, the Middle East, and Ukraine, as well as Armenia, Azerbaijan, Georgia, and Tajikistan. His advocacy has been on behalf of not only Christians but also Jews, Muslims, and Buddhists alike, along with other minority religious groups, for instance, within Turkey.

Throughout the centuries of Ottoman rule, there were undoubtedly gifted patriarchs who were skilled in negotiating relations with their Muslim overlords and others who reached out to other faith communities. A magnificent mosaic at the entrance to the patriarchal office at the Phanar depicts Patriarch Gennadios Scholarios receiving a pastoral staff and imperial edict (*firman*) from Sultan Mehmed II around the middle of the fifteenth century. Nonetheless, it is difficult to imagine any of Bartholomew's predecessors having both the personal resolve and the political resilience to accomplish this high level of interfaith encounter and exchange. In God's time, it would seem, Bartholomew was elected at a moment in history when openness and integrity between the great religions would most be needed—an era that has witnessed the brutal internecine war in the former Republic of Yugoslavia, the horror of 9/11 in the United States, and the ensuing bloodshed in Iraq, Afghanistan, and Syria, as well as the ever-intensifying current refugee crisis resulting from those wars.

Interfaith Conferences

As a child, Bartholomew developed a rudimentary regard for Muslims as well as an elementary respect for Jews. Growing up at Imvros, he would recite poems in Turkish and Greek on major holidays. When he was a seminarian at Halki, he loved to attend the stage theater in Istanbul. His favorite memories of *Fiddler on the Roof* and *The Diary of Anne Frank*—both plays relating to Jewish circumstances and suffering—early instilled in him admiration for resilience from oppression, the revulsion of prejudice, and the resolve to compassion.

Bartholomew's convictions have led him as the patriarch in the pioneering of interfaith projects and in the drafting of several significant declarations.

The Bosphorus Declaration: International Conference on Peace and Tolerance (1994)

The first of these came in 1994, from the International Conference on Peace and Tolerance I, cosponsored by the Ecumenical Patriarchate and the Appeal to Conscience Foundation; a second conference—Peace and Tolerance II—followed in November 2005. Meeting in Istanbul, delegates from all over the world succeeded in issuing a joint statement of common principles that came to be known as the "Bosphorus Declaration." The cornerstone of this document was a reaffirmation of the key tenet of the 1992 Berne Declaration, that "a crime committed in the name of religion is a crime against religion."

The Bosphorus Declaration proceeded to condemn all ethnic conflict as incompatible with the core values of Judaism, Islam, and Christianity:

We reject any attempt to corrupt the basic tenets of our faith by means of false interpretation and unchecked nationalism. We stand firmly against those who violate the sanctity of human life and pursue policies in defiance of moral values. We reject the concept that it is possible to justify one's actions in any armed conflict in the name of God.

In his personal statements Bartholomew has gone even further in distancing religion from violence, saying of terrorists that they are not religious prophets but, in fact, the falsest prophets of all:

When they inflict hurt, death, and destruction, they steal more than life; they undermine faith itself—although faith defiantly remains the only way to break the cycle of hatred and retribution.

The Brussels Declaration: International Conference on Peaceful Coexistence (2001)

The prophetic truth of his words became painfully apparent in the attacks of September 11, 2001. Without skipping a heartbeat, Bartholomew did not hesitate to accept an invitation to address a Conference on Peaceful Coexistence between Judaism, Christianity, and Islam. Meeting in Brussels in December, barely three months after 9/11, the conference issued a strong statement condemning actions of extremists as neither genuinely reflecting nor accurately representing the teachings of their own religions—despite their immoral actions being committed supposedly in the name of religion. Bartholomew spearheaded the joint statement declaring that "the will of God is for the peace of heaven to reign on earth." At the heart of the Brussels Declaration was the insistence that faith itself is not to blame for conflict and terror, contrary to the rising sentiment of the secular West that religion itself is to blame. Religion is called to heal, not a cause for hurt:

> We unanimously reject the assumption that religion contributes to an inevitable clash of civilizations. On the contrary we affirm the constructive and instructive role of religion in the dialogue among civilizations.

In other words, different creeds should never give rise to divisive conflict. Religion can never be justified if it is part of the problem, but essentially exists to be part of the solution.

The Bahrain Declaration: The Role of Religion in Peaceful Coexistence (2002)

The following year, Bartholomew was invited to a special session of the Christian-Muslim dialogue in Bahrain, celebrating the tenth such consultation organized by the Ecumenical Patriarchate since 1986. The Bahrain Declaration of 2002 stressed that both Christianity and Islam teach the core values of freedom of conscience, religious tolerance, and tangible compassion. The declaration was emphatic:

> Violence breeds violence, while suppression engenders animosity. So concerned authorities should stand up to address violence through constructive dialogue rather than repression.

For many Western Christians, it may come as a surprise to learn that there is common ground with Islam on the principle of religious tolerance and non-coercion in matters of faith. For this reason, the Bahrain Declaration also called for a greater commitment to spread "the right understanding of both Islam and Christianity to all concerned individuals and individuals of good will through education and mass media."

Indeed, this value of non-coercion as respect, tolerance, and understanding runs like a golden thread through the thoughts and writings of the patriarch. He often resorts to a line from one of the earliest postapostolic writings, the anonymous second-century *Epistle to Diognetus*: "God persuades; God does not compel. For violence is entirely foreign to God."

In the mind of the ecumenical patriarch, to coerce someone in matters of conscience is an assault on his very personhood, integrity, and humanity:

> For the Christian tradition, freedom—the ability to make decisions consciously and with a full sense of responsibility—is the most tremendous thing granted by God to human persons. Without liberty of choice there is no authentic personhood.

An Ongoing Legacy

In helping to shape the Bosphorus, Brussels, and Bahrain Declarations, His All-Holiness laid the foundation for a lasting legacy of interfaith cooperation and peace. However, his efforts were not exhausted in these few seminal, symbolic events. He has also initiated, organized, or spoken at numerous other interfaith encounters, covering such diverse topics as youth and education, culture and heritage, as well as tradition and law. During the period of his own patriarchal tenure alone, there have been formal conversations between Orthodoxy and Judaism—at least six conferences held in Israel and Greece; and there have been formal conversations between Orthodoxy and Islam—at least seven conferences held in Jordan, Greece, Turkey, and Bahrain. There have also been several joint ventures involving Judaism, Christianity, and Islam—in Greece and Turkey; and there has even been a conference "against violence in the name of religion"—held in Austria in 2014, an event assembling Christian, Mandaean, and Yazidi, as well as Sunni and Shiite leaders. Most recently, he delivered the keynote address at an interfaith conference focused on the plight of the Christians in the Middle East and North Africa, which was organized in Athens, Greece, in October 2015 and included religious and political leaders from all over the world.

Looking at One Another in the Eyes: The How of Encounter

There is an inevitable risk in situations of interfaith encounter: participants may not always be sincere in their professed openness to the other. Those who consider that they have a monopoly on "truth" or "right" can only play at trading freely in the marketplace of ideas. Scholars sometimes label this as "syncretism," which does not necessarily have the pejorative luggage it has acquired in certain periods and conservative circles. But Bartholomew plays no such games. He likes to quote the words of Patriarch Athenagoras: "Come, let us look one another in the eyes!" Bartholomew's participation in inter-religious dialogue is genuine and grounded. He is open to finding God's grace at work in all peoples and in all traditions. His attitude is expressed succinctly in the Amaroussion Declaration of 2004 in Athens, Greece:

> It is our common understanding that the divine and the human converge in all religions upholding the sanctity of human life, and therefore, each in its own special way emphasizes the values of liberty, justice, brotherhood, solidarity, and love, for peaceful coexistence amongst all human beings and all peoples, particularly in our modern multicultural global community.

The patriarch's premise is not just spiritual; it is deeply theological. On the one side, he believes and argues that every religion has profound insight to offer into the deeper realities of existence. On the other side, he is convinced and claims that no religion—not even his own—can adequately express the whole truth about God in dogmatic statements, liturgical utterances, or mystical experiences. This is precisely where his critics are quick to jump in and find fault. But they should understand that the patriarch, in doing so, embraces a fundamental aspect of Orthodox doctrine—namely, what is called the "apophatic" approach (roughly analogous to the "via negativa" in Western thought), the conviction that the human mind can never fully know or fully grasp, and certainly never fully define or even fully describe God.

"You cannot see My face; for no man shall see Me, and live," says the God of the Abrahamic faiths (Exodus 33:20). This statement intimates the ineffable transcendence of God, whose presence always remains beyond all conception, comprehension, or formulation. And so, in this sense especially, no religion is capable of either possessing or even expressing all that must be said about the infinite and divine. Without this profoundly provisional understanding of theological language, interfaith dialogue is impossible. As the patriarch likes to say, "Dialogue resists laying claim to a part of the truth as if it was the whole truth." The tyranny of fragmented truth blinds people to the fullness of truth. The peril of fundamental truth is ultimately an obsession about partial—even partisan—truth. Whereas if we humbly acknowledge that we can only grasp or experience truth incrementally and incompletely—"for now we see in a mirror, dimly. . . . Now [we] know in part" (1 Corinthians 13:12)—we will not presume to know the mind of God or express the will of God.

The patriarch is entirely uninhibited and unpretentious—even comfortable and fluent—in framing his ideas by employing the vocabulary of the other. For example, even beyond the Hebrew Scriptures that he embraces as his own in the Old Testament, he will cite the Qur'an with competence and confidence, as he repeatedly does in his book *Encountering the Mystery*, but especially during a speech in 2000 in the Kingdom of Bahrain:

All good deeds of humanity succeed in periods of peace, while many disasters occur at times of war. In view of this, it becomes clear that God is pleased by reconciliation, mutual understanding, and peaceful cooperation. However, this presupposes a mutual goodwill, which is dictated by both the Gospel through the commandment of love, as well as by the Qur'an through the commandment of doing good deeds. Indeed, as the Qur'an itself proclaims: "Christians are those most disposed to love the faithful; and this is because there are among them priests and monks, as well as because they are not proud" [chapter 5, verse 82]. Certainly, this does not pertain to all those bearing the name Christian, but only to those pious Christians who follow the commandments of God. Elsewhere in the Qur'an, we read: "Not all followers of the Scriptures share the same qualities; but some of them have pure hearts" [chapter 3, verses 113, 114]. And in another passage: "There are among the People of the Book, some who can be entrusted with a talent which they will return to you intact; there are others, however, who if they are not forced to do so, will not return to you even the deposit of a single dinar" [chapter 3, verse 75].

All Things to All People: The Why of Encounter

It bears noting that the patriarch faces intense, even extreme, resistance from some quarters within his own church for the sincerity of his interfaith efforts. As already noted, there are in the wider Orthodox community those who view such bridge building as a form of relativism or syncretism. Then there are others who dismiss religious tolerance as utterly powerless or fruitless. But for Bartholomew, open encounter and exchange between the world's great religions is not a personal option or fringe benefit; it is a moral imperative derived directly from fundamental dogmas of Christian Scripture and theology. During an address to the Second Congress of Leaders of World Religions held in 2006 at Kazakhstan, His All-Holiness declared:

> The Ecumenical Patriarchate is an eager participant in the interfaith dialogue and consultation, which strive to foster harmony, solidarity, and understanding between our Lord's warring children . . . irrespective of language and culture, and irrespective of religious and political convictions. Simply because all of us are created in the image of God and, therefore, profoundly integrated and equal.

This is how Bartholomew sees all people of every faith: we are all brothers and sisters *regardless* of our differences of creed, color, and culture. In fact, we are all brothers and sisters *even before* we discern or display differences of creed, color, and culture. Moreover, we are all brothers and sisters *above and beyond* any differences of creed, color, and culture. For Bartholomew, echoing the ancient rabbinic as well as the classical Hellenic tradition, the worst form of surrender to the devil is to forget that we are—all of us—children of the living God.

If Saint Paul, as the early "apostle to the nations," strove to be "all things to all men" (1 Corinthians 9:22), then surely the patriarch is merely following the apostolic way. This is why his interreligious work is characterized by a keen desire, not simply to speak the *truth*, but primarily to speak the truth in *love* (Ephesians 4:15)—in a

manner that seeks out the most congenial form of respectful atten-
tiveness and compassionate expression.

Building Bridges, Not Ramparts

Of course, Bartholomew is deeply conscious of and sensitive to his
status as a role model for other clergy and laypeople in his church
and beyond. Thus, his interreligious activities are at all times characterized by dignity, integrity, and responsibility. It would be easy for
him to use the many opportunities to speak before political bodies
and powerful rulers as occasions to grandstand the difficulties of the
minority Christian population in Turkey or the unjustifiable and
unforgivable curtailment of rights for the Ecumenical Patriarchate.
But he would never yield to such a temptation. He remains always
fixed on the task at hand: building bridges and not ramparts; extending open arms rather than a raised fist.

During the visit of Pope Francis to the Phanar in November
2014, the pontiff and the patriarch issued a joint declaration urging leaders around the world—and not only Christian leaders but
religious leaders more widely—to follow their example of fraternal
cooperation and friendship:

> The grave challenges facing the world in the present situa-
> tion require the solidarity of all people of good will, and so
> we also recognize the importance of promoting a constructive
> dialogue with Islam based on mutual respect and friendship.
> Inspired by common values and strengthened by genuine

fraternal sentiments, Muslims and Christians are called to work together for the sake of justice, peace and respect for the dignity and rights of every person, especially in those regions where they once lived for centuries in peaceful coexistence and now tragically suffer together the horrors of war. Moreover, as Christian leaders, we call on all religious leaders to pursue and to strengthen interreligious dialogue and to make every effort to build a culture of peace and solidarity between persons and between peoples.

No Bridge Too Far

One of the fastest-growing religious groups in the Western world are the so-called Nones—those who identify themselves as having no religious preference or affiliation. The patriarch recognizes and worries about this rising tide of nonbelief—though he avoids sweepingly or dismissively associating it with any single culture or with the West alone—and he diagnoses it as a symptom of secularism, which he would define as a heresy directly dependent on and deriving from the problem of fundamentalism. Where secularism perceives the earthly and human as absolute values, it is often a reaction to fundamentalism as the arrogant identification with the heavenly and divine. It is no wonder that the Nones prefer to identify with, well . . . *"none* of the above."

In fact, the patriarch would describe the encounter with the Nones of the West—with secularists and fundamentalists alike—as an interfaith dialogue in its own right. Speaking to the

US Congress on the occasion of receiving the US Congressional Gold Medal in 1997, he characterized secularism precisely as a faith unto itself:

> Since the Enlightenment, the spiritual bedrock of Western civilization has been eroded and undermined. Intelligent, well-intentioned people sincerely believed that the wonders of science could replace the miracles of faith. But these great minds missed one vital truth, namely that faith is not a garment, to be slipped on and off; it is a quality of the human spirit, from which it is inseparable. The modern era has not eliminated faith; one could no more eliminate faith than love. Even atheists believe in atheism. The modern era has simply replaced spiritual faith in God with secular faith in man. . . . Therein lie the lessons of Orthodoxy for America, that paradoxically, faith can endure without freedom, but freedom cannot long abide without faith. And while God has led us to reason, reason alone can never lead us back to God. Only faith can do that.

For Bartholomew, the great philosophical debate of the present age, between belief and unbelief, is a matter of opposing faiths. It will be resolved—as all religious controversies can only be resolved—by patient encounter and openness of mind. The gulf between faith and agnosticism or atheism is not unbridgeable—at least, not for the builder of bridges from the city of Constantine. The patriarch eloquently expressed this optimism before the Emir of Qatar during a conference on relations between Christians and Muslims at the University of Qatar in 2002, where he concluded with words

from thirteenth-century Sufi poet Jalal ad-Din Rumi, in a poem
entitled "Religious Strife":

> The blind religious practitioners are in a dilemma.
> But the worthy practitioners from the one
> > or the other side stand firm.
> Each side is happy with its way.
> Love alone can stop their strife.
> Love alone brings assistance
> > when you ask for it against their arguments.
> Eloquence is dumbfounded before love:
> It does not dare start a controversy.
> It is like a beautiful bird
> > that has perched on your shoulder
> And your soul is afraid in case it causes it to fall off:
> You do not dare either to move or to breathe.
> Love is like this bird: It makes you silent.
> It places the lid on the pan that is boiling.

We are called to love by a God who created the whole world. We
are commanded to love by a God who identifies with every single
person in the world. And we are judged on love by a God who is
revealed only in and through the other person.

Guided by such love, there is surely no bridge too far to be built
between groups of God's children. Love is clearly the plumb line
of Bartholomew's interfaith encounters as an advocate of tolerance
and dialogue but also an architect of peace and coexistence.

LOVE AND LAUGHTER

The patriarch shared a small anecdote that, for me, demonstrated how humanity and humility are so closely related, how love and laughter are two sides of the same coin, and how justice and charity go hand in hand.

In the next chapter I describe various aspects of the historical meeting between Patriarch Bartholomew and Pope Francis in Jerusalem on May 25–26, 2014. The two leaders undoubtedly shared a connection from the outset.

So when they traveled to Jerusalem—it was just the second time they had met in person—they nonetheless felt very comfortable in each other's presence and company. On May 25, they held a joint thanksgiving service in the Church of the Resurrection and then venerated the Holy Sepulcher, the tomb of Jesus Christ. The following day, the two leaders met at the residence of the Orthodox Patriarch of Jerusalem on the Mount of Olives, where Jesus Christ prayed on the night of his betrayal, adjacent to the walls of the old city.

During their cordial and genial private conversation, the pope turned to Bartholomew and confided that he was about to propose to Israeli president Shimon Peres and Palestinian president Mahmoud Abbas that they should visit the Vatican for a prayer for peace—which occurred just two weeks later, on June 9, 2014—in an effort to shake hands and demonstrate a symbolical gesture of reconciliation. Needless to say, the two rival presidents accepted; it's not that easy to decline a papal invitation.

The pope proceeded to ask the patriarch whether he would accept to extending this invitation jointly to the two political leaders. "Why should I invite them alone? It will be better for both of us to invite them," said the pope. Bartholomew replied that he was deeply touched by the generous thought and would accordingly consult the members of his synod; upon securing his synod's consent, the patriarch was prominently involved in the prayer invocation together with the pope and the two presidents.

In Rome, after the official ceremony of the peace summit—which was held in the gardens of the Vatican out of sensitivity toward the guests of honor; that is to say, not in a church, neither in a temple, nor in a mosque—Bartholomew bade farewell to Francis, who continued to greet the rest of his high guests. But as Bartholomew left the hall and entered his car, he noticed the pope hurrying toward him. The patriarch stepped out of the car and said, "Santità, please! You have honored me more than enough; you have spent so much time with me; we have said our good-byes." The pope embraced the patriarch and replied:

You don't understand. This is our protocol. When a special guest leaves, we escort them to the very end. And we do this for two reasons: first, to be sure they have departed safely; and second, to be sure they haven't departed *with* something!

They both laughed. "Then let me leave with your love," said the patriarch.

Humor helps; just as humor heals. Humor, too, can be an important part of harmony.

BENEDICT XVI

Pope Emeritus

MY FIRST CLOSE PERSONAL CONTACT WITH ECUMENICAL PATRIARCH Bartholomew was granted in the year 2002 on the way to the World Meeting of Prayer in Assisi. It was Saint Pope John Paul II's idea to travel together by train to Assisi in order to express our inner journey alongside the external trip. For me it was a joy to learn that the patriarch had invited me to sit with him for a while in the same compartment and, in this way, to become personally closer.

For me, this meeting—along the way—is more than an accidental expression for the state of the faith. I was also immediately moved by the personal openness and warmth of the patriarch. It required no great effort for us to become close to one another. His inner openness and simplicity immediately brought with it comfortable intimacy. Naturally, what also contributed to this feeling was the fact that he speaks all of the major European languages, not only French and English, but also Italian and

German. Even more surprising for me was the fact that he has mastery of Latin and knows how to express himself in that language. If one can converse with someone in one's own language, there is an immediacy of speaking heart to heart and thought to thought. The patriarch has studied not only in the realm of the Orthodox Church, but also in Munich and Rome. To the diversity of languages there also corresponds, in the process, a diversity of cultures in which he moves. In this way, from its very depths, his thought is a journey with others and toward others, which certainly does not degenerate into a lack of direction, in which "being on the road" would simply lead nowhere. Deep rootedness in faith in Jesus Christ, the Son of the living God and our Redeemer, does not stand in the way of openness to the other because Jesus Christ bears in himself all truth. At the same time, however, this rootedness protects us from slipping into triviality and from an empty play of vanity because it holds us in the truth, which belongs to all and desires to be the way for all.

Thus, I somehow see in this our first meeting a picture of the entire personality of the ecumenical patriarch: living on the road toward a goal; living in the many dimensions of the great cultures; living in encounter, borne by the fundamental encounter with the truth that is Jesus Christ. In the end, the goal in all of these encounters is unity in Jesus Christ.

Even if, of course, it cannot be the aim of this short reflection to delineate in some fashion the ministry of the patriarch in its entirety, I would at least like to underline a point that is important for the characterization of this great man of the Church of God: his love for creation and his advocacy that it be dealt with in accordance with this love, in matters big and small. A shepherd of the flock of Jesus Christ is never oriented merely to the circle of his own faithful. The community of the Church is universal also in the sense that it includes all of reality. That becomes evident, for example, in the liturgy, which signifies not only the commemoration and realization of the saving deeds of Jesus Christ. It is on the way toward the redemption of all creation. In the liturgy's orientation to the East, we see that Christians, together with the Lord, want to progress toward the salvation of creation in its entirety. Christ, the crucified and risen Lord, is at the same time also the "sun" that illumines the world. Faith is also always directed toward the totality of creation. Therefore, Patriarch Bartholomew fulfills an essential aspect of his priestly mission precisely with his commitment to creation.

My election as successor of Saint Peter naturally has given our personal meeting a new dimension. Responsibility for faith in the world and, simultaneously, responsibility for the unity of divided Christianity are part of the office that has been given us, but it is precisely also a personal obligation.

I feel it is particularly felicitous that, after my resignation, the patriarch has remained ever close to me personally and has even visited me in my little cloister. In many places in my apartment can be found memorable items from him. These items are not only endearing signs of our personal friendship, but also signposts toward unity between Constantinople and Rome, signs of hope that we are heading toward unity.

His All-Holiness Bartholomew is a truly ecumenical patriarch in every sense of this word. In fraternal solidarity with Pope

Francis, he is making additional important steps on the path to unity. Dear brother in Christ, may the Lord grant you many more years of blessed ministry as shepherd in God's Church. I greet you ἐν φιλήματι ἁγίῳ.

CHAPTER 2

HEART WIDE OPEN

Ecumenical Advocate to the Christian World

Orthodoxy must be in constant dialogue with the world. Otherwise,
it will no longer be the "catholic" and "ecumenical" church but
instead be reduced to a "ghetto" on the margins of history.
—ECUMENICAL PATRIARCH BARTHOLOMEW,
LENTEN ENCYCLICAL, 2010

THE LANGUAGE OF DIALOGUE

Dialogue is in the patriarch's blood. It is in the Ecumenical Patriarchate's DNA, the mother tongue of the Phanar. Frankly, it is an integral element of the Orthodox Church's identity. And it is quite undeniably—albeit very contentiously—Christianity's genuine apostolic and evangelical narrative. In recent years, the patriarch addressed the Orthodox faithful in a pastoral letter from the Phanar:

Beloved children in the Lord, Orthodoxy has no need of either fanaticism or bigotry to protect itself. Whoever believes that Orthodoxy has the truth does not fear dialogue, because truth has never been endangered by dialogue.

The unique personalities that loomed large in Bartholomew's childhood and formation—Metropolitan Meliton and Patriarch Athenagoras—shaped the historical opening of a church clearly steeped in a vibrant theological and spiritual tradition but also courageously standing at the threshold of ecumenical outreach and dialogue. In fact, Bartholomew was constantly at Meliton's side in ecumenical and inter-church meetings, and he would never leave Ecumenical Patriarch Demetrios's side in such events.

However, his own childhood already revealed glimpses of genuine openness and deep respect toward others: his school essays speak of "cultivating respect for all people irrespective of race, gender, language, and religion." Moreover, his graduate studies exposed him to the Roman Catholic Church in Rome, the Protestant world in Munich, and the World Council of Churches in Bossey. Finally, his long, personal experience over almost two decades in the private office of his beloved Patriarch Demetrios exposed him to heads of churches, theological dialogues, and the ecumenical movement.

He was a long-standing member of the Central and Executive Committees of the World Council of Churches. For fifteen years, he served as member and for eight years as vice president (1975–1983) of the Faith and Order Commission of the World Council of Churches, the only commission in which Roman Catholics also participate. Indeed, he was vice president during the development of the Baptism, Eucharist, and Ministry Document, on which the Orthodox presence and influence are demonstrably apparent. He participated—either as representative or head of the delegation of the Ecumenical Patriarchate—in three general assemblies of the World Council of Churches: in Uppsala (1968), Vancouver (1983), and Canberra (1991).

I recall sitting beside him for the duration of that general assembly in Australia in 1991, just months before he was elected patriarch: the alphabetical proximity of his title "Chalcedon" and my surname, Chryssavgis, providing for me a unique—my very first—opportunity, indeed privilege, to watch him in action. What has remained vividly in my mind is his concentration on and commitment to the slightest detail on the table for discussion. He read every document distributed, kept detailed notes on developments, and orchestrated a concerted and collaborative Orthodox response to issues raised. As a young theologian-clergyman at barely thirty-three years of age, I admit being hastily scandalized by many Orthodox delegates, who seemed more interested in touring the Australian capital and shopping at its malls. The patriarch did not leave his seat—which certainly made it embarrassing for me even to consider leaving my own—at any point of the plenary sessions. During a committee session discussing finances, he was obliged to step out for an interview on local television, and I remember how astounded I was that he asked me to take notes during his ten-minute absence—notes on budget numbers!

And it could not be otherwise. He recognized his role and responsibility—despite fierce and vociferous anti-ecumenical sentiment in some pockets of the Orthodox world—in witnessing to the Orthodox teaching, coordinating the message of the Orthodox churches, and maintaining a tradition of ecumenical leadership within the Ecumenical Patriarchate. After all, he had been trained and nurtured within that tradition from his student years under Patriarch Athenagoras.

ORTHODOX-CATHOLIC DIALOGUE: A MICROCOSM OF ECUMENICAL RELATIONS

A detailed survey of the evolving relationship between the Catholic and Orthodox Churches reflects the broader commitment of the patriarch to ecumenism and dialogue with all churches.

New Rome Meets Elder Rome

In December 1963, Athenagoras sent Meliton to the Vatican, where he addressed Pope Paul VI:

> Perhaps it is a matter of divine inspiration. . . . For centuries [we] have not communicated with one another. Behold, now [we] are revealing a mutual desire and wish for exchange and encounter. This wish is none other than the Lord's command and the Christian people's nostalgia.

Earlier, Athenagoras had commissioned Iakovos, newly elected and soon to be enthroned archbishop of North and South America, to travel to Rome to meet with Pope John XXIII, who had just months earlier announced the convocation of the Second Vatican

Council that later began in 1962. When Iakovos visited the pope on March 17, 1959, it was the first encounter between any representative of the ecumenical patriarch and the pope of Rome since May 1547. Bartholomew was studying in Rome at the time; he was personally present at this historical meeting. Both Iakovos and Bartholomew were, therefore, present at this pioneering, preliminary meeting that prepared the ground and set the pace for Orthodox-Catholic relations.

The Ecumenical Patriarchate has long been ahead of its time in the area of ecumenical openness. And it has consistently paid the price within an Orthodox Church often obsessed with and suppressed by a narrow interpretation of truth and tradition. It is a cost—frequently a consequence of ignorant misinformation, consistent misinterpretation, and malignant misrepresentation—that Patriarch Bartholomew is willing to pay out of a sense of Christian conviction and personal commitment. In an encyclical issued in 2010, at the outset of Great Lent, the patriarch boldly responded to his detractors:

> Critics of the restoration of unity among Christians do not hesitate to distort reality in order to deceive and arouse the faithful. Thus, they are silent about the fact that theological dialogues are conducted by unanimous decision of all Orthodox Churches. They disseminate false rumors that union between the Roman Catholic and Orthodox Churches is imminent. . . . They condemn those who conduct these dialogues as allegedly "heretics" and "traitors" of Orthodoxy, purely and simply because they converse with non-Orthodox, with whom they share the treasure

and truth of our Orthodox faith. They speak condescendingly of every effort for reconciliation among divided Christians and restoration of their unity as "the pan-heresy of ecumenism."

The patriarch knows very well that the sustained efforts of the Ecumenical Patriarchate for the reconciliation of all Christians and the restoration of church unity are ultimately a fundamental expression of obedience and loyalty to the exhortation and expectation of Christ immediately before his betrayal and crucifixion "that [his disciples] all may be one" (John 17:21). He is also well aware that these efforts have a long-standing history, especially during the twentieth century, sometimes called "the century of ecumenism."

The Way to Reconciliation

The twentieth century was a time of growing restoration of relationships among Christian churches. After almost a millennium of more or less total isolation from one another, the Churches of Rome and Constantinople broke through an unbecoming silence that tacitly also engendered suspicion and contempt.

However, in 1927, an archbishop by the name of Angelo Giuseppe Roncalli, later installed as Pope John XXIII, paid an unofficial, albeit unprecedented, visit to Ecumenical Patriarch Basil III in Constantinople. Roncalli would later also serve as the Vatican's representative in Turkey, where he became acquainted with Orthodox prelates and faithful, even attending the funeral of Ecumenical Patriarch Photius II in January 1936.

After the Second World War, and especially following the election of Ecumenical Patriarch Athenagoras, contacts between

Rome and Constantinople steadily increased. Already comfortable and confident in the presence of non-Orthodox leaders from his ministry in the United States, Athenagoras soon also met with Roman Catholic leaders in Turkey. Nevertheless, in October 1958, Athenagoras opened up a new and historic chapter in Orthodox-Catholic relations, when he addressed a simple word of concern about the illness of Pope Pius XII, followed by an expression of condolence upon the death of the pope only a few days later.

With the election of Pope John XXIII, the two churches began corresponding with one another, responding to each other's felicitations, and finally meeting formally. The meeting, then, between Iakovos and the pope would open up fresh possibilities and affirm ongoing bonds between the Elder Rome and New Rome.

These were exciting times for Bartholomew to be in Rome; the council for the Roman Catholic Church, convened by Pope John XXIII, had commenced in October 1962. Vatican II would reshape and reform the Catholic Church, a constructive and in many ways controversial process that is still ongoing more than fifty years since it was closed under Pope Paul VI. In fact, throughout his ministry, Bartholomew was privileged to meet four popes: Paul VI, John Paul II, Benedict XVI, and Francis. It is only John Paul I whom he did not have the opportunity to meet, though his mentor, Metropolitan Meliton, attended the inauguration of the short-lived pope. Bartholomew would meet at least once a year with Paul VI, who would invite the young Orthodox students of theology to the Vatican for a meal. Later, as metropolitan of Philadelphia, Bartholomew visited Paul on June 29, 1978—just five weeks before the pope died—when he accompanied Metropolitan Meliton on a trip that took him to Rome, Moscow, and Tiflis. He also attended Pope Paul's funeral with Metropolitan Meliton at St. Peter's Square in 1978. The patriarch remembers Paul VI as a dignified man:

> He had a noble stature and a refined nature; and he cared deeply about the dialogue with the Orthodox, for which John XXIII had paved the way. But Pope Paul is the one who moved the dialogue forward substantively.

Bartholomew was not present at the council in any official capacity, but he was definitely there "behind the scenes." The ensuing discussions among theologians—and of course the endless conversations among theological students—were constant, creative, and compelling. The greatest luminaries of Roman Catholic theology at the time were in attendance, their theological wisdom proving transformative. And a future generation of theologians—Roman Catholic, Orthodox, and Protestant—was also present at the sessions.

Invited to assign observers to the council, initially the Orthodox were not in unanimous agreement as to their response. Thus, no observer was present during the first session in 1962. Athenagoras sent a personal representative to the session in 1963. Finally, with the Orthodox Pre-conciliar process established around the same time by Athenagoras to set the scene for a Holy and Great Council of the Orthodox Church, the Ecumenical Patriarchate decided to appoint official observers to the third and fourth sessions of the council throughout 1964 and 1965. The presence of Orthodox clergy and theologians was instrumental and influential on decisions of the Vatican council, especially those pertaining to liturgy

and ecclesiology, which the Orthodox churches had uniquely preserved in their sacraments and structures through the centuries.

Bartholomew was still in Rome when the ongoing and growing
relations between Rome and Constantinople reached groundbreaking proportions in the pioneering steps taken by Patriarch
Athenagoras and Pope Paul VI, after the death of Pope John XXIII
in 1963. How could the two churches, formally separated since
1054, show the world that reunion was once again possible? Could
the two leaders demonstrate their commitment to a process of
reconciliation and dialogue?

Estrangement and Encounter

Previously, for many centuries, the two churches were not in
personal contact and shared very little official communication,
especially after what became known as the "Great Schism," or separation, of 1054—the final breaking apart of the church, with mutual
excommunications by Rome and Constantinople. There were two
brief occasions where reunification was debated in the thirteenth
and fifteenth centuries—at the Council of Lyons in 1274 and at the
Council of Ferrara-Florence in 1438–1439—but these encounters
probably left feelings of bitterness rather than hopefulness for the
Orthodox Christians of the East, especially after the tragic events
of the Crusades.

So when Pope Paul VI and Patriarch Athenagoras met on the
Mount of Olives in Jerusalem on January 5, 1964, it was, in fact,
the first time that a pope of Rome and a patriarch of New Rome
had met in more than five hundred years and possibly only the second time in history. Patriarch Athenagoras, famous for his ability

to charm people with his wit and wisdom, summarized the event memorably, stating to reporters that he had come to Jerusalem to see the pope because after so many centuries it was time at least to say "good morning to my brother."

Several decades later, after the historic and humble retirement of Pope Benedict XVI, Patriarch Bartholomew spontaneously decided to attend the inaugural mass of Pope Francis on March 19, 2013. He says, "I simply knew something was different about this man; from the very beginning, with his election, I sensed something very genuine."

Much of the mainstream media as well as most papal biographies reported that this was the first time in one thousand years that a primate of Constantinople attended the installation of the pontiff of Rome; in fact, it was the first time in recorded history that anything like this had occurred. On that day, in St. Peter's Square, Bartholomew was the only non-Catholic leader to be invited to the altar in order to exchange the kiss of peace with the new pope.

The close friendship between the two leaders has been attested to in papal interviews and biographies: "almost joined at the hip," observes one papal biographer—a serendipitous echo of a description by one of the greatest Orthodox theologians of the twentieth century, Fr. Georges Florovsky, of the Orthodox and Catholic churches as "conjoined" twins. Reflecting today on his relationship with Pope Francis, Bartholomew says,

> There is a chemistry between us. We feel comfortable in each other's presence. We trust one another. He has a sense of humor. He is simple and humble.

When I attended his inauguration, I stayed at Santa Marta House. I met the new pope in the lobby and he invited me to dinner. Our friendship was instantaneous and spontaneous.

I would always stay in a larger apartment with three rooms [an office, a lounge, and a bedroom] in Santa Marta's. That is where the pope chose to stay after declining to move into the papal palace. So after his election, I would stay in another room. When I met him afterward, I said: "Your Holiness, you took my place." And he remembered this; when, a couple of years later, I asked him whether he had moved into the papal palace, he replied: "No, I am still at your place!"

Hours after the inaugural papal mass, Bartholomew would invite Francis to celebrate the fiftieth anniversary of the meeting between their predecessors—Athenagoras and Paul—in Jerusalem. Indeed, the historic fiftieth anniversary was marked by a joint pilgrimage by the two leaders to the Holy Land in May 2014. Pope and patriarch bowed to enter the tomb of Jesus Christ inside the fourth-century church constructed by the Emperor Constantine and his mother, Helena. I was privileged to witness the meeting in Jerusalem; as I watched the two leaders approaching the Church of the Holy Sepulcher, I visualized two frail mortals bowing down to the God who alone could provide reconciliation and unity. Yet in our age—when religion is used and abused for political and other secular purposes, when there is so much suffering and persecution facing Christians all over the world (particularly in the Holy Land and the Middle East), when injustices are inflicted on the weak members of contemporary societies, and when an alarming refugee exodus and ecological crisis threaten the balance and very survival of God's creation—there is an urgent call and need for a common and collaborative solution to the problems that divide us. And the meeting between Bartholomew and Francis in Jerusalem was a sign that this was possible.

Almost two years later, in April 2016, in a joint effort to highlight the plight of refugees fleeing from the Middle East, northern Africa, and Central Asia, while also spotlighting the deplorable response—and inhumane rejection—to the humanitarian crisis on the part of the European Union and others, Patriarch Bartholomew convinced Pope Francis to visit the Greek island of Lesbos together—accompanied by Archbishop Ieronymos of Athens and All Greece—in order to stand where hundreds of thousands risked their lives in search of safety and in the hope of a better life.

"The world will be judged by the way it has treated you," the patriarch said to hundreds of refugees gathered in the detention camp. His words were quoted in the *New York Times* on April 16, 2016. "And we will all be accountable for the way we respond to the crisis and conflict in the regions that you come from. The Mediterranean Sea should not be a tomb. We assure you that we will do everything to open the eyes and hearts of the world."

The Dialogue of Love

The meeting in Jerusalem fifty years earlier marked the beginning of what Metropolitan Meliton of Chalcedon would coin as "the dialogue of love"—namely, the critical process of gradually softening relations and breaking down barriers created over centuries between the two churches. On November 21 of that year, the papal encyclical *Unitatis Redintegratio* declared Christian unity as "one of the principal concerns" of the Second Vatican Council and divisions among Christian churches as "clearly contrary to Christ's will."

The noise had not yet subsided from the momentous events of 1964 when, on December 7, 1965, another dramatic step occurred. Through their respective channels—a synodal decision in Constantinople and a papal proclamation in Rome—the two churches lifted the excommunications of separation dating from the tragic events of 1054. A common declaration between Pope Paul VI and Ecumenical Patriarch Athenagoras . . .

> condemned to oblivion and expressed regret and the desire to remove from memory and from the midst of the Church the sentences of excommunication . . . the remembrance of which acts right up to our own times as an obstacle to our mutual approach in charity.

At the time, cynical observers described the event as purely protocol gestures, while conservative circles feared that sentimentalism might trump doctrine. Neither was the case. At a conference held in Vienna in 1974, the then professor Joseph Ratzinger (who later became Pope Benedict XVI) emphasized the canonical validity and theological gravity of the eleventh-century excommunications that invariably resulted in tragic ramifications for the entire church.

There was also much historical confusion over the legitimate validity of the eleventh-century condemnations. For instance, it is curious that there was no discussion at the important union councils of reunion at Lyons in 1274 or Ferrara-Florence in 1438–1439 about what had actually transpired in 1054. Nonetheless, the mutual and progressive estrangement between Eastern and Western Christianity had deep roots in the religious culture of both worlds that developed over centuries—emerging long before 1054, while evolving into growing prejudice and misunderstanding; it was this alienation that caused both sides to accept the finality and irrevocability of the condemnations in 1054. Of course, the animosity and wrongdoing of Eastern Christians notwithstanding—for instance, calling to mind the discrimination against and decimation of Latins by Greeks in Constantinople at the end of the twelfth century—the pope-sanctioned Crusades and the election of a Latin patriarch in the same city at the outset of the thirteenth century certainly did not help. Thus, through the centuries, the two churches somehow lost their bearings and priorities with regard to dialogue and communion.

It is of course true that the "lifting of the anathemas" in 1965 could not—whether magically or mechanically—lay aside the differences between the two churches, nor could it reestablish sacramental communion between them. But it removed an embarrassing milestone that had been an obstacle for any genuine rapprochement and reconciliation. Indeed, beyond the reminiscence of a specific instance and incident in 1054, the anathemas were also symbolic of what is viewed today by scholars as mutual misconduct that should weigh heavily on the historical conscience of both sides. While the lifting of the anathemas could not resolve theological differences, it did pave the way for more positive and constructive relations between them. In this regard, it also prepared the ground for sincere and serious theological discussions on established, perhaps somewhat esoteric, disputes such as the procession of the Holy Spirit—whether from the Father alone, as in the original version of the fourth-century creed still recited by the Orthodox, or from both the Father and the Son (*filioque*: the addition of the words "and the Son") professed by the Roman Catholic—as well as the infallibility and primacy of the pope, all of which the East regarded as arbitrary, if evolutionary, developments.

Bartholomew remembers being privileged to attend the historical occasion of the lifting of the anathemas:

> I was still a student, a deacon. Archbishop Iakovos was there as head of the patriarchal delegation. Of course, I would always be vested formally, wearing my clerical hat. But on that day, Fr. Maximos Aghiorgoussis from America [later Metropolitan Maximos of Pittsburgh] was stressing about visiting the Vatican and forgot his hat. So he asked to borrow mine. As a result, in the official photographs, I am not wearing any hat. Metropolitan Meliton asked where my hat was and I told him. He retorted: "No wonder you look like a janitor!"

Bartholomew coedited the official volume entitled *Tomos Agapis: Vatican-Phanar (1958–1970)*, containing the original communications and official correspondence between the Vatican and the Phanar through this period. In fact, Bartholomew conceived the title of the book, which means "Volume of Charity" and which he borrowed from a phrase that he liked from Dositheos, an eighteenth-century theologian and patriarch of Jerusalem.

The Return of Relics

There were other important consequences to this reconciliatory approach. One such sign of restored relations was the return of relics of a number of saints by the Roman Catholic Church to the Orthodox Church. This was a significant, albeit sensitive, matter in relations between the two churches, especially since relics are an integral part of Orthodox liturgy and spirituality. Sacred relics underline the fullness of transfiguration of all creation—material and animal, human and environmental—by divine grace as well as serve as a reminder that the whole of humankind and the whole cosmos were fashioned by a loving God. As such, relics have been preserved and venerated by Orthodox faithful through the centuries—evidence of such popular reverence dates back to at least the middle of the second century—and are especially treasured and respected during times of trial.

Unfortunately, largely as a result of the looting of Jerusalem and Constantinople by crusaders from the eleventh through the thirteenth centuries—but also due to fraudulent exploitation and general superstition in the Middle Ages—numerous relics of highly revered saints had found their way to Rome. Returning these relics would serve as a concrete expression of remorse for wrongful acts of the past and respect for renewed relations in the present. Restoring such sacred items to their "rightful" or "original" owner would be a weighty and worthy step of good faith.

Thus, for example, in the mid-1960s, Pope Paul VI returned the sacred relics of Saint Andrew to the Church of Greece—where the disciple of Christ is said to have undergone martyrdom in the Peloponnesian city of Patras—just as he returned the relics of the evangelist Saint Mark to the Coptic Church in Egypt. (While the Copts are Oriental Orthodox, the act was seen as part of the general restoration of relations between Eastern and Western Christianity.) There have also been other similar and subsequent gestures of repentance and reconciliation, notably with the return of the relics of Saint Titus to the Church of Crete, where the disciple of Saint Paul had served as bishop in apostolic times.

However, it was Bartholomew who secured the most spectacular return of relics to the Church of Constantinople. In November 2004, remains of the two most renowned archbishops of Constantinople—Saint Gregory the Theologian (329–389) and Saint John Chrysostom (347–407)—were solemnly restored to the Ecumenical Patriarchate. Gregory was a remarkable poet and mystic; John was a fiery preacher and ascetic. Both served as archbishops of the capital of Byzantium, even before the See of Constantinople had exclusively adopted the title "ecumenical patriarch" in the sixth century.

The relics of these archbishops were formerly treasured in the Church of the Holy Apostles in Constantinople, where they lay side by side from the tenth century until the time of the Crusades. At some point during the early thirteenth century, the relics of the two saints were "relocated" to Rome by way of Venice, leaving a dour and deep wound in the memory of Orthodox Christians. Saint John Chrysostom's relics were placed inside St. Peter's at the Vatican; Saint Gregory the Theologian's were originally preserved in the convent of St. Maria in Campo Santo but later transferred to a side chapel—subsequently known as the Capella Gregoriana—in St. Peter's.

The relics of both saints remained in Rome until June 29, 2004, when Ecumenical Patriarch Bartholomew visited the Vatican. The particular occasion marked the fortieth anniversary since the "dialogue of love" was established in Jerusalem in 1964, as well as the eight-hundredth anniversary since the Fourth Crusade in 1204. In his address, Pope John Paul II officially apologized for the tragic events of the Fourth Crusade that sacked Constantinople, looting its invaluable spiritual and cultural treasures. In turn, Patriarch Bartholomew responded that no material compensation could possibly be appropriate after so many centuries, but the rightful return of the sacred relics of the two archbishops of Constantinople would certainly constitute "a tangible gesture of the acknowledgment of past errors, a moral restoration of the spiritual legacy of the East, and a significant step in the process of reconciliation."

Bartholomew was already acquainted with Pope John Paul II. He first met him at the Phanar, when the pope visited Patriarch Demetrios in 1979. Moreover, as patriarch, after formally traveling to the Orthodox patriarchates according to the tradition of "irenic visits," in 1995 he addressed an official letter, requesting to meet with the pope. Pope John Paul II received the patriarch very warmly, hosting him in the medieval St. John's Tower overlooking the Vatican Gardens. The patriarch remembers Pope John Paul II as a handsome, athletic man: "It was tragic to witness his health declining toward the end of his life."

Bartholomew's request regarding the return of the relics still came somewhat as a surprise to the Vatican; no one had really confirmed the existence of the relics in the chapels dedicated in their honor inside St. Peter's. Not long afterward, however,

Cardinal Walter Kasper, then president of the Pontifical Council for Promoting Christian Unity and cochairman of the official theological dialogue between the two churches, addressed a letter to the patriarch on July 15, 2004, confirming that the relics were indeed in St. Peter's, though the decision to return them was a papal prerogative.

On July 21, 2004, having secured the support and decision of his own synod, Bartholomew officially appealed "for the return of the Holy Relics of St. Gregory the Theologian and St. John Chrysostom to the Church of Constantinople, where they morally belong." On October 27, Pope John Paul II responded to the ecumenical patriarch, accepting the patriarch's request and stating that "the return of the relics to their home country . . . will become a new bridge between us."

Later in the same year Bartholomew returned to Rome in order to accompany the relics of his venerable predecessors to Istanbul on November 27, 2004, following a service of presentation and ceremony of procession led in person by Pope John Paul II at St. Peter's in Rome. Two cardinals accompanied the patriarch, who escorted the relics back to their home. It was one of the final and finest charitable acts—arguably the most memorable ecumenical gestures—by the elderly and frail pontiff.

Once in Istanbul, the saintly relics were respectfully escorted in a long motorcade from the airport to the Patriarchal Church of St. George. In accordance with ancient tradition and protocol—a practice whereby the ecumenical patriarch symbolically defers to the saints by reserving the throne in their honor—the crystal cases containing the relics of Saint John Chrysostom and Saint

Gregory the Theologian were prominently "seated" upon the patriarchal throne, while the patriarch himself sat on the side throne (*parathrónion*).

The return of relics is more than a purely spiritual milestone of historical importance; for the Orthodox Church, it is a liturgical event of great significance. There is even a new feast of "the translation of the relics" of the two saints, henceforth commemorated on November 30, which was the official date of their reinstallation and coincides with the patron feast of the Church of Constantinople, the Feast of Saint Andrew, the "First-called of the Apostles."

But for the patriarch, there is another, more personal reason for gratitude and gratification in securing the sacred relics of his bygone predecessors. Saint Gregory had presided over the Second Ecumenical Council in 381—it was this council that articulated the theology of the Holy Spirit and complemented the articles of the Nicene-Constantinopolitan Creed. How could Bartholomew not feel a connection with Saint Gregory the Theologian, who had undergone setbacks and trials to convene a council in the fourth century, just as he himself was hoping to convene in the modern era? And how could Bartholomew not seek the prayers of Saint John Chrysostom, who was often misunderstood and maligned, ultimately even exiled from the imperial city, just as his twentieth-century successor would himself frequently be called a "traitor" and even a "heretic" for engaging in a dialogue of love and a dialogue of truth?

In some ways, the return of the relics is a continuation or extension of the dialogue of love initiated by Athenagoras and Paul VI. But in other ways, it is the completion or consummation of this dialogue inasmuch as it is a material expression and tangible affirmation of the commitment on the part of both churches to reconciliation. If they could not yet be united in the same doctrine or share the same cup of communion at the altar in the present, they could at least kneel together in repentance and reparation for the wrongdoings of their respective churches in the past.

The Dialogue of Truth

It is in the same spirit of reconciliation and love as a prelude to dialogue and truth that the two churches established the custom of attending one another's patron feasts. Thus, without interruption since 1969, the two churches have exchanged formal annual delegations—in Rome on June 29 for the Feast of Saints Peter and Paul and in Istanbul on November 30 for the Feast of Saint Andrew the Apostle. Usually high-level bishops are assigned to lead this delegation. Even when Patriarch Bartholomew visited Rome on June 29, 2004, to request the relics of his predecessors, he was, in fact, there for the Feast of Saint Peter.

Thus, the return of relics may well be the culmination of the "dialogue of love," but it is infinitely uncomplicated and unchallenging when compared to the monumental task of restoring a common mind or understanding between the Roman Catholic and Orthodox Churches. When Patriarch Athenagoras and Pope Paul VI met in Jerusalem, they were fully aware of the long road that lay ahead. After the public dialogue had been broadcast throughout the world, few people realized that the microphones were not switched off. The transcription of the day's proceedings includes remarks by the pope seemingly oblivious to the fact that his voice could be heard: "It will take a long time to digest what my soul has received. I want to assure you at this moment of the absolute loyalty, with which I will henceforth relate to you."

The patriarch replied: "I will do exactly the same."

The way toward unity is long and fraught with difficulties. Nevertheless, this road inclines toward reconciliation and converges in the sources of the gospel. Both leaders recognized that they were faced with "a difficult task because of people's mentality and psychology," while pledging not to allow "questions of prestige and primacy, or matters related to discipline, honor, privilege, and ambition" to interfere with their goal "to discern the truth," but rather "to cherish the church." The meeting of the pope and the patriarch was a double reminder and a timely call: of the fact of separation and of the task of unity.

Only a few years later, in 1967, Pope Paul VI and Patriarch Athenagoras also met in Rome and Constantinople. Their sentiment was that theological dialogue was necessary and that the "lifting of the anathemas" made such dialogue possible. An international dialogue was important and imperative. Almost immediately after the lifting of the anathemas in 1965, a dialogue between Orthodox and Roman Catholic theologians began in North America; on the Orthodox side, it was Archbishop Iakovos, then chairman of the Standing Committee of Canonical Orthodox Bishops in the Americas, who assumed a leadership role. This was perhaps the first time in history that Orthodox and Roman Catholic theologians were engaging in official discussion of common theological issues since the Council of Florence in the fifteenth century. The North American consultation is the longest-standing theological dialogue between Orthodox and Roman Catholics in the world.

On the tenth anniversary of the lifting of the anathemas, Pope Paul VI and Patriarch Demetrios began to plan the international theological dialogue. In 1976, a commission was established to assess the possibility of theological dialogue between the Holy See and the fourteen autocephalous Orthodox churches; in 1978, an agenda of items for discussion at the dialogue was determined; and in November 1979, during the papal visit to Constantinople, Pope John Paul II announced with Patriarch Demetrios the creation of the Joint International Commission for Theological Dialogue between the Roman Catholic Church and the Orthodox Church.

Thus began the official theological "dialogue of truth" on May 29, 1980, during the tenure of the late Ecumenical Patriarch Demetrios and Pope John Paul II. It was to be "a dialogue on an equal footing," a process for examining jointly, diligently, and openly the doctrinal differences between the two sister churches. Behind the scenes—which "yéro-Meliton" continued to orchestrate—Bartholomew proved instrumental in paving the way for this ambitious and landmark initiative. Ever empowering and encouraging the finest theologians of the Ecumenical Patriarchate, he marshaled the erudition and expertise of Archbishop Stylianos [Harkianakis] of Australia, now senior Metropolitan John [Zizioulas] of Pergamon, and Metropolitan Kallistos [Ware] of Diokleia; the latter two of these distinguished bishop-theologians were also prominently involved in the Orthodox-Anglican dialogue.

The initial sessions of the theological dialogue went well. But by the time Bartholomew was elected ecumenical patriarch in late 1991, the process was slowing down. Moreover, in 1992, with communism collapsing in eastern Europe and the fall of the Soviet Union, Eastern

Catholic (so-called Uniate) churches had reemerged in the region, especially in Ukraine, after decades of suppression. Accordingly, a statement issued by the Joint Theological Commission at Balamand, Lebanon, entitled "Uniatism, Method of Union of the Past, and the Present Search for Full Communion," received a very mixed and less-than-enthusiastic reception. The Orthodox Church of Greece condemned the document, as did the monastic community on Mount Athos. The dialogue had reached an impasse. Knowing how much the two churches shared, Bartholomew worked intensively to resuscitate, restore, and resume the international dialogue with the Roman Catholic Church.

Thus, on June 29, 1995—again in Rome for the Feast of Saints Peter and Paul—Bartholomew signed a common declaration with Pope John Paul II affirming the importance of dialogue on all levels between the two churches, while only two weeks later, on July 13–14, 1995, at the invitation of the patriarch, the Joint Theological Commission met at the Phanar. Finding solid or sufficient common ground on the question of Uniatism was difficult. Even a new document, titled "Canonical and Ecclesiological Consequences of Uniatism," could not break the impasse. This would literally require another ten years of behind-the-scenes work.

Continuing the vision of his predecessors, Patriarchs Athenagoras and Demetrios, Bartholomew insisted on restoring dialogue between the two churches, no matter how challenging the obstacles. The fact that the joint commission was able to return to its theological agenda and make new progress after 2006 was due in no small part to the personal and persistent efforts of the patriarch, who revived the dialogue together with Pope Benedict XVI. In the face of strong objection, even opposition from some quarters, Bartholomew was able to forge an Orthodox consensus regarding the continuation of dialogue, while greatly increasing official participation by the individual Orthodox churches. Ever the spokesman for the Orthodox point of view on divisive questions, the patriarch remains an ardent advocate of dialogue as the only path toward greater respect for and understanding of one another's teaching and traditions and, at least in the case of the Roman Catholic Church, the possibility of reconciliation and restoration of full communion.

Upon the election and inauguration of Pope Benedict XVI in April 2005, Bartholomew invited the new pope to the Phanar; Benedict was eager to come, though his trip was delayed by Ankara, claiming that, as a head of state, the pope could only come to Turkey at the invitation of the government. When Turkey finally extended a formal invitation through President Abdullah Gül, the pope specifically asked to be there at the end of November in order to attend the patronal Feast of the Ecumenical Patriarchate, as he had promised the patriarch. Eighteen months later, Pope Benedict honored Bartholomew's invitation as well as his own pledge to visit the Phanar.

Just two years later, in October 2008, Benedict invited Bartholomew to deliver a formal lecture—titled "The Word of God in the Life and Mission of the Church"—to more than four hundred cardinals and bishops during the Twelfth General Ordinary Assembly of the Synod of Bishops of the Roman Catholic Church in the Sistine Chapel. There were several similar occasions and anniversaries—interfaith peace summits in 2002, 2007, and 2011; the opening of the Year of Saint Paul in 2009; the celebration of fifty years since the Second Vatican Council in 2012; and others.

Bartholomew has visited the Vatican more than a dozen times during his tenure.

So it was through the seeds of this friendship between Bartholomew and Benedict that, in 2006, the dialogue between the two churches finally recommenced in Belgrade, Serbia. All fourteen autocephalous Orthodox churches sent their representatives. The original agenda from 1978 was readopted, though a new document would be released in 2007, "Ecclesiological and Canonical Consequences of the Sacramental Nature of the Church: Ecclesial Communion, Conciliarity, and Authority." The text is better known for the site of its issue, Ravenna, Italy. The Ravenna Document raised many issues, but the most significant among these was the role of primacy in the church. Of course the Ravenna Document should be read in light of Roman Catholic–Orthodox relations. As a result, the document reveals a major new development in Roman Catholic as well as Orthodox thinking about the primacy of Rome, a long-standing sticking point in the relationship between the two churches as well as among the Orthodox themselves. What would recognition of Rome—traditionally first in the historic pentarchy—mean for the ranking of other churches? And what did recognition of a universal primacy mean for the Orthodox churches in the absence of Rome? Thus, within Orthodoxy the document was used to allege that Bartholomew was attempting to establish a "papal-like" primacy over the Orthodox Church. Wasn't primacy an anathema to the Orthodox Church that based its governance on conciliarity? Some Orthodox seemed all too quick to review primacy in the Roman Catholic Church but all too hesitant to reflect on how primacy might shape their own ecclesiology. The Ravenna Document was deeply, perhaps deliberately, misunderstood on the Orthodox side. These vital issues of primacy and conciliarity raised many questions.

Primacy and Conciliarity

In a sermon delivered at St. Peter's Basilica in Rome on June 29, 1997, Bartholomew spoke with the same openness that is characteristic of his ministry, addressing Pope John Paul II about the need for "a primacy of service" during a homily self-described as "a confession of the heart":

Fortunately—with God's assistance, albeit through numerous afflictions and humiliations—today we have reached the maturity of true apostolic awareness that seeks *primacy not so much among specific persons, but rather among ministries of service.* And we know how many urgent ministries of service confront us in the world at every moment, at least if we are truly concerned not with "being admired by men" but with "being pleasing to God." Today, we learn once again that the principal and queen of Christian virtues, the only virtue that can truly transform and save the world, is humility coupled with repentance. . . .

Great humility and constant repentance are necessary for pastors and flock alike. . . .

Your Holiness . . . may we also be permitted to declare in truth that, only when *the primacy of a kenotic ethos* prevails convincingly in the historical church will we not only be able to re-establish our deeply desired unity in faith, but also to render ourselves immediately worthy of experiencing all that God's revelation has promised to those who love the Lord: "a new heaven and a new earth."

So Bartholomew knows and acknowledges how primacy is perceived and practiced in the church. But is there a functional—and actual—primacy in the Orthodox Church? Or is this merely a manifestation of the Roman Catholic Church?

In the history of the church, there were never primates without synods; nor again were there synods without primates. However, the concept of primacy should not be connected or confused with the way it was normally perceived in the West, with the development of the papal primacy. Even in the Eastern Church, primacy constitutes an inherent and indispensable part of ecclesiology: there is always need of a "first" (*prótos*) in order to preserve and protect the order or structure of the church. In this regard, primacy is intrinsic and indispensable on all levels of ecclesiastical life: local, regional, and universal.

Even the fundamental and essential task of convening—or, indeed, enforcing—a council implies and involves the presence of a universal primate. Frequently, the argument is proposed that the early councils were convened and enforced by the emperor, that councils of bishops were ultimately instruments of the secular empire. But surely primacy and conciliarity, just as unity and communion, are an exclusive privilege of the church and never solely an affair of the state.

At the same time, however, primacy does not imply that the primate is merely a spokesman—or, as one theologian put it, like the sovereign in a constitutional monarchy, who reigns without governing. It involves far more than just an honorific status; it incorporates official privileges and prerogatives. In fact, much more than simply a "primacy of honor," it might be called the "honor of primacy." It is an exceptional, albeit essential, authority that guarantees the unity of the church in faith, liturgy, and practice.

A Dialogue Bears Fruit

The relationship between Rome and Constantinople has borne considerable fruit over the years. There has been a return of relics. Perhaps more important, we have seen change within the two churches themselves. Within the Roman Church, we see a new stance on issues of papal primacy. While the pope has not abandoned older positions, we have seen new styles in actualizing them. Under Pope Francis, we have witnessed a conciliar approach to leadership—such as with the Council of Cardinal Advisors, the nine cardinals from around the world who counsel the pope on various matters. Whenever representatives of the two churches meet and recite the creed, it is done without the *filioque*. In 2014, Pope Francis suspended the practice of obligatory celibacy for Eastern Catholic clergy, on the rationale that celibacy is not according to the tradition of the Eastern Church. Orthodoxy, too, has taken several steps, without compromising a single theological position. Relationships between Orthodox and Roman Catholic bishops generally are positive, with regular exchanges and visits among them. Orthodox theologians have realized that the issue of primacy is not as simple as an East-West difference or disagreement. And Orthodox scholars have found welcome homes in many Roman Catholic universities and faculties around the world. The old animosities between the two churches continue to decline, even disappear.

Bartholomew's personal and profound knowledge of Roman Catholic texts and thought is important to this process. He is well acquainted with Roman Catholic theology, having studied in Rome; he can readily critique and comment on Roman Catholic documents and papal encyclicals, including the Catechism of the Catholic Church, released in 1993. He also has an extraordinary understanding and sober analysis of developments in other Christian communions, which he can discern through the lens of the historical past, the critical present, and the distant future.

OTHER COMMUNIONS AND COUNCILS OF CHURCHES

A New Era for a New World

The early twentieth century opened numerous new relationships among the various Christian communities. The Oxford Movement in the late-nineteenth century created a renewed appreciation for the writings of the church fathers. It also caused a particularly warm fellowship between Orthodox and Anglicans at the time. In the 1920s, the Fellowship of Saint Alban and Saint Sergius brought Orthodox and Western Christians together in Great Britain for the first time in centuries for common study and conversation. The formal dialogue—or "joint doctrinal discussions"—with the Anglican Communion commenced in Oxford, UK, in 1975. It has produced several agreed-upon statements on Scripture and the councils, but also on doctrine and church. It continues to make positive progress, especially on matters related to Christian anthropology—including ethics and personhood, as well as bioethics and the sanctity of life.

The patriarch reminded the primate of the Anglican Communion and archbishop of Canterbury, Dr. Rowan Williams, of this evolution during the latter's first official visit to the Phanar in 2003:

> It is, indeed, a remarkable gift of divine grace that there has never been any cause of conflict or bitterness between Anglicans and Orthodox in the course of history. Our relations have always been marked with mutual respect, while there have been occasions when the Anglican Church supported and assisted the Ecumenical Patriarchate during difficult times. We acknowledge this with deep appreciation. In the context of this long history of fraternal relations, our two churches have also engaged in official theological dialogue from as early as the nineteenth century, before the appearance of the ecumenical movement, of which they have been founders and supporters ever since.

Earlier patriarchal encyclicals of 1902 and 1920 had also paved the way for greater Orthodox involvement with the churches of the Reformation. In 1910, the World Missionary Conference took place in Edinburgh. In 1925, the World Conference on Life and Work in Stockholm renewed Christian efforts for peace and justice in the aftermath of the First World War. In 1927, a similar conference, Faith and Order, was held in Lausanne to discuss theological issues dividing Christians and to work for Christian unity. These were the first threads of what would later be known as the "ecumenical movement." They would lead to the eventual creation of a global fellowship of Christian communities, as called for in the Ecumenical Patriarchate's ingenious encyclical of 1920. That encyclical boldly called upon "the churches of Christ everywhere" to overcome dissension, obey the Lord's commandment to love one another, and work toward Christian unity. Earlier, in 1902, the Ecumenical Patriarchate had urged the Orthodox churches and its own faithful to renew communications and contacts with other Christian churches, especially the Roman Catholic, Anglican, and Protestant communions.

So while the initial stages of the ecumenical movement were largely a Protestant campaign, the Orthodox churches, nonetheless, soon became actively involved. The global depression and the Second World War required that these efforts be suspended somewhat. But after the war and the excitement about creating the United Nations, the idea of a global Christian body returned. In 1948, the World Council of Churches was formed, and the Ecumenical Patriarchate was among its first and founding members. One of the greatest Orthodox theologians of the twentieth century, Fr. Georges Florovsky, was convinced that the role of the Orthodox Church in the ecumenical movement was both decisive and definitive.

WCC Engagement and Experience

As Metropolitan of Philadelphia, Bartholomew was involved with the World Council of Church's Faith and Order Commission, where he represented the Ecumenical Patriarchate. This was a natural place for him to offer his considerable intellectual gifts to the study and conversation of theological issues. Such gatherings are "multilateral" discussions, with the fullest diversity of Christian communities and traditions at the table—from the larger mainline communions to the smaller Protestant confessions. Protestants and Orthodox are the main participants in most of the WCC's work;

Faith and Order is unique in that it includes Roman Catholics, who do not participate in other aspects of the WCC's life. This makes for a very engaging, albeit sometimes messy, conversation.

Yet Bartholomew served during a very exciting period for the WCC and Faith and Order. The document "Baptism, Eucharist, and Ministry" (BEM), also known as the Lima Document—finally adopted in Lima, Peru, in 1982—was being composed and revised. During this process, many Christian communions from across the spectrum of theological positions for the first time were exposed to and understood the nature of baptism, the place of the Eucharist, and the role of the priesthood. The document explores areas of convergence and divergence among the Christian communions. At meeting after meeting, Christians strove to build new bridges and discover common ground.

Bartholomew also shaped the future direction of Faith and Order, encouraging the commission to concentrate its attention on "the apostolic faith" and center its study on the role of the Nicene-Constantinopolitan Creed in the Christian Church. Formulated at the First Ecumenical Council of 325 in Nicaea and then amended at the Second Council in 381 in Constantinople, this creed had been recited by Orthodox and Roman Catholic Christians for centuries. For the Orthodox, it is the preeminent statement of doctrine, the essential symbol of faith. But in some Protestant churches there are no creeds, or else there is only an occasional use of one of many briefer creeds, such as the Apostles' Creed, which probably dates after the Nicene-Constantinopolitan Creed. However, all Christians claim—in one way or another—to be faithful to the apostolic faith. So Faith and Order undertook a study entitled

"Towards a Common Expression of the Apostolic Faith Today."
Bartholomew participated in the early stages of this work, until his
election as ecumenical patriarch.

Ecumenical participation, especially through the World
Council of Churches and Faith and Order, involves a great
deal of travel. The diverse locations and the diversity of delegates broaden the perspectives of participants. The witness of
Christian faith and life among individuals and within communities challenges personal assumptions about other Christian
confessions. The experience of common study, shared meals, and
parish visits renders it increasingly difficult to stereotype those
belonging to a different faith community. It is much harder to
call someone a "heretic" or "apostate" after learning about his
life, sharing family photos, and understanding his joys and sor-
rows while witnessing his faithfulness to the way of the gospel,
especially amid extreme poverty or persecution. Even the meeting venues can challenge one's presumptions or prejudices.

No doubt these experiences influenced Bartholomew and
increased the fervor with which he seeks genuine fellowship
and visible unity for Christians. His commitment to dialogue
and contact with organizations such as the World Council of
Churches and the Conference of European Churches—as well as
other international inter-Christian organizations and ecumenical bodies—are evident from the First Synaxis of Primates (an
assembly of the heads of all the fourteen independent Orthodox
churches), which he convened just weeks after his election and
enthronement as ecumenical patriarch. The message of that historic meeting declared:

Moved by the spirit of reconciliation, the Orthodox Church has participated actively for many decades in the effort to restore Christian unity, which constitutes the express and inviolable command of the Lord (John 17:21). The participation of the Orthodox Church as a whole in the World Council of Churches aims precisely at this.

In Pursuit of Unity

Bartholomew has offered his vision for visible unity among Christians to many and various Protestant audiences. In an address at Westminster Abbey in December 1995, he outlined the contours of this vision. For him, visible unity is conceived in theological, biblical, and spiritual perspective as the great gift that Jesus Christ desires for and the Holy Spirit grants to the entire church. "Division is dishonorable to God and shameful to us," he said. As an antidote, Bartholomew pointed to the unity within the Orthodox Church as a model for all Christians to consider, stating:

> The subsisting unbroken internal unity of the Orthodox churches in different places offers a promising ecumenical perspective. . . . Our hope flows from the firm conviction that Orthodoxy, adhering to the witness of the one, undivided, church of the apostles, the fathers, and the ecumenical councils, shows the way not to the past but to the future.

What is significant about this statement is not that it promotes Orthodox unity in a triumphant manner—in the next chapter, we shall see that Bartholomew was first to censure the Orthodox themselves for their sanctimonious profession of unity—but that he shuts the door to any caricature of Christian unity as sweepingly blending all Christian teachings into one or as superficially rendering everyone uniform. Dialogue and reconciliation do not imply parity among denominations or unity as confessional adjustment. Nor again do they entail acquiescence to doctrinal relativism or resignation to denominational minimalism.

But the path to Christian unity has been neither peaceful nor painless. On the occasion of the sixtieth anniversary of the World Council of Churches, in the first decade of the third millennium, ecumenical agents and their respective agencies were under severe stress—there were budget reductions, organizational restructuring, and institutional downsizing. Some spoke of an "ecumenical winter"; no issue seemed to raise much enthusiasm or interest. People appeared less concerned about visible unity and instead emphasized common action. The World Council of Churches had grown to more than 350 communions and confessions, from more than one hundred countries, incorporating more than 550 million faithful. It was under this overwhelming and ominous cloud that Bartholomew was invited to address the World Council of Churches for its official sixtieth anniversary celebration in 2008 at Geneva's St. Pierre Cathedral. He reminded his audience of their central mission: unity.

It is a task that still remains difficult to fulfill. But the bonds of friendship among divided churches and the bridges by which we can overcome our divisions are indispensable, now more than ever. Love is essential, so that dialogue between our churches can occur in all freedom and trust. Then, we will acknowledge that the divergences originating from different ways in which churches respond to moral problems are not necessarily insurmountable, since churches witness to the gospel in different contexts. We will also recognize that dialogue on ethical and moral questions should proceed on the assumption that churches are not content to "agree to disagree" on moral teaching but that they are prepared to confront their divergences honestly, examining them in the light of doctrine, worship, and holy Scripture. Let us, therefore, proceed with hope along the path that we have trodden.

A Breath of Fresh Air

This is why—in addition to the formal dialogues with the Roman Catholic Church and the Anglican Communion, as well as its presence and participation in the World Council of Churches—the Ecumenical Patriarchate has persistently pursued dialogue with other mainstream churches and confessions. Indeed, the reinforcement of dialogue with these and the fostering of dialogue with other Christian confessions was yet another initiative envisioned and encouraged from as early as the Fourth Pan-Orthodox Conference at Chambésy, Geneva, in 1968. In some ways, it's much like opening up the church windows for fresh air. For example, the dialogue with the Lutheran World Federation began in 1981—though some claim that this dialogue dates to the sixteenth century, when Ecumenical Patriarch Jeremiah II exchanged correspondence with theologians at Tübingen. Like the dialogue with the Roman Catholics and Anglicans, the dialogue with the Lutherans is ongoing and regular.

Other dialogues have started and come to a standstill, or else started and nearly concluded. For instance, the dialogue with the Old Catholic Church (or the Union of Utrecht) commenced in the 1960s and continued through the 1980s, progressing relatively quickly—with numerous agreements signed and hopes expressed for a possible reconciliation in the near future. Unfortunately, for various reasons and diverging developments in the Old Catholic Church, this did not ultimately come to fruition, and the dialogue stopped in the 1990s. Likewise, the dialogue with the World Alliance of Reformed Churches completed its first phase of conversations and awaits a new expression following the merging of the World Alliance of Reformed Churches and the World Reformed Council. Other requests for dialogue were also explored, with varied results, by the Ecumenical Patriarchate—less formally or bilaterally, rather than as official, multilateral, and international dialogues with the Orthodox churches as a whole—with the Baptists, Methodists, Seventh-day Adventists, Pentecostals, and the Evangelical Church in Germany.

Arguably the closest family to the Orthodox Church includes the pre-Chalcedonian churches, sometimes also called the Ancient Oriental churches. This dialogue began informally in the 1960s and formally in the 1980s, grinding to a standstill in the 1990s—although, once again, there were fervent hopes of possible union. These ancient churches include a group of seven communions, such as the Copts, Armenians, Syro-Jacobites, and Malankara Orthodox. Unfortunately, geopolitical developments in the regions where these ancient churches struggle and survive— Egypt, Syria, Armenia, and India—as well as complications pertaining to the coordination of the communions involved, have all but frozen the official conversations. However, the ecumenical patriarch is keen to revive this dialogue.

Speaking the Truth in Love

At the same time, as already hinted, Bartholomew is swift and stern in his censure of his own sister Orthodox churches. For instance, at the Sixth Synaxis of Primates in January 2016, the patriarch replied to criticism by certain of his brother hierarchs against the un-Christian attitudes that characterize Europe and America, observing that "it is easy complacently and conveniently to condemn the West as sinking in sin," but, he added, "we must be more honest with ourselves and our faithful to admit that our own cultures and regions are not exactly basking in holiness."

The patriarch knows that any kind of "piecemeal" truth ultimately idolizes the formalism of dogmas and canons. The church is neither a sect nor a denomination. It is the one, holy, catholic, and apostolic church. And this is precisely what defines and prescribes the parameters of ecumenical dialogue. Moreover, this is exactly what affirms and accentuates the solemn responsibility of the Orthodox Church to bear witness to the gospel truth in the world. The church is concerned with the whole truth about the whole of humanity within the whole created cosmos—to the last speck of dust. And when a church lays claims to the fullness of truth, then its obligation to enter into dialogue and collaboration with all other Christian denominations in a spirit of love, humility, and service is also greater. If Orthodox Christians ignore or condemn the life and beliefs of other Christians or other churches, then not only will their understanding be deficient and defective, but their vocation and responsibility to Christ and his gospel will be found to be untruthful and unfaithful.

The patriarch is convinced—heart, mind, and soul—that to "remain indifferent about the unity of all Christians . . . would constitute crude betrayal and criminal transgression of our Lord's divine commandment that his disciples may be one." Are we first of all open to dialogue with others? Or do we begin with a closed-heart policy? It's as simple as that.

Rabbi David Rosen, KSG, CBE

International Director of Interreligious Affairs, American Jewish Committee

THE THIRD VERSE OF THE FIRST PSALM DESCRIBES THE RIGHTEOUS paragon with the image of a luxuriant tree with deep roots planted by the streams of waters, "that brings forth its fruit in its season, / whose leaf also shall not wither; / and whatever he does shall prosper."

There is an understandable but regrettable tendency among those who are deeply rooted in a religious tradition to be insular and exclusive in their world outlook. While on the other hand, all too often those who are more open to engagement with those different from themselves reflect a superficiality lacking substance.

However, the ideal as reflected in the above biblical image is of one profoundly rooted within his own heritage and yet whose branches reach out as widely as possible, providing fruit for all. Such is the blessing, intellectual and spiritual, that His All-Holiness Patriarch Bartholomew brings both to his own community and also to the world at large.

From the outset of his patriarchate, he has advanced inter-religious dialogue, especially within the Abrahamic family, but also beyond it, expressing his recognition that the Divine Presence is to be found within the diversity of human religious experience.

Indeed, his leadership in the environmental movement, long before it became fashionable, is a reflection of his sincere and genuine care for the cosmos as a whole. Particularly important has been his commitment to combatting the terrible abuse of religion and striving to ensure that it be the force for good that is its purpose.

Time and again he has declared that "war in the name of religion is war against religion;" and as has been noted by Archbishop Demetrios of America, "Patriarch Bartholomew has been at the forefront of organizing international inter-religious conferences to confront the evils of religious fanaticism and intolerance."

At the gathering of religious leaders from the Jewish, Christian, and Muslim communities that he convened in Brussels in the wake of the September 11, 2001, attacks, His All-Holiness declared: "We do not consider it necessary to have (religious) differences extinguished in order to achieve social peace. We respect our fellow human beings and their convictions, and it is exactly on this basis that we engage in dialogue and peaceful cooperation with them."

Patriarch Bartholomew accordingly serves as an inspiring example not only for his own flock and faith, but indeed for all religious communities and for all of society—a model and inspiration for which we give thanks to the One Creator and Guide of the universe.

CHAPTER 3

From Imvros to Istanbul

Childhood, Education, Ordination

Imvros is my home, my heart, and my memory.
—Ecumenical Patriarch Bartholomew, interview, 2016

It Really Does Take a Village

He is a leapling, born on February 29, 1940, virtually at the beginning of World War II, in the Republic of Turkey, which had been founded less than two decades earlier and managed to stay out of the war, without taking sides, until it joined the Allies in February 1945.

His name is Bartholomew. But he was born Demétrios; Bartholomew is his church name.

The year 2016 marked the seventy-sixth since he was born, the nineteenth celebration of his actual "leapling" birthday, the fifty-fifth year since entering the priesthood, and the twenty-fifth anniversary of his tenure as archbishop of Constantinople–New

Rome and ecumenical patriarch, leader of the worldwide Orthodox Christian Church.

His birthplace is a tiny, pristine village called Haghioi Theodoroi (Saints Theodores), one of six villages on the Aegean island of Imvros (İmroz or Gökçeada), just off the coast of Turkey, near the Dardanelles, the strait connecting the Aegean and the Sea of Marmara. The name Haghioi Theodoroi derives from two horse-riding military saints of the early church, Theodore Teron (the "recruit") and Theodore Stratelates (the "general")—always mentioned together because both appeared in a vision to a fourth-century patriarch warning him of contaminated Lenten food.

The village is nestled at the foot of Mount Kastrí—or Arasiá, as they call it. While looming large when Demetrios was growing up, the village, in fact, had only two churches (one dedicated to Saint George, the other to the Dormition of our Lady) and a primary school, narrow streets with many water fountains, six grocery stores, and five or six cafés. He remembers the stone houses as well as olive trees—lots of olive trees!—and almond trees marching up and over the mountainside, while also sprawling in backyards to give shade to the residents in the summer heat. At the time there were 800 to 850 residents, most of them farmers and shepherds; but there were also shoemakers, traders, builders, and carpenters. There were even a few beekeepers—their hives supplying the sweetness for pastries dripping with honey. And the village abounded in oil and cheese, as well as a little wool. It was—at least in the memory of young Demetrios—an idyllic setting in an idyllic time. Today the island is known for its fishing and tourism, but in those previous years there was far less fishing and certainly no tourism. In fact, it was a rarity for fish even to be available in the markets.

As a child, and even after trips to the sophisticated city of Istanbul, Demetrios thought the villagers were shrewd and sharp. Without a doubt they were hardy and tough, albeit healthy and robust from their rigorous and natural lifestyle. Many of them would spend entire months in their farmsteads on the other side of the island, tending sheep and crops, returning to the village only for the major festivals or cold winter months.

But it was the olives that were the gold currency—literally the fortune—of the village and of the entire island. There were even two oil presses. In the fall, Demetrios would enjoy going with his friends to the presses, carrying some warm bread to dip in the oil. The Turkish name for Saints Theodores is Zeytinliköy (or Zeitinli), which means "olive-tree village." Bartholomew recalls the women and men rising early to collect the olives—some reaching high on ladders, others sorting on the ground. They would break for lunch consisting of bread and cheese, olives, and sardines, then return home late, burdened with large canvas catching frames. The routine of collecting and returning home would be repeated every day, except Sundays, for two months.

In January, he says, the two oil presses would operate without interruption until the oil filled the barrels to the brim and its unmistakable fragrance filled the air. They would sell the oil in the spring so they could enjoy first-class coffee in the fall.

Overwhelmingly inhabited by Greeks from ancient times until around 1960, Imvros's original residents may have dwindled but never disappeared. In book 13 of *The Iliad*, Homer describes a cave in the deep seas between Imvros and Tenedos (its neighboring sister island) as the place where Poseidon kept his winged horses. In fact, the island features in *The Histories* of Herodotus and *The Peloponnesian War* of Thucydides. History records inhabitants on the island since at least the fifth century before the Christian era. In the golden age of Byzantium, as after the fall of Constantinople, islanders lived in relative peace and prosperity until the early twentieth century. I remember learning at school in Sydney, Australia, that ANZAC (Australian and New Zealand Army Corps) forces were based in nearby Gallipoli during the dark months of a campaign there in World War I (1915–1916).

According to the 1893 Ottoman census, the island had 9,456 residents, two hundred of which were official Turkish authorities and six Armenians; the rest were Greeks. Although the 1923 Treaty of Lausanne (Article 14) excluded its Greek residents from the population exchange of the time and permitted "non-Muslim" residents of the island to remain without disturbance or disruption, the Turkish government never really adhered to the provision for autonomous administration; and in 1927, Turkish civil law revoked the rights of the inhabitants of Imvros and Tenedos and closed schools. Hundreds of residents emigrated—some voluntarily, most forcibly—to Europe, America, and Australia. While census statistics of 1927 record almost seven thousand Greeks in Imvros and fewer than two hundred Turkish people, in the year 2000 the ratio was reversed: there were no more than a few hundred Greeks living year-round on the island and eight thousand Turks.

The pogrom of 1955 did not really affect the islanders, who were far away from the pressures and problems faced by the Greek communities in Istanbul. Bartholomew remembers hearing about the intimidation of Greeks in the city, but the repercussions were not felt on Imvros. In any case, he was far too young: "The island felt very distant from the city," he recalls. "We would hear the news of all that was happening on the mainland and certainly feel very sad about it; but because we were somewhat separated from it, we weren't directly affected and consequently weren't really afraid." He was on summer vacation at the time; he remembers writing to the high school at Halki to ask if classes would resume in the fall and then receiving a form letter in return, saying that it would reopen as scheduled. Kyra-Panagiotí, a woman just a few years older than the patriarch, lived a few doors away in the same village. She recalls being pregnant at the time: "It's funny what one remembers. For some reason, I remember the chapel of St. Demetrios was having its windows replaced. So, yes, we felt a little afraid; but, unlike elsewhere, we did not suffer persecution." Later, in 1964, Greek inhabitants on the island began to sense financial and emotional pressure, including the closure of the Greek schools that had reopened in 1952. The idyllic period of Demetrios's childhood was coming to an end.

But it was around the time of the Turkish invasion of Cyprus in 1974 that the Turkish government resettled thousands of Turkish citizens on the island, creating five new Turkish villages. Most Greeks then left Imvros and other places in Turkey in the early 1970s, which is also when the famous Theological School of Halki was forcibly closed.

Regrettably, only three hundred or so year-round Greek residents live on the island today; most young people have moved to the mainland cities or abroad. Well over fifteen thousand Greek Imvrians live overseas, although many of them continue to maintain strong ties with the island, returning regularly for vacations. In fact, every summer the island comes to life, offering its vacationers glimpses into a golden era of old. In September 2015, the first Greek secondary school, reconstructed from ruins, reopened its doors in the village of Panaghía, with just fourteen pupils, following the courageous example of a smaller primary school that had already opened the previous year with just a handful of pupils in the village of Haghioi Theodoroi. Much of this recent resurgence of Greek residents and institutions springs from the efforts—and personal visits—of the current ecumenical patriarch, Bartholomew. But what was it like for the patriarch before this "paradise was lost"?

Childhood Years

On May 8, 1940, Bartholomew was baptized Demétrios, the third of four children born to Chrístos and Merōpi Archondónis: Zakharō, the eldest and a girl; little Demétrios—or Dimitráki, as he was known—was the second of three boys, with Nikólaos (or Níkos) his senior and Andónios (or Andóni) his younger.

Of his four grandparents, Bartholomew only remembers his paternal grandfather (or *pappoú*) Demétrios, after whom the future patriarch was named to follow the Greek tradition of respecting one's roots and naming children after the grandparents. Pappoú Demétrios was a carpenter and basket weaver who died at the ripe age of one hundred.

His father was austere, though attentive; his mother was gentle, though firm. But somehow the children knew it was easier to put one past their unsuspecting, trusting mother. In order to make ends meet, young Demetrios's father operated the village café and also served as the local barber in the right corner by the entrance to the café that had a couch and a hanging mirror. His elder brother, Nikos, migrated for work to Australia, where today his son runs a popular café called Uncle Bart; the patriarch smirks: "They're exploiting the trade name!" His younger brother, Andonios, became a hairdresser in France; to this day, whenever the patriarch gets a haircut there, he jokes: "I tell him to put it on the tab. It's been over forty years now."

The family had a donkey, sometimes a horse, along with goats for milk and cheese, and a small garden for vegetables. Like everyone else, they had olive groves and some property; if any oil remained, it would be sold for secondary income.

His father worked very hard at the family store and as a barber. Like other men of his village, he had learned his trade from a young age, ironically on Mount Athos in Greece, the world-famous monastic center where the monks are known for their long hair and beards. During school holidays, the other children would help with the livestock and fields. But Demetrios mostly helped in the café— where he also acquired his social skills and delighted in reciting poetry for the regulars—keeping the fire burning, washing coffee cups, fetching fresh water, sweeping hair off the floor, and crossing the modest square to deposit trash in a small Dumpster.

His father's café mostly sold coffee and *rakí* (anise-flavored alcohol), as well as *vyssináda* (Morello cherry juice) and *lemonáda* (homemade lemon juice). They didn't have many sweets available; there was just some *loukoúmi* (Turkish delight). A budding and imaginative entrepreneur, Demetrios would sometimes slice the piece of *loukoúmi* into two and sprinkle icing sugar in order for it to look untouched. He still chuckles: "I knew how hard my dad used to work; I thought that I could perhaps make a little more money for him this way." But the patriarch still recalls his father's tirelessness: Christos Archondonis would never enjoy much sleep; he would be up early to light the fire and prepare coffee for the morning farmers.

The family of six managed to live "well" despite its limited resources and the town's lack of what today we might consider basic necessities, such as running water and electricity. Stretched between schoolwork, the café, and helping at the church, the young Demetrios still carried water from the fountain at a nearby spring and studied with a kerosene lamp; even when electricity came to the capital, "it was never on past midnight," he explains. It was at the same spring that families would gather to wash clothes in two large stone sinks that were carved in the ground. Bartholomew remembers how white the sheets and shirts would look as they hung to dry—the lye from finely sieved white ashes serving as the bleaching ingredient for "the whites." In order for Demetrios to bathe, his mother would burn wood beneath a stove and pour the heated water with a small casserole dish. The patriarch's brother was moved to tears when he remembered their mother's charity and courage. Though their family was relatively poor, every week their mother would take cigarettes and sweets sold in the family café and hand them out to inmates at the local prison.

On a few occasions during the summer, Demetrios would go swimming with his friends, but the mountain village was somewhat remote from the seaside, and transportation was sparse. (He has not been swimming since being elected patriarch.) In any case, there was a lot of work to be done planting and maintaining the fields in the spring and summer, while preparing for the olive harvest during the fall and winter months. The only people spending time at the seaside were a handful of fishermen and some sponge divers.

Demetrios's affinity to the church may have been "inherited" from his father's uncle, Photios, an archimandrite (celibate priest), and his mother's uncle, Joseph, also an archimandrite—in fact, a monk at Vatopedi Monastery on Mount Athos. His brother Andonios still remembers a bronze pitcher in the kitchen inscribed with Father Joseph's name. It was the same pitcher that young Demetrios would use to fetch water. So there was priestly blood in the family line.

However, during his elementary school years, Demetrios became attached to the village priest, Father Asterios, a simple but good and upright man, for whom he quickly developed into a companion, helping out at the altar or serving as cantor as required. Father Asterios was the village priest for forty years without interruption—performing his duties day in and out, come rain or snow, all summer and winter. He also baptized all of the Archondonis children and gifted Demetrios with the fabric to make his first set of vestments when he was ordained to the priesthood. His son, Father George, succeeded him, and his grandson, Father Asterios (named for his grandfather, of course), serves as the village priest today.

Sometimes after a liturgy with Father Asterios, the two would visit the family coffee shop of Demetrios's father; Father Asterios would look at his pocket watch and say: "Mr. Archondonis, bring us some coffee. Demetrios and I are exhausted," and then offer

Demetrios *vyssináda* and *loukoúmi*, while he enjoyed a coffee—and then perhaps a *rakí*.

Demetrios loved to visit the countless chapels scattered in the countryside; he knew each and every one of them—where they were and to whom they were dedicated. Years later Bartholomew would approach the local authorities to stop the desecration of a tiny seaside chapel that local Turks degraded by using it as an outhouse. The authorities complied.

He would also eagerly accompany Father Asterios for house blessings. Sometimes families would ask for the incredible commitment of conducting forty liturgies to be held over forty days in mountain chapels, as a kind of vow (*táma* in Greek) that combines prayer to Christ and a promise to a saint while appealing for assistance or guidance. Demetrios would light the *thurible* (censer) and often recite the epistle reading (that precedes the gospel reading by the priest). On most occasions, however, it would be only Father Asterios and Demetrios in the chapel, offering liturgies that lasted for ninety minutes or more; yet Father Asterios—in keeping strictly to proper procedure, and perhaps the hope that some parishioner might come—would always check his pocket watch before asking the young Demetrios to ring the bell letting the whole village know that the service was beginning.

He explored every hill and valley in the region. Some of the dozens of chapels were aloft on crags; Demetrios considered them as "eagle nests"—even the donkey carrying the church vessels would stop at a certain point when the mountain pathway became too rocky and rough, especially on Mount Arasiá, which towered over the village. But the indescribable view more than compensated for the prolonged and precarious climb. "Whenever I had—indeed, whenever I still have—the chance to return, I would love to hike the surrounding terrain. I worship that island," he says. In a small container in his office, he still cherishes some soil from a property where his parents built and tended a small chapel dedicated to Saint Marina.

The quiet services in the remote chapels contrasted with those on major holidays at the village church dedicated to the Theotokos (Mary, the Mother of God), where Demetrios would assist the village priest during school holidays and at its annual feast on August 22. When he was older, he would walk each day to the diocese to help the local metropolitan bishop; in fact, it was here, not in school, where he first learned to use a typewriter.

Demetrios considered his church and school, located close to each other at the northern fringe of the village, as twin guides, both of them looking after the formation of its entrusted pupils. The church looked out across a valley of olive groves; in the far distance, you could even distinguish the island's capital, Panaghía. The schoolhouse, built with a grant from a celebrated Imvrian, Kosta Eliades, had six rooms and a long, rectangular hall.

Every Monday morning, the pupils—about seventy-five of them when the patriarch was growing up—would line up to take off their shoes and socks for the teachers to inspect whether their feet were clean. Hair was kept short; if the teacher could pull your hair, then it was clearly too long. And every morning during the winter months, every pupil was expected to bring along some firewood for the heating stoves inside each classroom. During play or rest, they would stand and respectfully cross their arms as the priest walked by.

One corridor served as the school spine: As you entered, first grade was on the right while second and third grades were on the left. Farther along the corridor, there were another two rooms for fourth and fifth grades. The last room was for sixth grade, but also accommodated the headmaster's office and the teachers' common room. The school clock commanded the scene in the hall, together with photos of the school's founder and Mustafa Kemal Atatürk, founder of the Republic of Turkey.

The patriarch remembers the young headmaster walking the streets in casual attire, without a tie, though pretending to look prim and proper. His arithmetic teacher, however, was very strict, always carrying a walking stick made of a branch. And there was the Turkish teacher, an elderly woman who had also learned just enough Greek to get by. Every Thursday afternoon, all the pupils would head over to the church for religious classes. When Turkish authorities recently granted permission for community schools to reopen, Bartholomew restored the elementary school in his village, maintaining the exact footprint and design of the original structure—one straight corridor to show the way of learning and life.

His favorite teacher at school was Kostis Terzis, himself an Imvrian. Terzis lived at Panaghía and loved his educational vocation. He would walk for an hour each day, for years, despite weather conditions, to get to the village school at Haghioi Theodoroi from the island capital. "It's my obligation and responsibility," he would say. When he died, he was buried on the island of Lemnos, Greece, where as a bishop Bartholomew made a point of visiting his grave to perform a memorial service.

As for games, Bartholomew's brother told me that they would

play an equivalent of the French *petanque,* where one throws a hollow ball to see who comes the closest to a smaller ball in the distance. Demetrios and his brother used rocks and stones since owning a ball was a rare luxury. Leisure time was all about using their imagination to create fun activities. The patriarch recalls burning dead olive branches at Easter so they could jump over the fires and searching for frogs in the nearby streams in spring.

Holy Days and Holidays

The patriarch's favorite feast was Easter (*Páscha* in Greek). Demetrios loved the resounding difference in the tone of the bells that tolled mournfully on Good Friday and joyfully on Easter Sunday. Actually, the residents of his village were not known for their piety; other islanders even affectionately referred to the village as "Capernaum"—a biblical reference to the ancient Palestinian city that was not moved by the miracles performed by Christ. By comparison, other villages were indeed distinguished for their piety: in one village, called Skhinoúdi, whenever women had difficulties conceiving, they would dedicate their children to the parents of the Virgin Mary—naming them either Joachim or Anna.

Still, everyone in the village of Saints Theodores would be in church for the Easter Vigil. Demetrios, serving as altar boy, remembers the bell summoning the villagers just before midnight. He remembers the jubilant singing of the Paschal anthem "Christ Is Risen!" as well as the candlelight that brightened the streets and the fireworks that lit up the sky at midnight. Each year, his parents brought home a lit candle directly from the service, marking the sign of the cross on the doorway lintel next to crosses from previous years; people greeted one another with the Easter salutation: "Christ is risen!" "He is risen indeed!"

Christmas was his second favorite holiday. Just before Christmas, Demetrios brought home his report card; in return for good grades, he would plead for new clothes or new shoes. The village custom from ancient times was to slaughter pigs for the festive meal on Christmas Day. On Christmas Eve, the children would go to bed early, while their mother would prepare the meal for the next day. At 2 a.m. on Christmas Eve, the bell would ring and villagers would stream to the church to "greet" the newborn Jesus and return home after the service to a "breakfast" of warm soup and chicken. The patriarch still remembers vividly that, while gifts were not normally exchanged on Christmas Day (that was done on New Year's Day), there was not a single poor family that did not receive food, clothes, and firewood from the whole village.

Bartholomew tells a story later related by his mother. Every year, many guests dropped by their home on Christmas Day because it was the nameday of his father, Christos. (Greeks often hold open houses on the feast day of the saint for whom they were named.) They would always be received in the formal living room, which they called "the good lounge." The next morning, skilled at serving in the café, the young Demetrios would tell his mother how many guests had been in and out of the open house. "How do you know?" his mother would ask. Astute and observant, he had served the houseguests himself and knew exactly how many pieces of *baklavá* had been handed out. "We didn't have many sweets," he says, "so my mother's homemade sweets were a treat, and I counted every one!"

New Year's Eve was another holiday that Demetrios eagerly anticipated. Since there was no school, he would help his mother with the house chores, including setting a splendid and abundant dining table filled with fruit and trays of sweets. And of course there was the *vasilópitta*, the New Year's sweet bread dedicated to Saint Basil, a bishop from Caesarea in Turkey. The tradition honors a miracle by the saint one thousand years earlier when valuables stolen from a village were baked into a large, circular loaf of bread, and when the slices were distributed, each family received their valuables back. His father would slice the bread that contained a coin baked somewhere inside. The first portion was always placed aside for Saint Basil, the second for his father, the third for his mother, and the fourth for guests, even if there were none. There followed pieces for the children in order of age, each child unabashedly hoping to get the coin in his or her piece of bread. Demetrios was no different. Whoever got the coin received good luck for the year. Gifts were exchanged also in honor of Saint Basil (the equivalent of Santa Claus in the West), a lover of children and charity. Finally, late in the evening, carol singers would knock on the door, until at midnight the children would kiss their father's hand out of respect and head off to bed.

The village also observed the national holidays, primarily at school with flags and songs. Demetrios learned from a young age the importance of civil responsibility and global concern. In an essay penned during his final year at school, he wrote:

As citizens of Turkey, we have the sacred obligation to care with all our might for our country's society and for the community of nations. We should never utter words that might offend people or authorities. The slightest grain of sand can damage our eyes.

May 19 is Independence Day, celebrating the beginning of liberation of the region in 1919 by Atatürk, and the schoolchildren would wear their clean uniforms and gather to sing the hymn of independence. Above all, there was respect and honor toward the "eternal father" and "courageous founder" of Turkey, Kemal Atatürk, who was born in Thessalonika in 1881 and died in Istanbul in 1938 at the age of fifty-seven. And on Republic Day, October 29, classrooms would be colorfully decorated to celebrate the new Turkish republic established in 1923.

Metropolitan Meliton

Bishop and Mentor

For the young Demetrios, a genuine child of Imvros, the local bishop was an inspiration and support, someone to whom he looked up and someone who looked after him. Melíton Hatzís (born 1913, died 1989)—subsequently Meliton of Chalcedon (1966–1989)—served as metropolitan of Imvros from 1950 to 1963. On feast days, the village children would ring the bells as soon as they saw the bishop's car approaching from a distance. They were welcoming a prince of the church, but for the children it was like welcoming Santa Claus because the bishop would always bring a satchel of gifts: often caps for the boys and dolls for the girls. Once, Bartholomew's brother received a balloon; on another occasion, he was given a whistle.

It was Meliton, who knew all his faithful personally, who recognized the potential in Bartholomew; it was at Meliton's expense that Bartholomew left Imvros for secondary studies at the famous Zográfeion Lyceum (with a scholarship from the Imvrian Society of Istanbul), which still functions in Istanbul and, later, priestly formation at the renowned seminary of Halki (with a scholarship from the Ecumenical Patriarchate).

Away at school at the tender age of eleven, Bartholomew felt homesick and regularly corresponded with his parents, who would send him money and sweets, but he would reassure them that he was studying hard to pass his grade. Istanbul felt like a distant foreign land to the young Demetrios. The journey by boat could take up to twenty-four hours, with endless stops and the risk of storms. Today it only takes six hours, from door to door, by bus and ferry; and there are even regular flights from Istanbul to the tiny island airstrip.

As the young Demetrios traveled from Imvros to school in Istanbul, he would have felt the surroundings becoming increasingly stifling and industrialized. By contrast, as he returned from Istanbul to Imvros, he would have admired the green hills and valleys, the coastline and its small rock islands, as well as the slopes and fields studded with pine trees and almond trees, until he reached the welcoming blue waters of the Aegean Sea from where the Greek islands were also clearly visible. (His love for nature would manifest itself many years later in one of his most significant ministries: creation care.) Each time, he also would have passed along the beautiful strait, Dardanelles.

However, during Demetrios's first year of middle school, Meliton opened a new school—the Central School or Semi-Secondary

School, as they referred to it—in Panaghía and invited him to return to his home island in September 1952 to continue his education. Demetrios was delighted to hear the news from his parents:

> I didn't even a stay a minute longer than I had to away from my home. I would continue school near my parents, my siblings, and my friends. Everything would be perfect.

He loved the new building, his new teachers, and his classmates. The teenage Demetrios would walk close to an hour—over three miles each way—every day from the village of Saints Theodores to the island capital of Panaghía. He reminisces:

> You can't imagine my joy at returning home after spending a year in Istanbul, where I felt as if I was in a foreign land. For me, the new school was the ultimate; it was all that I could dream of! Because it was close to home.

He prepared with food and an umbrella, in case it rained, and he remembers every turn in the road. One morning, as he pondered the material to be covered in a test later that day, he stopped to look at his study notes; he still recalls the exact spot and the very topic of the test. His memory for details still applies to people, places, and events: from priests to popes, from the Black Sea to the Mississippi River.

That daily routine planted the seed for the priestly calling of the young Demetrios because Fr. Spyridon Damthás (or "Papa Spíros")—a Halki graduate and married clergyman at the local diocese in Panaghía, who also served as secretary to the local bishop and taught Sunday school to the Archondonis children—would talk to Demetrios about Halki while accompanying him to and from the capital. Once he stopped to mark the soil with his walking stick, sketching on the ground the shape of the seminary grounds (constructed in the form of the Greek letter *pi* [π], indicating the church in the center with a dot).

When Demetrios's shoes wore out from the walking, Metropolitan Meliton replaced them with sturdy boots. The patriarch recalls that from January 1951 until July 1984, Meliton was his "guardian angel" and spiritual father. Imagine the pride of the teenage Demetrios Archondonis upon receiving personal letters from his revered bishop. On March 14, 1956, one such letter read:

> My dear Demetrios, thank you for your wishes on my nameday.
> I hope you are sound in health and marking constant progress. I always think of you; and in my prayers I ask the Lord to be your illumination and consolation during your high-school years.

Prince of the Church

Well-educated, a prolific and imposing preacher, Meliton was the heart and mind of the Ecumenical Patriarchate for almost three decades—both during the pioneering tenure of Patriarch Athenagoras [Spyrou] (1948–1972) but especially during the pastoral tenure of Patriarch Demetrios [Papadopoulos] (1972–1991). Meliton was a unique churchman, near statesman. He was a caring pastor and experienced administrator, a bold advocate for Orthodox unity and Christian reconciliation.

However, it was the difficult post–World War II years that

proved tragic for the Orthodox community, particularly in Istanbul and more generally in Turkey, that saw the rise of Meliton within the ranks—indeed, within the "holy of holies"—of the Ecumenical Patriarchate: from deacon to senior bishop, from deputy secretary of the Holy and Sacred Synod to grand chancellor under Patriarch Maximos V (1946–1948), and then bishop (first of Imvros, later of Elioupolis, from 1963 to 1966, and finally of Chalcedon). And it was the difficult years for the Greek community in Imvros during the 1950s through the early 1960s that molded and proved the charismatic Meliton as a caring minister as well as a skillful diplomat, promoting the spiritual, social, educational, and cultural needs of his flock. He established schools and a hospital while also organizing pedagogical and artistic programs for the islanders, who to this day remember him as their "great benefactor."

Patriarch Athenagoras, who had previously served as archbishop of America from 1930 to 1948 and was familiar with the art of advancing excellence in his coworkers, recognized Meliton's gifts and charged him with the task of fostering inter-Orthodox and inter-Christian relations, as well as cultivating the organization of the Orthodox diaspora—namely, the numerous communities within and beyond the jurisdiction of the Ecumenical Patriarchate throughout the world. In a remarkable transition of mentor and pupil, Meliton later continued these roles and responsibilities under Patriarch Demetrios, who succeeded Patriarch Athenagoras in 1972. A simple survey of the archdioceses under the Ecumenical Patriarchate in the United States, Australasia, and Europe from 1963 until Meliton's death in 1989, reveals the silent, albeit stunning, success of his efforts.

Meliton was also a pivotal figure in realizing the Holy and Great

Council, a hallmark presence and influence in the preparatory process from 1961 to 1984. He revived the collapsed discussions about a Pan-Orthodox council from the 1930s. He firmly believed that the Great Council could and would be a credible and collective witness of the diverse Orthodox churches to their own faithful and the rest of the world. His contributions are palpably evident in conferences and consultations held on the Greek island of Rhodes (1961, 1963, and 1964) and in Chambésy, Geneva (1968), which he presided over as the representative of the Ecumenical Patriarchate. It was during one of these meetings—at the Third Pan-Orthodox Conference in Rhodes (1964)—that Meliton proved instrumental in decisions pertaining to relations with the Roman Catholic Church, which in turn led to the unprecedented exchanges and encounters between Patriarch Athenagoras and Pope Paul VI.

Meliton was the indispensable, even if invisible, protagonist behind the spectacular events in association with the Vatican, including the first meeting in 1964 between the pope of Rome and patriarch of Constantinople since the Great Schism of 1054 and the attendant lifting of excommunications between the two churches in 1965 that resulted from that schism. Meliton was also the judicious mind behind the texts drafted and agreed upon, inasmuch as these had significant theological and ecclesiological implications. This was especially crucial in the latter instance, where Meliton achieved what was nearly impossible at the time—before the digital and virtual era—namely, the simultaneous recitation of the lifting of the anathemas in St. Peter's Basilica in Rome and at St. George's Patriarchal Church in Istanbul on December 7, 1965. For Western minds not as familiar with this vast history, it is difficult to comprehend just how significant this act was in altering the perception of something that had been in place for more than nine hundred years.

Following the death of Patriarch Athenagoras, Meliton invariably served as the indisputable responsible advisor and principal co-administrator of the patriarchate until the morning of July 28, 1984, when he suffered a severe stroke that caused disabilities he endured for five and a half years and from which he never recovered.

Bartholomew still remembers Meliton affectionately and respectfully—Meliton's close circle and protégés referred to him as "yéro-Meliton" ("old Meliton"). He shaped so many, affectionately calling them "young leaders." In a sermon delivered on November 1, 1964, on the Greek island of Rhodes, he would say:

> The church is not just a historical event; it is not only a divinely established, albeit static institution; it is not a lifeless rule of faith. It is more than these. It is the dynamism of history. It is life.

Meliton was an aristocrat, though engaging. He was a gastronome, albeit frugal. He was an orator, but revered silence. He once wrote:

> Silence attends every great value in life: there is the silence of holiness, the silence of wisdom, the silence of courage, the silence of patience, the silence of love. . . . Silence guards the doors of the altar, the vigilance of the sage, the resolve of sacrifice. . . . Silence belongs to eternity.

For Bartholomew, Meliton was "an exceptional, historical, and unique example of church statesmanship." He refers to him as "the incarnation and interpretation of the ethos of the Phanar" precisely because "he could see far and wide!" The influence of Meliton on Bartholomew and his part in making him the man and leader he is today cannot be overstated.

After the last two years of middle school at Panaghía, Meliton transferred Demetrios to Halki for the remaining three years of high school and four years of seminary. It was Meliton who provided Bartholomew with the official letter of recommendation for his application:

Your All-Holiness,

I hereby faithfully present to Your All-Holiness a student from my humble diocese, Demetrios Archondonis, from the village of Saints Theodores, who has completed his preliminary secondary schooling in Imvros, and who desires to enter our mother school [of Halki].

In submitting to Your All-Holiness his relevant application, along with all the necessary certificates, I would like to inform you with particular and wholehearted joy that this student comes from a very good and pious family, has received meticulous upbringing, and has distinguished himself in education, exceling in his classes and character.

I am convinced that this student, upon entering our mother school, will be a model of studious and upright character, and will herald a bright development for the benefit of the Mother Church, which he will be called to serve.

At the Holy Metropolis of Imvros
September 18, 1954

The letter of recommendation by Metropolitan Meliton of Imvros for Demetrios Archondonis's three years of high school and four years of seminary at Halki.

Ἀριθ. Πρωτ. 1519

Τῇ Αὐτοῦ Θειοτάτῃ Παναγιότητι,
τῷ Οἰκουμενικῷ Πατριάρχῃ
Κυρίῳ κυρίῳ Ἀθηναγόρᾳ τῷ Α:

Παναγιώτατε Δέσποτα,

Διὰ τῆς παρούσης μου εὐλαβῶς παρουσιάζω τῇ Ὑμετέρᾳ Θειοτάτῃ Παναγιότητι τὸν ἐκ τοῦ χωρίου Ἁγίων Θεοδώρων τῆς ταπεινῆς μου παροικίας μαθητὴν Δημήτριον Ἀρχοντώνην τοῦ Χρήστου, ἀπόφοιτον τοῦ Ἡμι-γυμνασίου Ἴμβρου, ὅστις ἐπιθυμεῖ ὅπως εἰσαχθῇ εἰς τὴν Τροφὸν Σχολήν.

Ὑποβάλλων τῇ Σεπτῇ Αὐτῆς Κορυφῇ τὴν σχετικὴν αἴτησιν τοῦ ἐξομολογηθέντος μεθ' ὅλων τῶν ἀπαιτουμένων πιστοποιητικῶν, μετ' ἰδιαιτέρας ὅλως χαρᾶς πληροφορῶ Αὐτὴν, ὅτι ὁ μαθητὴς οὗτος, προερχόμενος ἐκ λίαν καλῆς καὶ εὐσεβοῦς οἰκογενείας, ἔτυχε ἐπιμεμελημένης κατ' οἶκον ἀνατροφῆς, διεκρίθη δὲ καὶ κατὰ τὴν ἐνταῦθα μαθητείαν του, ἀριστεύσας καθ' τε τὴν ἐπίδοσιν εἰς τὰ μαθήματα καὶ τὸ ἦθος.

Πεποιθὼς ὅτι ὁ εἰρημένος μαθητὴς εἰσαγόμενος εἰς τὴν Τροφὸν Σχολὴν θὰ ἀποτελέσῃ ὑπὸ στίγμα ἐπιμελείας καὶ χρηστοηθείας καὶ θὰ σημειώσῃ λαμπρὰν ἐξέλιξιν, ἐπ' ὠφελείᾳ τῆς μητρὸς Ἐκκλησίας ἣν θὰ κληθῇ νὰ ὑπηρετήσῃ, συνιστῶ αὐτὸν εἰς τὴν πατρικὴν εὔνοιαν τῆς Ὑμετέρας Παναγιότητος καὶ παρακαλῶ Αὐτὴν ὅπως, ἀποδεχομένη τὴν αἴτησιν αὐτοῦ, διατάξῃ τὴν παροχὴν αὐτῷ πάσης εὐκολίας πρὸς ἐγκατάστασίν του ἐν τῇ Σχολῇ.

Ἐπὶ δὲ τούτοις ἀσπαζόμενος τὴν παναγίαν Αὐτῆς δεξιάν, διατελῶ μετὰ βαθυτάτου σεβασμοῦ.

Ἐν τῇ Ἱερᾷ μητροπόλει τῇ 18ῃ Σεπτεμβρίου 1954,

Συνημμένα: 7
1. Αἴτησις
2. Δέσκληψα
3. Πιστοποιητικὸν ὑγείας
4. Πιστοποιητικὸν προελεύσεως ἐκ νομίμου γάμου
5. Πιστοποιητικὸν ἤθους καὶ φρονημάτων
6. Ἐγγυητικὸν
7. Φωτογραφίαι.

The practice of identifying and mentoring young Orthodox Christian boys with potential in the church was vital to ensure well-educated, pious men who could someday even become ecumenical patriarch. Turkey requires that an ecumenical patriarch be a Turkish citizen, and the Turkish authorities scrutinize the final list of candidates proposed by the Holy Synod of the Ecumenical Patriarchate.

HALKI: HILL OF HOPE

Completing Secondary Education

Halki—today known as Heybeliada—is one of nine in a charming and natural constellation of islands known as the Princes' Islands in the Sea of Marmara. Byzantine empresses vacationed here, while disgraced princes understandably chose the island as their preferred place of exile. Indeed, during the golden age of Byzantium, the island was a place of seclusion and a literary hub.

The monastery of the Holy Trinity that houses the theological school was established around the ninth century; the great and controversial Patriarch Photius is recorded as its founder and to this day commemorated as its patron.

The restoration of the monastery and establishment of the seminary are associated with Ecumenical Patriarch Germanos IV, who succeeded in having the school accredited by the Turkish authorities. The school was officially opened on September 13, 1844, and classes commenced on October 8, 1844. Known variously as the "Theological School of the Great Church of Christ" or the "Theological School of Halki," the seminary is located at the top of Ümit Tepesi ("Hill of

Hope"), also known as Papaz Dağı, or the "Mount of Priests," still offering a breathtaking view of Istanbul, despite today's seemingly impenetrable air pollution. As early as 1856, French historian and journalist Abdolonyme Ubicini described it as the only establishment of its kind in the whole empire, annually furnishing countless leaders to the church. Destiny would have the current Ecumenical Patriarch Bartholomew celebrate the 150th anniversary of the school on August 28–31, 1994.

In 1971, a new law issued by the Turkish ministry of education abolished private higher education, requiring direct supervision of schools by the state or affiliation with a state-operated university. The school at Halki was obliged to suspend operation as a seminary, functioning only as a secondary school that eventually closed in 1984. Today, the institution functions as a monastic brotherhood and conference center.

Such then was the historical and prestigious school where Bartholomew was to complete secondary and seminary studies. He transitioned very smoothly into his new school, writing to his parents at age fourteen:

> I left our home and your love to come to my second home, where Christian love prevails. Everyone here makes sure to welcome new students, helping them forget about missing their parents and family, assimilating them to their new environment. Classes have started, and I am enjoying them.
>
> Respectfully, your son.
> Demetrios Archondonis

Bartholomew still recalls the day he started school at Halki, if for no other reason than the fact that he wore his first long trousers. He used to envy his elder brother, Nikos, who wore long pants, and would implore his parents to let him wear them as well; but they would say he was too young and pants didn't suit him.

But the time came when they made my first suit with long trousers. Not because I was now considered "big," but because . . . circumstances demanded it. I was going to enter the Theological School of Halki. I gave up my "little" clothes . . . and one Sunday morning, on October 31, 1955, I received my suit and long pants. For me, it was cause for celebration! I had grown up; I was no longer in junior high or middle school. My classmates might make fun of me, but I didn't care. My dream had come true. I walked about like a general ready to conquer the world. From now on, I could keep company with adults. When I sat down, I was careful not to crease my trousers; so I would raise them a little, just as I would see the adults doing. And when I folded them at the end of my bed, I treated them almost like something sacred.

Of course, that craze passed, just as it did the first time that I shaved . . . except in that case, that I knew that one day I wouldn't need to shave; and then, I'd also be wearing a clergyman's cassock over my long pants.

At Halki, during his first of the remaining three years of high school, his favorite teacher was his literature master, Athanásios Tsernóglou, himself formerly an infant refugee from the exchange of populations in Asia Minor during the 1920s. Bartholomew still recalls how Tsernóglou would bring them to the well at the entrance of the theological school in order to read and recite the inscription around the well that is dated 1777:

ὕδωρ ἀρίσασθαι γλυκύ, πίετε, δροσισθῆτε . . .

[DRAW FROM THIS SWEET WATER; DRINK AND REFRESH YOURSELVES. YOU SHOULD ALL COMMEMORATE ABBOT SAMUEL AND ASK FOR THE FORGIVENESS OF ITS MERCIFUL FOUNDERS, WHOSE INSPIRATIONAL LABOR YOU SHOULD ALSO IMITATE.]

Bartholomew can still recite the classical Greek text in its entirety by heart.

Alas, the young teacher left after only a year at this post, but Bartholomew retained close contact and exchanged regular correspondence with him through the years until Tsernóglou's death. His respected teacher would sign off his letters to Bartholomew with the words: "I venerate the cheek of my pupil and the hand of my bishop [or, later, patriarch]." Tsernóglou is buried on the island of Lesbos, Greece, where Bartholomew visited his grave several times to perform a memorial service.

Commencing Seminary Formation

Halki was a remarkable place. No more appropriate site could be found for a theological school that shaped the leaders of the church for nearly two centuries. "The most affluent king in the world could never match the blessings and benefits of the island," Demetrios wrote in his journal, now published in Greek and entitled *When I Was a Child, School Essays.*

The island is small and green; the skyline is dominated by two pine-covered hills; the fragrance of pines is pervading. There is no traffic noise or city bustle; people travel by foot or horse carriage. Its beauty is uncommon and picturesque; its scenery is conducive to scholarship and spirituality. And the pine forests protect the island and especially the school from the southern gales and northern winds.

Behind the barricade of pine trees, a wall surrounds the seminary grounds. But "inside the walls, it was like a piece of paradise," the young Demetrios wrote in his journal. There were plentiful waters and flowers, a myriad of colors and scents, even vegetables and vines. And there was the tree of knowledge: the source of sacred education and spiritual formation. Bartholomew is still said by his former classmates, as well as generations of contemporary and later students, to have been the brightest in his class. His love for poetry remained with him, and he would retain a composition book with his favorite poems and those of his friends, mostly from contemporary Greek laureates and authors. Each seminarian would have committee obligations; Bartholomew was a member of the library committee and president of the canteen committee, responsible for stocking and distributing such "necessities" as composition books, toothbrushes, and shoe polish.

Each day after the evening vespers, students were free to visit the magnificent library with its five spectacular successive rooms or, especially around dusk, to roam the seminary gardens and walk through the surrounding forest. The library inside the magnificent nineteenth-century building once boasted more than one hundred thousand volumes and rare manuscripts; today it contains more than forty thousand books; most are preserved at the patriarchate. The seminary grounds include burial sites of patriarchs, metropolitan bishops, clergy, and faculty; some twenty ecumenical patriarchs are buried on the island of Halki, with the graves of two patriarchs behind the altar of the Holy Trinity Monastery. As for the Church of the Holy Trinity, it lay between the two legs of the Greek letter *pi*, just as the young Demetrios had learned from Papa Spíros years before on the island of Imvros.

Students played football or handball, Ping-Pong or chess. Or else they sat daydreaming, as they watched the fishing boats and ferryboats moving to and from the other major islands among the Princes' Islands: Prinkipos, Antigone, and Proti. The landscape was charming and the air magical. *No wonder,* he would think, *they call this the hill of hope!* Some would talk about classes or teachers; others would philosophize about nature. Sometimes they would descend all the way to the harbor, deep in conversation, until it was time—refreshed and reanimated—to return to the school. In his notebook he would record:

> It was time for students to ascend the carriage road toward the seminary, just as they would one day ascend the way of life toward perfection.

Graduates were awarded their degrees during a special ceremony, which took place annually on the first Sunday of July in the chapel, with the ecumenical patriarch always in attendance.

Indeed, the school dominated the more recent history of the island. It remains a place of international pilgrimage and scholarship, also serving as a personal retreat for patriarchs—Bartholomew himself regularly withdraws there for reading and reflection.

Pursuing a Priestly Vocation

At the age of fifteen, three years before even commencing seminary classes, Demetrios penned a lengthy entry into his essay journal, entitled "My Biography." He wrote of his carefree days at Imvros, his "zeal for the priesthood from a young age, which would ultimately lead [him] to the sacred school at Halki in order later to fulfill a noble commission." As a young boy his life was centered on a minuscule corner of the earth, the village of Haghioi Theodoroi; later he learned that God's blessings were generously and judiciously dispersed throughout the universe:

> I consider the present moment as the happiest of my life. . . . Sometimes I reflect on my future. I see it as being filled with toil and pain. But at the end, I can discern a moral fulfillment concealed. I am making my way on the straight path and I hope to reach my desired goal.
>
> I pray that my dreams will be realized so that I may leave this transient world with the righteous conviction that I have accomplished all my duties—personal, social, national, and religious—in the assurance that I will gain the kingdom of God.

It was Bartholomew's mentor, Meliton, who ordained him to the diaconate on August 13, 1961, the day on which the Orthodox

A page from Demetrios Archondronis's high school journal describing pre-seminary life at Halki.

Church celebrated the culmination—also called the "taking leave"—
of the Feast of the Transfiguration of Christ on Mount Tabor.
The service took place at the Cathedral of Imvros at Panaghía.
Bartholomew still vividly recalls the advice offered by Meliton on
that day:

> Stand still, stand in silence, stand with awe before the glorious light
> of the Transfiguration. Never take your eyes from the transfig-
> ured Lord; always convey this light that never wanes for all people.

It was on that same day that he received a new name—his name
as a celibate clergyman, his "monastic" name—Bartholomew, the
name of one of Christ's twelve disciples and also an erudite monk
from Imvros who taught in Thessaloniki and Venice, later settling
at Koutloumoúsi Monastery on Mount Athos, where he edited
liturgical texts. The learned monk Bartholomew hailed from the
village of Glykí (which means "sweet"), to this day one of the pretti-
est mountain spots on the entire island. At the foothill of the village,
the ecumenical patriarch is erecting a small monastery in memory
of his namesake Athonite monk.

Bartholomew's parents were proud of their son: his mother did
not seem to mind the change of name. But his aunt Olympia, who
was already heartbroken that the young Demetrios would not be
married and raise a family, reacted differently: "The bishop couldn't
find a different name? I can't even pronounce this one!"

A few years later, on October 19, 1969, the same Meliton also
ordained Bartholomew to the priesthood, this time in the chapel
of the Holy Trinity at the Theological School of Halki, where

Bartholomew would begin his ministry. The prelate addressed the young ordinand:

> You are approaching to receive God's grace. That is all that matters. That is what is ultimately decisive. But in order for this to occur, you must first empty yourself, you must make space for grace. Empty yourself, humble yourself, and above all make room for divine grace.

On the same day, Meliton prayed that Bartholomew would remain "graceful" (filled with the grace of God) and "gracious" (recognized for his generous charisma). His words echoed the description of a priest by the "golden-mouthed" preacher and former archbishop of Constantinople, Saint John Chrysostom, almost sixteen centuries before:

> Be serious but gracious, commanding but compassionate, unwavering but reconciliatory, unassertive but unyielding, compelling yet calm.

They were also a prophetic observation about a young man, barely thirty, who would guide the entire Christian East only twenty-two years later.

Bartholomew grew up to trust the far-reaching and outreaching discernment of yéro-Meliton, while the latter grew to trust his protégé unequivocally. In fact, before any important document left the office, Meliton would always ask: "Has Bartholomew seen it?" A positive response was as good as Meliton's signature.

Through the years that followed, Meliton groomed the young clergyman to incarnate the vision of the Ecumenical Patriarchate, to adopt a spirit of ecumenical openness, and ultimately to stand at the helm of Orthodox unity as ecumenical patriarch with the resolute conviction and diplomatic charm of a world leader.

It was Bartholomew who assumed responsibility for Meliton's care when his mentor suffered the stroke. He accompanied him to New York for two months in December 1984 and January 1985 for specialized therapy at Burke Rehabilitation Center in White Plains, New York, looking after him from early morning till late night. A few months later, when visiting New York, Bartholomew took the time to stop by the hospital to offer sweets to the doctors and nurses.

Cosmopolitan Experience and Education

Bartholomew received his theological licentiate in 1961 from Halki, whereupon he fulfilled his reserve military service for the next two years, from 1961 to 1963. Even these years were not spent very far from Imvros, with his base located in the small town of Demirtepe on the mainland, near the city of Gallipoli. It was during this period that—with the spiritual and personal direction of Meliton—Bartholomew also grew close to the great Patriarch Athenagoras. In fact, both Meliton and Athenagoras insisted that Bartholomew should be ordained before commencing his military service; Bartholomew was thinking of delaying his ordination. While neither party expressly revealed the intention behind his preference, it is clear to the patriarch today that his mentors wanted to secure a celibate ordination as early as possible in case the young ordinand decided to choose marriage. The fact is that Bartholomew was still considering marriage during the final years of seminary. "And the rest is history," he says with a twinkle in his eye.

It was Athenagoras who provided Bartholomew with a scholarship for further studies abroad. It would come as no surprise that church unity was deeply embedded in the heart of the young clergyman, shaped by Meliton and Athenagoras. Bartholomew chose to pursue a doctoral program starting in the fall of 1963 in Rome, where the Second Vatican Council was already in full swing. He decided to apply to the Gregorian University and specifically to the well-known Pontifical Oriental Institute located opposite the famous Santa Maria Maggiore, a major papal basilica in Rome. The Oriental Institute was and remains a renowned center of study for Eastern Christianity, with established publications such as *Orientalia Christiana Analecta* (with books specializing on Eastern Christianity) and *Orientalia Christiana Periodica* (with academic articles and book reviews on Eastern Christianity), as well as noted Jesuit scholars, such as Tomáš Špidlík (famous for his formative work on Orthodox spirituality) and Robert Taft (acclaimed for his seminal work on Orthodox liturgy).

Classes at the institute were in Latin, so Bartholomew devoted much of his early time and attention to learning Latin, as well as Italian and French, the language of the French Seminary that accommodated him during his studies. At the same time, Bartholomew would frequent and follow the open sessions of the Vatican Council, which had invited an Orthodox presence for the first time in centuries. Joseph Lécuyer, a specialist on ordination and teacher at the French Seminary, served as one of the *periti* (experts for the council); Lécuyer was, in fact, secretary to the commission that drafted the council's text entitled *Presbyterorum Ordinis* ("The Priesthood in the Ministry of the Church").

So Bartholomew had firsthand experience and access to discussions and decisions of Vatican II. Indeed, through his interactions with council delegates, Bartholomew met and became acquainted with influential Roman Catholic and Orthodox ecclesiastical leaders and theological figures, including German Jesuit Karl Rahner and German professor Joseph Ratzinger (later Pope Benedict XVI), as well as French Dominican Yves Congar and French Jesuit Henri de Lubac. Moreover, while in Rome as a young deacon, he performed volunteer work with the Little Sisters of Jesus, who are inspired by the writings and work of Charles de Foucauld. He also crossed paths with such ecumenical pioneers as German biblical scholar Cardinal Augustin Bea, French academician Cardinal Jean Daniélou, and Benedictine monk Emmanuel Lanne, while coming to know Pope Paul VI quite intimately.

Bartholomew studied with a scholarship from the ecumenical patriarch, which would be mailed—albeit irregularly and behind schedule—from the church in America; however, even when pressed financially, he would respectfully decline any scholarship assistance offered by the Vatican, so as not to feel any sense of obligation to anyone beyond his own church. Bartholomew completed his doctoral thesis in canon law on the subject and with the title *The Codification of the Holy Canons and the Canonical Constitutions in the Orthodox Church.* The dissertation was successfully defended for the requirements toward a PhD at the Pontifical Oriental Institute in the spring of 1966 and subsequently published by the Patriarchal Institute of Patristic Studies in Thessaloniki in 1970.

Before heading for Munich in Germany—where he added another language to his long repertoire, which now included classical and ecclesiastical Greek, Turkish, English, and Latin, as well as Italian, French, and German—by way of Geneva, Switzerland, during the two academic years from 1966 to 1967, Bartholomew pursued a postgraduate program at the Ecumenical Institute at Bossey, near Geneva. At this educational center of the World Council of Churches, he met Nikos Nissiotis and was exposed to the contemporary philosophical trends of personalism and existentialism. Nissiotis was professor of psychology and philosophy of religion at the University of Athens, having studied in Zürich under psychoanalysts Emil Brunner and Carl Jung, as well as in Basel under theologians Karl Barth and Karl Jaspers. A highly prominent and respected interpreter of Orthodox theology and spirituality in language accessible to Western students, serving as a permanent observer at Vatican II, Nissiotis was a soccer aficionado and was a member of the International Olympic Committee.

After his time in Geneva, from 1967 to 1968, Bartholomew spent three academic semesters pursuing postdoctoral studies at the University of Munich, where he not only cultivated his scholarly appreciation of canon law but also increased his ecumenical understanding of Protestant theology.

Patriarch Demetrios

Unassuming "Saint"

Upon completing his studies abroad, Bartholomew returned to Constantinople in 1968 and was appointed assistant dean at the Theological School of Halki, where he had received his priestly formation. He was now in a position to teach canon law and provide spiritual guidance to younger seminarians. But the plan never came to fruition: while awaiting his formal appointment there, the school closed in 1971. Bartholomew remained at Halki as the assistant dean—involved in administrative matters but, sadly, not in academic teaching—until the death, in July 1972, of Ecumenical Patriarch Athenagoras, the longest-serving ecumenical patriarch at that time since the twelfth century. Athenagoras's successor, the similarly named Demetrios, was elected on July 16, 1972.

Ecumenical Patriarch Demetrios was by all accounts a humble man and a kind pastor. Born in 1914 in Istanbul, he dutifully served the same community parish there, in Feriköy, for almost twenty-five years, with a brief postwar appointment to the Greek Orthodox Church in Iran from 1945 to 1950, even teaching ancient Greek at the University of Tehran with the approval of the shah. His silent and sacrificial service to the church was rewarded when he was ordained titular bishop and later elevated to Metropolitan of Imvros in February 1972.

However, with the passing of Athenagoras, the sympathetic Metropolitan Demetrios was suddenly and unexpectedly thrust to the forefront of church administration and the center of church politics. The person intended—and, indeed, expected—to succeed Athenagoras was Meliton, Bartholomew's childhood bishop and longtime mentor. However, Meliton's name was deleted from the list of candidates by the Turkish authorities, who always approve the final list proposed by the Holy and Sacred Synod, the highest governing and decision-making body of the Ecumenical Patriarchate—at the time composed of twelve bishops living at the Phanar. While Turkish authorities rarely, if ever, intervened and the practice was almost always considered standard procedure in order to comply with the regulation that heads of church should be Turkish citizens, Meliton's name was nonetheless expunged. This was doubtless because of Meliton's ecumenical and international reputation as the driving force behind the unparalleled development of the patriarchate in the years leading up to the election.

In the case of Athenagoras, who was a citizen of the United States, it was pressure from the American government that ultimately enabled him to be considered a candidate for the position and subsequently elected patriarch. Athenagoras traveled to Constantinople on President Harry Truman's Air Force One, receiving Turkish citizenship upon landing and before disembarking at Atatürk Airport. But that was exceptional—and historical.

Unintended Patriarch

To the surprise of the world, the hitherto unknown Metropolitan Demetrios was enthroned on July 18, 1972. It was at this same time that Bartholomew assumed charge of a newly established personal office of the patriarch in order to attend and assist Patriarch Demetrios in the immense task that lay before him. Bartholomew continued to direct this office for eighteen years until he was elected Metropolitan of Chalcedon in early 1990, just over a year before the passing of Ecumenical Patriarch Demetrios.

From that position, already two decades before his election as ecumenical patriarch, there is no doubt that he organized (even orchestrated) and envisioned (even enabled) significant milestones of the Orthodox Church. In many ways he was already being groomed for the patriarchal throne. Although Metropolitan Meliton of Chalcedon was living at the time, remember: Bartholomew was in that central and critical office for the commencement of such events as the major theological dialogues with the Roman Catholic Church (1980), the Anglican Communion (1973), and the Ancient Oriental Churches (1985), as well as the conversations with both Judaism (1977) and Islam (1986); he was also instrumental in the establishment of September 1 as the "day of prayer for the natural environment" (1989).

Moreover, it was during the tenure of Patriarch Demetrios that the Ecumenical Patriarchate organized the first three Pan-Orthodox meetings at Chambésy, Geneva, in preparation for the Holy and Great Council. It was during the same time that two archbishops of Canterbury (Donald Coggan and Robert Runcie) as well as Pope John Paul II were received at the Phanar, while Patriarch Demetrios himself was invited to the Vatican in 1987, where, at a solemn ceremony at St. Peter's Basilica, the pope and the patriarch together recited the original text of the fourth-century Nicene-Constantinopolitan Creed. Above the entrance to St. Peter's Basilica in Rome, a marble inscription, written in Latin and Greek, reads:

For the reconciliation of full communion between the Orthodox and Roman Catholic Churches, there was a meeting of prayer in this basilica between Pope Paul VI and Patriarch Athenagoras I on October 26, 1967, and between Pope John Paul II and Patriarch Demetrios I on December 6, 1987. To God alone is due honor and worship to the ages.

The Private Patriarchal Office

As Metropolitan of Philadelphia (elevated in late 1973) and youngest member of the Holy and Sacred Synod (at the tender age of barely thirty-three), but also as Metropolitan of Chalcedon (elevated in early 1990) and still the youngest, albeit senior-ranking, member of the synod (at age fifty), Bartholomew represented the ecumenical patriarch and the patriarchate itself on the highest levels at various commissions of inter-church and interreligious relations. He continue to accompany Patriarch Demetrios on numerous visits to Orthodox churches and nations, as well as several ecumenical organizations, including the World Council of Churches, where Bartholomew was elected member of its Executive and Central Committees while serving as vice president of its Faith and Order Commission.

Some sources claim that the Private Patriarchal Office, which Bartholomew served as director from 1972 to 1990, was created to protect the new Patriarch Demetrios, who was unexpectedly elected patriarch; but others speculate that it was minted—perhaps even conceived by yéro-Meliton—to prepare the future Patriarch Bartholomew, who was already a rising, promising leader. The truth is that Patriarch Demetrios tearfully resisted his election; he was a meek and peace-loving man. "Genuinely and unassumingly humble," says Bartholomew:

> Patriarch Demetrios was guileless and unostentatious, authentic and without hypocrisy. He would promote even those who had hurt him.
>
> He was very simple; once he was outside the patriarchal church, when a few pilgrims from Greece asked to meet the patriarch. Dressed plainly, with just his cassock and without his *engólpion* [pectoral medallion] or staff, he replied: "You are looking at him." Exasperated, they shrugged him off and walked away.

I can certainly attest to that myself. When I first visited the late Patriarch Demetrios with my brother, very soon after the patriarch's election, as we walked into the office and came upon the saintly prelate, my brother whispered, "Where's the patriarch?" Bartholomew added, "That's the sort of person he was. I know for sure that he is in heaven, interceding for us."

Demetrios accepted to serve as patriarch only when Meliton insisted that the church was conscripting his service and assured him that he would have the necessary support. Patriarch Demetrios trusted Meliton blindly; Bartholomew was a mediator between the two—being formed and informed by the experience of both.

From this office and position then, Bartholomew accompanied Patriarch Demetrios on countless official visits, supporting and sheltering the patriarch with utmost dedication and admiration. For his part, Patriarch Demetrios felt safe in Bartholomew's presence;

he trusted and relied on Bartholomew, who worked indefatigably—administering the patriarchal office, checking or revising drafts of patriarchal letters and texts. Emotional, the patriarch recalls:

> He treated me like his son. He was nurturing. Sometimes he would say: "Bartholomew, if I knew for certain that the Turks wouldn't delete your name, I would step down and have you elected. I could stay home and you could just come and tell me the news." I was just thirty-two years old; I simply admired his meekness and modesty.

Patriarch Demetrios would come to the office three days each week; the remainder of the time, Bartholomew was authorized to manage and supervise—everything. At the Phanar, after lunch, Patriarch Demetrios would visit Bartholomew's office—literally next door to the patriarchal office—to have a coffee; every time, he would drink only half the cup, chatting with Bartholomew while the latter was working. In the nineteen years and a few months that Bartholomew was at the patriarch's side, never once was there any expression of disappointment between them; never once was there any personal disagreement.

It would be a smooth transition when Bartholomew was elected patriarch. In many ways, Bartholomew landed with his feet running.

The experience with Patriarch Demetrios was nothing short of a "postdoctoral" education for the young bishop Bartholomew. I have found myself hoping and wishing that Bartholomew might be equally deliberate in taking steps to groom his own successor. I honestly don't think he ever reveals his innermost thoughts on this;

he trusts that an institution sustained for centuries by a divine spirit "shall prevail against the gates of Hades" (see Matthew 16:18). But I do suspect that he is carefully preparing the ground for the smooth transition and election of the next patriarch. One remarkable achievement in this regard has been the guaranteeing of Turkish citizenship by naturalization to clergy from all over the world who apply for priestly vocation or synodal tenure at the Phanar. With dozens of bishops acquiring citizenship over the last few years—from France, Austria, Greece, Italy, Argentina, New Zealand, and America—this has ensured a wide spectrum of individuals eligible to vote and even serve as candidates for the next patriarch.

"It's a different time and a different world," he told me. "But I know that the Holy Spirit will provide the right person for the throne. I'm not anxious about it, just as I wasn't anxious at the time of my own election." However, the election of Bartholomew to ecumenical patriarch after the falling asleep of Ecumenical Patriarch Demetrios was more complicated than that.

The American Connection

Patriarch Athenagoras

In a July 6, 1972 article, *Newsweek* magazine announced the passing of Ecumenical Patriarch Athenagoras, who died of kidney failure at the age of eighty-six while hospitalized for a broken hip. The article noted, "The Greek-born, white-bearded, 6-foot 4-inch prelate became ecumenical patriarch in 1948 after seventeen years in New York as Greek Orthodox Archbishop of North and South America."

When Athenagoras was elected Greek Orthodox archbishop of North and South America on August 13, 1930, his appointment marked the end of a long era of instability and the beginning of a new era of growth. In many ways, the history of the Greek Orthodox Church in America is intimately connected to the personality and vision of Archbishop Athenagoras. Born in an area of northern Greece that was still under the Ottoman Empire, and a graduate of Halki Theological School, Athenagoras had served the Church of Greece in various capacities, including Metropolitan of Kerkyra (Corfu) before arriving in New York. He was a discerning and dynamic leader with farsightedness and open-mindedness. Through his diplomacy and persuasiveness, most of the dissident congregations joined or returned to the ranks of the archdiocese. Moreover, his early experience in Kerkyra with people of other Christian confessions and faith communities enabled Athenagoras to converse and collaborate with the wider American society.

He established five diocesan districts, each with an assistant bishop: in New York, Boston, Chicago, San Francisco, and Charlotte. He also recognized the importance of a new constitution for the church, adopted in 1931. The biennial Clergy-Laity Congresses became the highest legislative body of the archdiocese, its regulations binding for the church. Having arrived during the Great Depression, Athenagoras strengthened the finances of the church, and in 1942 moved the archdiocesan headquarters from an inadequate wooden edifice in Astoria to its present offices at 10 East Seventy-Ninth Street in Manhattan. Apart from instituting an archdiocesan registry and prompting parishes to do likewise for births, marriages, and deaths, Athenagoras also encouraged the formation of the National Clergy Association, whose priorities included the creation of a pension fund and medical insurance for clergy. He also founded the charitable arm of the church (the Ladies Philoptochos Society) in 1931, established a seminary (Holy Cross Greek Orthodox School of Theology) in 1937, and founded a school for teachers (St. Basil's Academy) in 1944. Before his election to the Patriarchal Throne of Constantinople on November 1, 1948, Archbishop Athenagoras had developed close relations with presidents Franklin D. Roosevelt and Harry S. Truman, while also inspiring the creation of a Federation of Orthodox Churches.

Archbishop Iakovos

The principal protégé of the great Athenagoras was Iakovos [Koukoúzis], formerly permanent patriarchal representative at the World Council of Churches in Geneva and subsequently archbishop of North and South America from 1959 to 1996. Iakovos had served as archdeacon to Archbishop Athenagoras and as priest at several parishes in New England as well as assistant dean at Holy Cross School of Theology, spending twelve years at Annunciation Cathedral in Boston, where he also graduated from Harvard Divinity School.

Archbishop Iakovos was one of very few non-African-American Christian leaders to walk in solidarity with civil rights activist Rev. Dr. Martin Luther King Jr. during the famous march in Selma, Alabama—a courageous act for which he went out on a limb, not least among his own Greek Orthodox faithful, and which was captured on the cover of *Life* magazine on March 26, 1965. I have long believed that, had Iakovos achieved nothing else in his lifetime, this valor alone would suffice for him to be chronicled in the history books. Iakovos met with every US president from Dwight Eisenhower to Bill Clinton; in 1980, President Jimmy Carter awarded him the Presidential Medal of Freedom. And he was the first Orthodox archbishop to meet with a pope in more than 350 years, as the personal emissary of Athenagoras to Pope John XXIII in 1959.

Exactly one year after marching with Dr. Martin Luther King Jr., and in the same spirit of championing human rights and religious freedom, on March 10, 1966, Archbishop Iakovos established the Order of Saint Andrew the Apostle: The Archons of the Ecumenical Patriarchate, conferring on thirty distinguished laypersons of his archdiocese various "offices" (*offikia*) and reviving the ancient Greek and Byzantine tradition of prestigious civic patrons to serve and support religious institutions of the Roman Empire. The Order of Archons is the oldest honor bestowed on a layperson in the entire Christian world. Whether collectively or individually, the archons have magnanimously promoted general programs of the patriarchate, procured a dignified patriarchal residence, as well as aided in both securing the return of the Prinkipos Orphanage and sustaining the issue of reopening Halki seminary in the political forefront (see chapter 1).

I mention Archbishop Iakovos because this historic leader was born on July 29, 1911, in the very same tiny village of Saints Theodores on the very same small island of Imvros as Patriarch Bartholomew. (There are, in fact, six bishops from Imvros serving the Ecumenical Patriarchate today. As the saying goes, there must have been something in the water of those village fountains.) Their respective childhood homes still stand within close walking distance—Bartholomew's house was closer to the village center; Iakovos lived just five or six minutes by foot higher up on the hill. Iakovos's parents are buried in the same local cemetery as Bartholomew's relatives. He attended the same local church, visited the same nearby diocese, and studied at the same Halki seminary as the current ecumenical patriarch. Both had the good fortune to be identified and mentored by outstanding bishops, who cared not only for their own legacies but also for the survival of the church, which needs solid, visionary leaders. Iakovos was mentored and sponsored by an earlier Metropolitan Iakovos of Imvros, who was later promoted to Metropolitan of Derkoi and was the ordaining bishop of the later archbishop of North and South America.

In fact—and how could it be otherwise in a sparsely populated community—Iakovos's sister, Chrysánthē, was the godmother of Bartholomew, serving as the spiritual sponsor for the infant Bartholomew; or as the villagers would say, Iakovos and Bartholomew shared the same baptismal oil. Both served the church under the same patriarch, Athenagoras—Iakovos as the archbishop who transformed the church in America, Bartholomew as the upcoming and promising leader at the Phanar. Although a generation apart—Iakovos was seventy-nine and Bartholomew fifty—both were potential candidates for the ecumenical throne after the passing of Patriarch Demetrios.

Election of a New Patriarch

When electing a pope, the Roman Catholic Church convenes a closed meeting of the College of Cardinals at the Vatican in the

Sistine Chapel, where a two-thirds vote is required. While the world watches on television, ballots are burned, creating black smoke when agreement is insufficient and white smoke when two-thirds or more have agreed on the same candidate. At the Ecumenical Patriarchate, electing a patriarch follows a different procedure—quiet, modest, and sacramental.

The members of the Holy and Sacred Synod propose three names from the list of candidates, which has already been vetted by the Turkish authorities. When Patriarch Demetrios was elected, four names were deleted from the list; when Bartholomew was elected, no names were deleted. The synod then proceeds to the patriarchal church, where each member inscribes the name of his choice on a piece of paper on the altar and then casts his ballot in a silver receptacle before the patriarchal throne in the center of the church. Two proclaimers draw the ballots and read aloud the names that are inscribed. In Bartholomew's case, on November 2, 1991, where the vote was unanimous, after the sixth ballot was read, there was an outbreak of applause, and the expectant crowd cried out: *"Axios!"* "He is worthy!"

Bartholomew's election as ecumenical patriarch appeared almost foreordained—perhaps even a straightforward path: his idyllic childhood with family and clergy, his privileged education at Halki and abroad, his prominent mentor, and service to a patriarch. But now many challenges lay before him in a rapidly changing world with countless complex paths: the rapid rise of radical Islam, the expanding dialogues with other Christian communions, the momentous changes within the Orthodox Church itself, as well as the campaign to sound the alarm about the environmental crisis. He would need to prove himself a worthy leader at the helm of a global church.

Rowan Williams

Master of Magdalene College, Cambridge,
and Former Archbishop of Canterbury

THE ROLE OF THE ECUMENICAL PATRIARCH IS OFTEN HARD FOR non-Orthodox to understand. He has oversight of a large network of local churches outside the traditional homelands of Orthodoxy; but he has no vast international secretariat or curia, and his universal authority does not go without challenge. The patriarchal establishment is painfully modest and exists in what has regularly been the most precarious of conditions in the midst of an Islamic society that has not always been friendly, to put it mildly.

This is the situation that a contemporary patriarch inhabits. And for some this suggests that the ecumenical throne is at best a historical anomaly, the last faint survival of Byzantine glories, and that it would make more sense to let go, once and for all, of the fiction of a special status for the patriarch. But there is another perspective, and it is this that has been highlighted by the exceptional personality who now occupies the throne.

131

Bringing to the office a profound spiritual maturity and theological sophistication, His All-Holiness Patriarch Bartholomew has shown how a hierarchical office that is without most of the conventional trappings of executive power can act as a means of theological witness, a potent sign, an office that holds up before the world (Orthodox and non-Orthodox) the central vision of faith—a vision, for Patriarch Bartholomew, that is rooted in the great patristic conviction of the coherence of all things, all material as well as spiritual reality, in the crucified and glorified Word of God. Deprived of any means of universal canonical control, any claims to be a final court of appeal, the patriarchal office can speak for an Orthodox Christian identity in precisely the way that Orthodox theology at its best seeks to work. It *manifests* something rather than arguing for it or enforcing it. The apparent "weakness" of the patriarchal office is, in fact, its freedom to be more and more simply a location for this theological witness, a witness to the continuity of the Body of Christ through the most disruptive and violent history, through power and weakness alike. The spiritual energy that is associated with the office does not at all depend on the power to compel and control.

In embodying in this way the complex history of Orthodoxy, the tragic story of a loss of historic splendor and security, the patriarchal office acts as a reminder that the purposes of God in his church do not depend on numbers, material resources, cultural hegemony, or whatever; these come and go, but the essential identity remains—liturgical, spiritual, in the service of the world. Patriarch Bartholomew has helped all of us see what this great position can mean in a world where integrity in manifesting the truth is increasingly more significant than any purported means of spiritual control. He speaks in freedom in the fullest theological sense—a freedom like that of the apostle Paul, to whom Christ says, "My strength is made perfect in weakness" (2 Corinthians 12:9).

CHAPTER 4

A Culture of Communion

Visionary Facilitator of Orthodox Unity

Our unity transcends the narrow limits of any nationalism or racism; may it also offer to those near and far a sense of hope that the world cannot provide—hope for a world of peace and love.

—Ecumenical Patriarch Bartholomew,

address at the Phanar, 2009

When Time Stood Still

October 10, 2008. The moment was piercing, the atmosphere virtually paralyzed with tension. Bishops, priests, and deacons were nervously gathered in the courtyard of the Phanar, just outside the Patriarchal Church of St. George, where the leaders of the Orthodox world had assembled in anticipation of the second day's session of the Fourth Synaxis of Primates that was about to commence; the opening session had already taken place the previous day, but with one glaring absence. This particular assembly was the hinge upon

135

which would turn the course of the much-longed-for Holy and Great Council, which had been through intermittent preparations over at least fifty years.

Ecumenical Patriarch Bartholomew was also waiting. He was in his office, preparing for the last of the hierarchs, Patriarch Alexei of Moscow and All Russia, who was supposed to travel on a Russian Federation aircraft at the last minute to attend the Synaxis of Primates. He had missed the first session, but would he, in fact, even arrive?

The previous encounter between the two patriarchs just three months earlier had proved challenging, if not charged. Alexei's tenure as head of his local church was only slightly longer than Bartholomew's, but the relationship between the two sees—one was the largest and wealthiest in the Orthodox world; the other was "apostolic" and considered "first among equals"—was tenuous at best. At that time, they were both in Kiev, celebrating 1,020 years since the conversion of the Slavic peoples in 988, the anniversary of the "baptism of Rus'"—its people and Prince Vladimir—by clergy from the Church of Constantinople.

The Moscow Patriarchate is—ironically, albeit in reality—a daughter church of its Kievan mother. Nonetheless, for centuries, since the fall of the Byzantine Empire, those roles had been reversed—a result of the harrowing exigencies of history. The Ecumenical Patriarchate in Constantinople had been repressed under the Islamic Ottoman Empire from 1453 until 1922. The Moscow Patriarchate ascended during the same period, but suffered horrendous setbacks during the Soviet era (1917–1991), notorious for its atheism and suppression of the church. Now, in the aftermath of the fall of the Soviet Union and the "Orange Revolution" in Ukraine from November 2004 to January 2005, its people were pressing for religious independence from the Moscow Patriarchate and looking to Constantinople for guidance and support. Complicating the patriarchal tenure of Alexei was the presence of the former Metropolitan Filaret [Denysenko] of Kiev, at one time a senior prelate of the Russian Church, who had been Alexei's chief rival to the patriarchal throne of Moscow in 1990. Filaret ultimately led and to this day continues to lead a nationalistic revival of the rival Ukrainian Church, which was created following the independence of Ukraine from Russia on August 24, 1991. The divisions within Ukraine itself were, and remain, the most sensitive issues and priorities of the Patriarchate of Moscow, which is dependent on Ukraine for close to half of its faithful and institutions—including legendary monasteries and enormous parishes.

In those late days of July 2008, Bartholomew decided to join Alexei in Kiev for the celebrations of the anniversary. The Russians were displeased and let that be known through ecclesiastical and secular avenues. Kiev, they felt, was Alexei's home turf; Bartholomew had no place there. But why should the ecumenical patriarch, whose own daughter was the Church of Kiev, not attend such a glorious observance? To be honest, if Constantinople was the "mother church" of Kiev and Ukraine, then it was also the "grandmother church" of Moscow and Russia.

Bartholomew (received at the airport with full state honors by

President Viktor Yushchenko) was under intense pressure from the Ukrainian government to proclaim the deeply politically divided Ukrainian Orthodox Church—to this day conveniently labeled "uncanonical" and critically dismissed as "schismatic" by the Church of Russia—an autocephalous, equal with the other fourteen independent Orthodox churches, thereby delivering Ukraine from jurisdictional domination by Russia. Navigating between what was no less than a land mine of the Ukrainian government and the Moscow Patriarchate was diplomatically delicate, if not dangerous; either side could throw the country into religious conflict and further division. Yet Bartholomew, a steady and skillful helmsman of the church, steered straight and true through—without declaring autocephaly—and any menacing crisis was averted. It may be tempting to dismiss disagreements between the various Orthodox churches as ecclesiastical competition or conflict, but the truth is that it frequently conceals a more nuanced relationship and methodology.

This most recent encounter must have been on the mind of Alexei as he headed to Constantinople, one day after the Fourth Synaxis had already commenced deliberations. His health was known to be failing—in fact, physicans had warned him that this mission to Constantinople could cost him his life. Still, Alexei was unrelenting about joining his fellow first hierarchs of Orthodoxy. Perhaps unstable of body but definitely resolute of mind and spirit, the Russian patriarch arrived amid the commotion of assembled clergy and international press covering this critical meeting.

Slowly, but deliberately and surely, Alexei was escorted by

the official reception committee of Orthodox hierarchs to Bartholomew's office on the third floor of the Phanar. When the two patriarchs emerged walking arm in arm through the courtyard, the crowds parted—literally like the waters of the Red Sea. Jittery clergy clamored behind them; anxious press snapped photographs as the two proceeded slowly toward the church.

And then the whole moment was transformed. What was formerly piercing became almost playful, as a little girl holding a single red flower leapt onto the scene. She could not have been more than six. The young girl just stood there silently before the two—for her—towering figures in their religious regalia. The attending subordinate clergy bumped into one another as the procession came to an unexpected and unintelligible halt. Both patriarchs stopped to look down at this child of God with an unmistakable gift in her hands.

They smiled and simply stood there, motionless in the presence of this young girl as if she were at that very moment the center of the world, the source of their deepest and common joy. It was as if time stood still. They stooped to bless her, patting her on the head and thanking her for her gift—surely more generous and suggestive than she could ever have imagined. There was a knowing look between the two patriarchs: whatever lay before them inside the doors of the church, they both knew what they had to do and for whom they had to do it.

Two months later, Patriarch Alexei passed away. Together, however, the two leaders had cleared the path to convening the Holy and Great Council of the Orthodox Church.

A FORTY-YEAR QUEST

As already indicated in earlier chapters, Bartholomew's hand at the helm of world Orthodoxy is no accident. The trajectory of his life—as humble and unpresuming as his beginnings were—has always pointed to and sharpened his unique sense of leadership. He had witnessed in the story of his home island of Imvros just how important the human rights and religious freedom of minority populations were, even as he witnessed the diminishment of the liberties and privileges of the Greek community of Turkey throughout every stage of his life. It is hardly surprising that social justice—human rights, civil rights, and religious rights—would prove key to understanding his model and method of leadership within the Orthodox Church over the past twenty-five years.

His sense of fairness and respect also became apparent in the first decade of his tenure in the churches within the immediate jurisdiction of the Ecumenical Patriarchate, especially with the unprecedented restructuring of the new synod and its regional representation (see chapter 6).

However, on a global level, Bartholomew's relentless outreach and righteous commitment within the modern movement to enact a Pan-Orthodox council is equally remarkable. No other prelate has had this at once supervisory perspective and ground-level perception of the entire process, which has moved in copious twists and various turns. No other hierarch has developed the flexibility to adapt to the utterly unforeseen circumstances shaping the spiritual odyssey that would ultimately lead to convening the Holy and Great Council on the island of Crete in June 2016.

Fourteen autocephalous Orthodox churches agreed to attend: the ancient Patriarchates of Constantinople, Alexandria, Antioch, and Jerusalem; the modern Patriarchates of Russia, Serbia, Romania, Bulgaria, and Georgia; and the Churches of Cyprus, Greece, Poland, Albania, and the Czech Lands and Slovakia. Years after the close of the Second Vatican Council by Pope Paul VI, Bartholomew would respond to a journalist from the *National Catholic Reporter*:

> You could compare the Orthodox Church's situation to that of the Catholic Church when Pope John XXIII convoked the Vatican Council—insofar as our aims are like John's: to update the church and promote Christian unity. Announcement of the upcoming Pan-Orthodox council has aroused high hopes. . . . The council will also signify an opening to non-Christian religions, to humanity as a whole, which in turn means a new attitude toward Islam, Buddhism, and contemporary culture, a renewed aspiration for a just society free of racial discrimination.

This was almost forty years ago. This was the Bartholomew who committed his life to the unity of the Orthodox Church and, as ecumenical patriarch, for the last twenty-five years to the historic singularity of the Holy and Great Council. Then as now, his voice was always consistent with his vision of Orthodox—indeed, Christian—unity. Ironically, when Bartholomew spoke those words to the *National Catholic Reporter* in 1977, he fully expected the Holy and Great Council to occur within a few years, an expectation long obstructed and procrastinated. Still, there is no way that he—or, indeed, his mentor, Meliton—could possibly have imagined that he would be the one to convene this council as a matter of personal destiny.

In the Gale Winds of History

Twentieth-Century Turmoil

The process whereby the Orthodox churches finally managed to convene this first Holy and Great Council in more than a thousand years was tortuous and riddled with land mines. The greatest challenges that would plague the entire twentieth century were a direct result of the Russian Revolution and the genocidal world wars that ultimately erected the Iron Curtain of the Cold War around more than two-thirds of the worldwide Orthodox Christian population. Orthodox churches became trapped under Soviet control: Russia (including Ukraine and, at that time, also Georgia), Serbia (formerly Yugoslavia), Romania, Bulgaria, Poland, Albania, and what was then Czechoslovakia. The Soviet principle of atheism deprecated and diminished all of the churches in these countries to one degree or another.

Secular authorities turned many monasteries into prison camps and neglected church structures. Clergy and laity suffered persecution and pressure from the oppressive state machine; although some of these were able to travel and speak in the West, it always remained a matter of suspicion just how far up the chain of ecclesiastical hierarchy the state had actually infiltrated. The Autocephalous Orthodox Church of Albania, which had been established by the Ecumenical Patriarchate in 1937, suffered heinous extinction at the hands of the militantly atheistic Enver Hoxha. It was only the Autonomous Church of Finland that seemed to have escaped harm's way.

Of particular note, the Church of Estonia—which had been granted autonomy in 1923 by the Ecumenical Patriarchate following its partition from Russia on the heels of the 1917 Bolshevik Revolution—was swallowed up with the other Baltic states in the aftermath of World War II and subsequently absorbed into the Moscow Patriarchate. Indeed, it was originally recognized by Moscow in 1920 by the saintly Patriarch Tikhon in an effort to protect it from the web of atheism that was spinning out of control at the time throughout the new Soviet Union. However, after its subsequent recognition by Constantinople as an independent Orthodox church, the Church of Estonia was subordinated to a diocese within the Church of Russia in 1945. The original autonomy of the Church of Estonia was formally reinstated by the Ecumenical Patriarchate in 1996, receiving its first permanent resident hierarch in 1999. The same Patriarch Alexei who was born of Russian heritage in Estonia would contend with Bartholomew over the restoration of the Estonian Church, a dispute that would later serve as a prologue to the ongoing struggle over the future of the Ukrainian Church. But there were decades of further change that would precede.

Byzantine Prehistory of a Modern Council

Under Bartholomew's predecessor, Ecumenical Patriarch Athenagoras, the first Pan-Orthodox Conference was held in 1961 on the island of Rhodes, as the ecumenical patriarch sought to move Eastern Orthodoxy in the same direction that Pope John XXIII was moving Roman Catholicism. This consultation was the beginning of a succession of conversations and conferences that would eventually lead to the Holy and Great Council. However, the conversation was contrived and constrained. It could not possibly proceed smoothly. The priorities of the autocephalous churches were quite different at the time. The motivations of those churches locked behind the Iron Curtain were not clear. So the consultations continued in Rhodes in 1963 and 1964, and later in Geneva in 1968, repeatedly bringing together delegations from the fourteen autocephalous Orthodox churches in order to seek and secure common ground for an agenda that was as manageable as it was feasible. Overshadowing these early consultations was the fear among many of the Orthodox churches of the reformation, even revolution, that was taking place within the Roman Catholic Church as well as a deeper mistrust of the Vatican in general.

Ever since the formal schism and conventional separation of the churches in the middle of the eleventh century, the Orthodox Church has held its Western "sister church" at a distance—for the most part at a very wide distance. This distance began with differences in language and culture, while being solidified with the pillage and rape of Constantinople in 1204, during the Fourth Crusade. The subsequent sixty-year tenure of a "Latin Kingdom" in Constantinople sealed the great divorce between Christian East and West. Moreover, Turkic tribes had been advancing west for some time since the critical Battle of Manzikert in 1071.

In the intervening centuries leading to the conquest of Constantinople by Mehmet II on May 29, 1453, there were several failed attempts to reconcile East and West, most notably at the Council of Ferrara-Florence in 1438–1439. Ranked as seventeenth among the Ecumenical Councils for the Church of Rome, the Florence council proclaimed a "union" that was fiercely rejected by the people of Constantinople, though the motivation of the Eastern Church may have been much more spiritual than political—the East would sooner submit to the prophet of Islam than the pope of Rome.

Nonetheless, securing military aid to repulse the ever-expanding Ottoman Turkish presence throughout Asia Minor was indispensable for Christian survival. When the Orthodox people of Constantinople rejected the council, they also sealed their fate. New Rome, founded by Constantine the Great in 330, fell one thousand years later but fewer than fifteen years since this last failed attempt to reunite the churches. Relations were severed and the era of the Byzantine Empire came to an abrupt end—forever.

The previous paragraphs are not simply a history lesson. The fall of Constantinople on May 29, 1453, cannot be overstated in understanding how Bartholomew has guided the Christian East to its present state. The fall of the Byzantine Empire meant the dissolution of Constantinople's governance over the Orthodox Slavic peoples, who had been increasing in number and power since the first missionary journeys of the siblings from Thessaloniki, Saints Cyril and Methodius, in the ninth century. The powerful center in Constantinople shattered, and the Church of Rus' would now shift its focus of authority and influence from Kiev to the center of the tsarist universe emerging around Moscow. Thus, the role of the "mother church" seemed to be matched, even snatched, by the daughter, a change whose consequences resonate powerfully to the present day.

How Many Romes Are There, Anyway?

During this period, throughout the Balkans, the local churches either fell under direct Ottoman rule or else were subject to Ottoman suzerainty. Between the utopian ambition of Moscow to be a "third Rome"—entirely missing the point that there was never any such enumeration but only an evolution from "elder" Rome to "new" Rome—and the escalation of nationalism in the Balkans around a shared language, ethnicity, and Orthodoxy, the influence of the Ecumenical Patriarchate began to wane.

By contrast, in the Greek-speaking world and among the ancient Patriarchates of Constantinople, Alexandria, Antioch, and Jerusalem—all of whom were subjects of an expanding Ottoman Empire—the role of Constantinople remained important and influential since the sultan recognized the ecumenical patriarch as leader of all Orthodox—an "ethnarch" with cultural authority, albeit without ethnic boundary. Of course, the history of the Ottoman era is far too complex to be reduced to a simple formula, but its effect on the Church of Constantinople was undeniably profound. In his masterful account, *The Great Church in Captivity*, Sir Steven Runciman observed how the Greeks are wrong to neglect their history under Turkish domination. For while it contains a great deal of suffering and pain, it also bears witness to the indomitable prominence of Hellenism and the spiritual resilience of the Orthodox Church.

No more appropriate or accurate words could be adopted of Ecumenical Patriarch Bartholomew, who exemplifies and expresses the spiritual strength of the Orthodox Church, all the while exhibiting the unquenchable vitality of Hellenism. He is often falsely accused of attempting to create a parallel "Vatican-style" rule of Orthodoxy—a dangerous canard arbitrarily cast around through surrogates and in the irresponsible blogosphere for years. In fact, Bartholomew is unrelenting in his defense of all minorities—religious, racial, and ethnic—while he has always maintained that the mission of the Ecumenical Patriarchate is solely spiritual, without pretensions to any kind of political presence. This, too, he had mapped out from his enthronement address in November 1991:

> We deem it our responsible obligation to state clearly that the Ecumenical Patriarchate shall remain a purely spiritual institution, a symbol of reconciliation and an unarmed force. Exercising the components of our holy Orthodox faith, safeguarding and conducting itself with regard to Pan-Orthodox jurisdictions, the Ecumenical Patriarchate is detached from all politics, keeping itself far from the smoky hubris of secular authority.

As the current occupant then of the first throne of the Orthodox Church, Bartholomew is charged with the responsibility to convene and coordinate the synergy of the Orthodox Church worldwide, to protect and preserve the principle of the church's unity. He cannot afford to experiment with petty expansionist ambitions. He feels a weighty responsibility to ensure that the historical developments that have brought the church to its current reality never mitigate the spiritual reality of the church as the body of Christ. Yet by what authority does the ecumenical patriarch have this primacy or privilege?

First Among Equals

A Paradoxical Approach

Bartholomew understands very well that the model of imperial and ecclesiastical authorities existing in parallel from the
fourth through the fifteenth centuries is gone forever, never to
be replaced. He appreciates how the loss of communion with the
pope of "elder Rome" has left an indelible impact on his own see of
"new Rome." Yet Canon 3 of the Second Ecumenical Council (381)
names the bishop of Constantinople second rank after Rome; and
the Fourth Ecumenical Council of 451, through Canon 28, elevates
the ranking of the Church of Constantinople in the new imperial
capital to second position after Rome—with equal prominence and
privilege—thus casting the die for Constantinople to inherit by
default the role of leadership after the Schism of 1054: to be "first
among equals."

Yet there is a paradox in this canonical approach to power in the
gospel, where the force of authority is conceived as a primacy of service and where the weakness of the cross is a symbol of love through
sacrifice. "The first will be last" (Matthew 20:16 NAB); for "the Son
of Man did not come to be served, but to serve" (Matthew 20:28).
An ecumenical patriarch's primacy rests both in the shepherd's
cloak of service and sacrifice as well as in the institutional authority
of canons. However, understanding the precise meaning and true
source of primacy continues to be debated among Orthodox theologians as mentioned in chapter 2. The glaring differences of opinion
and interpretation erupted with the Ravenna Document produced
by the Orthodox-Catholic theological dialogue. The Moscow

Patriarchate did not sign that document, choosing instead to submit a separate position paper.

Despite such disagreements, dialogue and bridge building define Bartholomew's service and authority—among the various religious communities, among the Christian communions, and especially among the Orthodox churches. His leadership mirrors the pontifical work of his contemporary, Pope Francis, who reminded the world that the radical meaning and etymological root of the Latin word *pontifex* is "bridge builder" (*pons* = bridge; and *fex*, from *facere* = make).

Now, as first among equals (*primus inter pares*) for the remaining autocephalous churches, Bartholomew has the vocation and obligation to lead his brother primates, and that is by no means an easy task. He understands the transition to the modern reality of autocephalous churches—churches with changing national, and sometimes seeming imperial identity. Even under intense pressure from the Turkish state, he has never failed to act in this role as arbiter and convener of world Orthodoxy.

In this context, the innovative approach that Bartholomew has brought to the governance of worldwide Orthodoxy in order to advance greater communion and cooperation is precisely the institution of the Synaxis of Primates—the first time that the heads of the Orthodox churches have gathered informally to discuss matters of common concern. However, already from the convocation of the First Synaxis of Primates in 1992—which also marked the beginning of Bartholomew's steady navigation of the Orthodox Church toward the Holy and Great Council—his vision and ministry dovetailed with the already initiated and ongoing process of four Pan-Orthodox Conferences started by Patriarch Athenagoras (three at Rhodes in 1961, 1963, and 1964; the fourth at Chambésy, Geneva, in 1968), five Pan-Orthodox Pre-Conciliar Conferences begun under Patriarch Demetrios (at Chambésy,-Geneva in 1976, 1982, 1986, 2009, and 2015), and a series of Inter-Orthodox Preparatory Commissions (at Chambésy, Geneva, in 1971, 1986, 1990, 1993, and 2009—the last two during Bartholomew's patriarchal tenure). Moreover, Bartholomew significantly accelerated the pace of preparation with six Synaxes of Primates: in March 1992 (Istanbul), September 1995 (Patmos), January and December 2000 (two sessions: Jerusalem-Bethlehem and Istanbul-Nicaea [modern İznik]), October 2008 (Istanbul), March 2014 (Istanbul), and January 2016 (Chambésy, Geneva).

In addition, two Special Congresses were organized at Chambésy, Geneva, in 1977, when a group of scientists and theologians discussed the calculation and common celebration of Easter; and in 1995, when a meeting of canon law specialists gathered to discuss regulations for the operation of so-called regional assemblies of bishops in the diaspora sometime in the future. Therefore, Bartholomew's institution of the Synaxis of Primates (leading to six meetings) was insightful and farsighted inasmuch as it inaugurated and inspired greater Orthodox cooperation, serving to facilitate and finalize the substantial work of the previous Pan-Orthodox consultations and commissions, even in the face of tremendous obstacles.

Chief among these obstacles, paradoxical as it may seem, was the fall of the Soviet Union and the restoration of the Orthodox churches in Russia and the Balkans. Churches that were for decades either suppressed or exploited by their governments suddenly found themselves liberated but now forced to confront their own institutional compromises of the past. No church was more affected by this new reality than the Moscow Patriarchate.

Bartholomew, a youthful but insightful patriarch at the time, did not hesitate to turn the rudder of the church directly into the roiling waters of the new world order. When Patriarch Alexei of Moscow faced enormous pressure about his record under the old Soviet regime, and particularly accusations pertaining to KGB affiliation, Bartholomew took the most unusual and daring step to visit Moscow in 1993. Standing with his new brother, Bartholomew bestowed the Ecumenical Patriarchate's seal of approval on the new patriarch of Moscow. This early intuitive intervention proved critical to Alexei's perception of legitimacy, preceding the ascendancy of Vladimir Putin and the enormous growth of the Moscow Patriarchate's financial power and political prestige.

Of course, as Moscow has increased, it is no secret that it has sought the diminishment of the Ecumenical Patriarchate, asserting that its own size and strength dwarf that of the first throne of Orthodoxy. As true as the numbers might be—much like the fiction of a "third Rome"—they nonetheless belie a deeper issue of contention: autocephaly.

The Ins and Outs of Autocephaly

In his address to the assembled heads of the Orthodox churches at the Fourth Synaxis of Primates in October 2008—the same assembly where Russian Patriarch Alexei would make his last public stand for the unity of the Orthodox Church—Bartholomew expressed how autocephaly should be perceived and how it has been misconceived in the Orthodox Church:

> This institution of autocephaly dates back to the early church, when the so-called "Pentarchy" of the ancient Apostolic Sees and Churches—namely, of Rome, Constantinople, Alexandria, Antioch, and Jerusalem—was still valid. The communion or "symphony" of these sees expressed the unity of the universal church throughout the *oikoumene*. However, this pentarchy was severed after the tragic schism of 1054 AD between Rome and Constantinople originally, and afterward between Rome and the other patriarchates. Subsequently, to the four Orthodox patriarchates that remained after the Schism, from the middle of the second millennium to our day, other autocephalous churches were added until we arrived at the prevailing organization of the Orthodox Church throughout the world today.
>
> Yet . . . the overall system of autocephaly was encroached in recent years, through secular influences, by the spirit of ethnophyletism or, still worse, of state nationalism, to the degree that the basis for autocephaly now became the local secular nation, whose boundaries, as we all know, do not remain stable but depend on historical circumstance. . . . So has Orthodoxy been divided?
>
> The response commonly proffered is that, despite administrational division, Orthodoxy remains united in faith and the sacraments. But is this sufficient? . . .
>
> When we fail to constitute a single Orthodox Church in the so-called diaspora in accordance with the ecclesiological and

canonical principles of our church—how can we avoid the image of division in Orthodoxy? . . .

This is the healthy significance of the institution of auto-cephaly: While it assures the self-governance of each church with regard to its internal life and organization, nonetheless on matters affecting the entire Orthodox Church and its rela-tions with the outside world, each autocephalous church does not act alone but in coordination with the rest of the Orthodox churches. If this coordination either disappears or diminishes, then autocephaly becomes "autocephalism"—a kind of radical independence—namely, a factor of division rather than unity within the Orthodox Church.

Case Studies: Albania and the OCA

As ecumenical patriarch, it falls to Bartholomew to recognize the validity of any autocephaly, so that it may be determined and executed in accordance with the canonical regulations and eccle-siological principles of the church as well as in concord with the whole of Orthodoxy. This is no small or simple matter. It was the prevailing tradition that, even when self-declared, the autocephaly of a particular church was not validated until Constantinople for-mally recognized it. The churches that emerged from the death throes of the Ottoman Empire self-declared their autocephaly in their own national and often narrow interests, frequently creating schisms before Constantinople was able to provide the healing balm of restoring peace and order to the body ecclesiastic.

When Bartholomew became ecumenical patriarch, even as the Iron Curtain rusted to nothing, he discerned the injustices perpetrated by the Communist tyranny on Orthodoxy that needed attention. With remarkable adeptness and foresight, he completely revived—resurrecting literally from the ashes—the virtually obliterated Albanian Orthodox Church. He embarked upon sensitive and skillful negotiations with the government in the Republic of Albania, selecting for the task a substantive hierarch in the open-minded, widely educated, and mission-experienced Anastasios [Yannoulatos] to serve as its new primate, while at the same time pastorally and paternally preparing the faithful of Albania for a renewed autocephalous church. Bartholomew's right to recognize—or, indeed, in this case to revive—the independence of a church has become one of the most contentious issues facing the Orthodox Church today.

There also remains the thorny issue of the "granting" of autocephaly by a church other than Constantinople. In perhaps the most conspicuous of these instances, the Patriarchate of Moscow attempted such a declaration in 1970, when it unilaterally created the Orthodox Church in America (OCA) out of diverse communities of immigrants and converts torn between their loyalty to mother Russia, their discomfort with the atheist Soviet state, and their allegiance to their new homeland in America. Before this, the OCA was a mission diocese of the Russian Orthodox Church that declared itself temporarily autonomous in the 1920s due to the massive persecutions by the Communist regime. By the 1950s the mission diocese had grown to several dioceses and was known as the "Metropolia." Only six years into the reign of Leonid Brezhnev, the Moscow Patriarchate proclaimed this minority body in the United States—though there were also anomalous cases where the Orthodox Church in America had parishes in Australia and elsewhere—as a completely independent autocephalous church, of equal standing with the other autocephalous churches. The autocephaly of the OCA was recognized by churches under the Soviet sphere of influence, but not by others, including Constantinople.

Nonetheless, Constantinople has responded not by shunning the clergy or faithful of the OCA, but by insisting that the order of the Orthodox Church must be observed by not recognizing or approving an anomaly. As Bartholomew noted in 2008, "the autocephaly of later churches grew out of respect for the cultural identity of nations," but the OCA represented less than 20 percent of the Orthodox Christians in North America.

Bartholomew was already involved in and supportive of dialogue with the OCA from the outset. And when he ascended the first throne of Orthodoxy, he took special steps to reach out to the OCA, even accepting an honorary doctorate in 1997 from its flagship seminary, St. Vladimir's in New York. More recently, as the patriarch told the Executive Committee of the Assembly of Bishops of North America in 2010, "We love the OCA." Love is never the issue with Bartholomew; his heart is always ready to reach out across any and all divides to embrace the individual or community in his presence. And he is unequivocal in recognizing OCA clergy as "full concelebrants." On the Sunday of Orthodoxy 2016, at the outset of Great Lent, Metropolitan Tikhon was invited by Bartholomew to concelebrate the Divine Liturgy at the Phanar—the third time that Metropolitan Tikhon had been invited by the ecumenical patriarch, but the first time that any metropolitan head of the OCA had ever concelebrated with the ecumenical patriarch.

For its part, the OCA would argue that the purpose of its autocephaly was not simply to acquire independence but primarily to witness to and work for Orthodox unity in North America. However, Bartholomew's faithfulness to the history and tradition of Orthodoxy is also beyond reproach. Thus, while he has embraced the OCA personally and continues to initiate avenues of communication as well as pursue methods for resolving the situation, he has nevertheless addressed the anomaly caused by the capricious actions of the Moscow Patriarchate. As he declared openly to Metropolitan Tikhon, "While differences in understanding remain with regard to the nature of autocephaly, this does not present an impediment to communion and concelebration." At Bartholomew's initiative, a canonical process for resolving the problem has now been instituted—perhaps for the first time—with the Assembly of Bishops; and the patriarch has clearly opened wide the doors of communication. The response will be indicative of the desire—and humility—to proceed with the same benevolence.

The OCA issue remains unresolved and is especially painful for those of us in the United States, who recognize and respect while also concelebrating and cooperating with many of its distinguished representatives—in the present as in the past: suffice it to mention clergy-theologians such as Fr. Alexander Schmemann and Fr. John Meyendorff. Both toiled to retain unity and mission as the principal vision for the church. In the 1960s, Schmemann and the Greek Orthodox Archbishop Iakovos had even imagined a joint property for their two flagship seminaries (St. Vladimir's in New York and Holy Cross in Massachusetts); it might well have proved an organic and grassroots approach to unity. And, as a phil-hellene, Meyendorff made no secret of his desire for dialogue with the Ecumenical Patriarchate to resolve the canonical situation in America; he spoke warmly of the intentions of and reception at the Phanar, convinced that the Ecumenical Patriarchate wanted to reach a resolution.

Bartholomew is casually criticized for interfering in local church affairs, particularly when it comes to the so-called diaspora—namely, regions outside of the traditional territories of the "mother" or "auto-cephalous" churches. Ironically, the late Fr. John Meyendorff—who died prematurely, just months after Bartholomew was elected patriarch—wrote prophetically in 1978 in the pages of the OCA's publication, *The Orthodox Church*:

It is unquestionable that the Orthodox conception of the church recognizes the need for a leadership of the world episcopate, for a certain spokesmanship by the first patriarch, for a ministry of coordination without which conciliarity is impossible. Because Constantinople, also called "New Rome," was the capital of the empire, the ecumenical council designated its bishop—in accord-ance with the practical realities of that day—for this position of leadership, which he has kept until this day, even if the empire does not exist anymore . . . and the Patriarchate of Constantinople was not deprived of its "ecumenicity," being always answerable to the conciliar consciousness of the church. In the present chaotic years, the Orthodox Church could indeed use wise, objective, and authoritative leadership from the Ecumenical Patriarchate.

More Fish to Fry: Autonomy and Annexation

Few then may appreciate Bartholomew's concern for advancing Orthodox unity in the correct, canonical fashion. Still fewer are aware that he has even more fish to fry. Bartholomew has also taken it upon himself to right additional, arguably more agonizing, wrongs of history.

As already noted, when the Moscow Patriarchate annexed—actually reabsorbed—the Estonian Church in 1945, the national aspirations of its people were dashed against the newly raised Iron Curtain. Many may still remember the "Singing Revolution" that began in 1987 with spontaneous mass demonstrations chanting banned national songs. With the fall of the Berlin Wall on November 9, 1989, it was clear to everyone within and without the Soviet Union that the end was here and near. The Singing Revolution continued for four years until, in the face of invading Soviet tanks, the courageous people of Estonia shielded their institutions with their bodies. Estonia became independent on August 21, 1991, without the shedding of a single drop of blood. This new reality posed a quandary for the Orthodox Christians of Estonia, whose own church had been suppressed and whose own citizens had been "russified" over many years of population exchange and drain. Moreover, the current patriarch of Moscow was none other than Alexei [Ridiger], born in Estonia and serving as the bishop of the Russian Orthodox Church in Estonia from 1961 to 1986.

Bartholomew knew all too well what it was like to suffer as a minority in one's own land; he had seen the cultural devastation that proceeds from forced population exchanges. However, in Estonia's case, the precedent was already set; Estonia had received an autonomous status under the Ecumenical Patriarchate in 1923 and the restoration of the Orthodox Church in Estonia was not only his right, but his responsibility. The patriarch of Moscow would not be pleased; even seemingly informed critics would not understand. They would regard this as much more than a mere incursion into Moscow's presumed zone of jurisdictional control and canonical authority. This was a personal affront to Alexei; it was also a portent of things to come in Ukraine.

However, Bartholomew understood the insecurity of the Russian Orthodox Patriarchate, which was still trying to assert an expansionist, territorial sway corresponding and equal to that of the borders of the former Soviet Union. No one truly knows how much pressure had been exerted on the Russian Church to help cement the position of the Russian Federation. But what had not gone unnoticed was how much attention was being paid to the Russian diaspora, who lived in lands that comprised the canonical privilege of the Ecumenical Patriarchate. Bartholomew understood very well how personal this was for Alexei but, as in all things, the ecumenical patriarch chose justice over indifference and the disenfranchised over the power hungry. Thus, in a letter to Alexei of February 24, 1996, Bartholomew wrote:

> The most holy Church of Russia is not at all justified in accusing the Ecumenical Patriarchate of encroaching in the internal affairs of the Church of Russia while transgressing the sacred canons. On the contrary, the Patriarchate of Russia during those years trespassed in countries under the spiritual jurisdiction of the Ecumenical Patriarchate—namely, Estonia, Hungary, and

elsewhere—always by the power of the Soviet army. The Church of Russia did not at any time seek the opinion of the Ecumenical Patriarchate, nor was any respect shown it. The annexation of the Orthodox Church of Estonia into the Most Holy Church of Russia happened arbitrarily and uncanonically. And it is certain that events that are uncanonical at one particular time are never blessed, never seen as efficacious, and could never set a precedent.

Nonetheless, even if the issue were not one of a territory belonging to the spiritual jurisdiction of the Ecumenical Patriarchate according to the strict interpretation of the canons, it was still duty-bound to intervene; of course, not of its own volition, but if invited to do so by someone who has been wronged. In Canons 9 and 17 of the holy Fourth Ecumenical Council in Chalcedon, the holy and God-bearing fathers placed upon the Church of Constantinople the most onerous responsibility of adjudicating cases of other local churches when called upon to do so. The immense weight of this responsibility is demonstrated by the issue at hand, when in defense of a small number of people who are Orthodox Estonians, the Ecumenical Patriarchate has to displease the most holy and cherished daughter Church of Russia. It does this precisely in defense of this small flock, not for personal gain, since the Ecumenical Patriarchate stands to gain nothing from this situation apart from the moral reward that comes from the gratitude of the Orthodox Estonians. . . .

We declare, then, before God and man, that the Orthodox faithful of Russian descent constitute for us beloved children of the church, the same as are the Orthodox Estonians, and we are ready to protect them also, if necessary.

The Archondónis family (center, age 5)

Demétrios
Archondónis
(age 5)

On completing
elementary school
(top right, age 11)

With friends
at Haghioi
Theodoroi
(far left, early
teens)

As a seminarian at
the Phanar (1961)

Demétrios Archondónis
(age 16)

The Patriarchal Theological School
and Monastery at Halki

With his parents (1970)

On the day of his ordination
to deacon, with Metropolitan
Meliton at Imvros (1961)

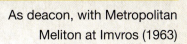

As deacon, with Metropolitan
Meliton at Imvros (1963)

With Ecumenical Patriarch
Athenagoras at Halki (1970)

His ordination
to bishop, with
Metropolitan
Meliton leading
(1973)

With Ecumenical Patriarch
Demetrios at the Phanar (1973)

With Ecumenical Patriarch
Demetrios in Geneva (1982)

At his enthronement
ceremony (1992)

On the day of his
enthronement, with
his mother (1992)

Consecration of the Holy Myron
at the Phanar (2002)

As Metropolitan of
Philadelphia (1973)

The return of the relics of Saints Gregory the
Theologian and John Chrysostom at the Phanar (2004)

With Archbishop
Iakovos (center)
and Archbishop
Demetrios of
America (right) in
New York (2004)

As a deacon, with Pope Paul VI at the Vatican (second from right, 1965)

With Pope Paul VI at the Vatican (1978)

With Pope John Paul II at the Vatican (1995)

With Pope Benedict at the Phanar (2006)

With Archbishop Rowan Williams of Canterbury at Lambeth Palace (2005)

With Archbishop Justin Welby of Canterbury at the Phanar (2014)

With Pope Francis and Presidents Peres and Abbas at the Vatican (2014)

With Pope Francis at the Phanar (2014)

In his office at the Phanar

With crowds at the annual
pilgrimage to Panaghia
Soumela (2010)

The compound at
the Phanar, with the
Patriarchal Church of
St. George, offices,
and dormitories

Holding the title of the Prinkipos
Orphanage at the Phanar (2010)

With Bob Simon on *60 Minutes* at Halki (2009)

Receiving the Congressional Gold Medal from Senator Strom Thurmond and Speaker Newt Gingrich (1997)

At Ground Zero, New York City (2004)

In New Orleans after Hurricane Katrina (2006)

As priest (top, third from left) at the Inter-Orthodox Preparatory Commission for the Great Council in Chambésy, Geneva (1971)

The First Synaxis of Primates at the Phanar (1992)

The Fourth Synaxis of Primates at the Phanar (2008)

Opening session of the Holy and Great Council (June 2016)

With Jane Goodall at the
First Halki Summit (2012)

With Prince Philip at Buckingham
Palace (1993)

Recording the opening
of the church year and
the day of prayer for the
environment on September 1

With Vice President
Al Gore at the
Phanar (2007)

With Secretary-General Ban Ki Moon at the United Nations (2009)

At the ecological symposium in the Arctic (2007)

PEACE AND TOLERANCE II

The Second Peace and Tolerance Conference in Istanbul (2005)

With Australian Prime Minister Julia Gillard at the Phanar (2012)

With President Fidel Castro in Cuba (2004)

With German Chancellor Angela Merkel at the Phanar (2006)

With Turkish President Recep Tayyip Erdoğan in Prinkipos (2011)

With Russian President Dmitry Medvedev and Patriarch Kirill of Moscow at the Kremlin (2010)

As Metropolitan of Philadelphia (center) with US President Jimmy Carter at the Phanar (1985)

With US President Bill Clinton at the White House (1997)

With US President George H. W. Bush at the Metropolitan Museum, New York (2004)

With US President George W. Bush at the White House (2004)

With Senator
Hillary Clinton in
New York (2004)

With Austrian President Heinz
Fischer at the Phanar (2008)

With French President
François Hollande at the
Élysée Palace (2012)

With US President
Barack Obama at the
White House (2009)

The opening liturgy of the Holy and Great Council (June 2016)

Holding a refugee baby, with Pope Francis in Lesbos (2016)

Visiting the nursing home at Baloukli, Istanbul

Celebrating the Feast of the Exultation of the Holy Cross on September 14 at the Phanar

When Rivalry Reverts to Relationship

Bartholomew was right. This has been the traditional practice of the Orthodox Church uninterruptedly and consistently, while these specific canons have remained permanent and unchanged in the conscience of the church from the earliest and formative years. This is true not only in the first fifteen centuries until the fall of Constantinople, but it has also proved valid from 1453 to our days. There are more than sixty instances in the history of Constantinopolitan initiatives and conciliar interventions from 1575 to the early twentieth century—ironically, though not surprisingly, a large number of these relate to the Church of Moscow. Moreover, there are more than forty historical examples to the same effect, related to activities in the diaspora from the beginning of the twentieth century to the present.

Still, even with such assurances, Alexei removed Bartholomew's name from his diptychs for a short time—the severest form of institutional censure in the Orthodox Church—thereby causing a brief rupture in the communion of the Orthodox world. Yet Alexei's wrath could not endure against the integrity of Bartholomew's stance. Years would go by before any accommodation was made, to allow the presence of both churches inside Estonia.

At the historic Synaxis of Primates in 2008, Bartholomew had also invited both the heads of the Estonian Church and of the Finnish Church—another autonomous church, formerly under the Moscow Patriarchate until 1923 (like Estonia) and subsequently under the Ecumenical Patriarchate—to be present at the proceedings. This was particularly sensitive for Alexei, as he had never been put into a public situation in which he had to interact with the head of the Estonian

Church. As during every synaxis, the event concluded with two formal events: first, a solemn concelebration of the Divine Liturgy by all the heads of churches, and second, a fellowship dinner for all involved.

During the Divine Liturgy, the moment came for the hierarchs to respond to the exhortation: "Let us love one another that in one mind we may confess." Each primate, starting from Bartholomew as the first in rank, in turn embraced his fellow hierarchs with the "kiss of peace." The head of the Estonian Church, Metropolitan Stephanos, was included in the liturgical celebration of the day; he would also have to pass by Patriarch Alexei. When the moment came, the two smiled and embraced, and all who looked on realized that an enormous hurdle had been overcome. Bartholomew had—by his mere presence as ecumenical patriarch, as the father of worldwide Orthodoxy—at the very least bandaged a wound whose depth reached back nearly one hundred years. Later that day, in an address during the closing luncheon, Alexei would heartily praise Bartholomew for his wisdom in bringing the synaxis together, as he raised his glass to toast his host and brother.

Entering the Final Stretch

Toward the Holy and Great Council

The Synaxis of Primates in 2008 was the turning point for closing the gap to the Holy and Great Council. Scheduled within the context of the year dedicated to two millennia since the birth of Saint Paul, Apostle to the Gentiles, the synaxis was followed by a scholarly and spiritual symposium on October 11–17, 2008, with a unique pilgrimage to some of the cities of Asia Minor and Greece visited by Saint Paul during his missionary journeys. In his address to the Synaxis of the Primates on October 10, 2008, Bartholomew clearly laid out the reasons for convening the Holy and Great Council, which would address such issues as theological dialogues with the non-Orthodox, the environment, bioethics, and, above all, the diaspora. With the decision to resume the Pre-Conciliar Conferences, especially with the objective of eventually forming the Assemblies of Bishops throughout the diaspora, a huge obstacle was within reach of being overcome. As the primates declared in their final message of the 2008 synaxis:

> As primates and representatives of the most holy Orthodox churches—fully aware of the gravity of the problems [of unity] and laboring to confront them directly as "servants of Christ and stewards of the mysteries of God" (1 Corinthians 4:1)—we proclaim and reaffirm:

> 1. Our unswerving position and obligation to safeguard the unity of the Orthodox Church in "the faith which was once for all delivered to the saints" (Jude 3), the faith of our fathers, in the common Divine Eucharist and in the faithful observance of the canonical system of church governance by settling any problems that arise from time to time in relations among us with a spirit of love and peace.

2. Our desire for the swift healing of every canonical anomaly that has arisen from historical circumstances and pastoral requirements, such as in the so-called Orthodox diaspora, with a view to overcoming every possible influence that is foreign to Orthodox ecclesiology. In this respect we welcome the proposal by the Ecumenical Patriarchate to convene Pan-Orthodox conferences within the coming year 2009 on this subject, as well as for the continuation of preparations for the Holy and Great Council.

The Assemblies of Bishops

During the days from June 6 to June 13, 2009, the representatives of all autocephalous churches gathered at the Orthodox Center of the Ecumenical Patriarchate in Chambésy, Geneva, and a momentous decision was unanimously taken to create the Assemblies of Bishops in countries with overlapping jurisdictions. In fact, the clear and explicit mandate of the Assemblies of Bishops, their "unswerving obligation" (to cite their "Rules of Operation," Article 5.1a) is to safeguard the unity of the church and (to quote the primates' Message of 2008) to advance "the swift healing" of the canonical anomalies, especially the problem of the parallel presence of multiple bishops in one and the same city.

At the same meeting, the representatives created—originally twelve but, at a subsequent meeting, thirteen—assemblies in the following regions: (1) North America, Canada, and Central America; (2) Latin America; (3) Australia, New Zealand, and Oceania; (4) Great Britain and Ireland; (5) France; (6) Belgium, Holland, and Luxembourg; (7) Austria; (8) Italy and Malta; (9) Switzerland and

Liechtenstein; (10) Germany; (11) Scandinavian countries (except Finland); and (12) Spain and Portugal. (In 2014, the United States and Canada were recognized as a distinct assembly, while Central America joined the Assembly of Bishops in Latin America.)

These regions represented more than one hundred bishops around the world and, for the first time in the modern era, brought together hierarchs of the diaspora to discuss common concerns under the umbrella of a Pan-Orthodox process that would lead to the first Holy and Great Council of the Orthodox Church in more than a thousand years. From this perspective, in the lead-up to as in the wake of the council, perhaps the most consequential and enduring pronouncement of this council will be its deliberation and determination regarding the organization and administration of the Orthodox Church throughout the world. The question is whether churches, such as in the United States, western Europe, and Australasia—composed of Orthodox immigrants and converts long established in their new homelands, miles away and cultures apart from their "mother churches" of origin—have reached the maturity or acquired the single-mindedness and commitment to minister to their people in harmony and manage their affairs in unity.

Regrettably, many Orthodox churches seem to be retreating into a stifling, sheltered, and safe provincialism, which they explain—or excuse—as attending to internal affairs that are in turn reckoned as more important pastorally than concerns for collegiality and communion. What is again unfortunate is that contemporary church leaders, who have been exposed to and educated in the modern world and its global challenges—at least by comparison with their predecessors, who were perhaps restricted by the Iron Curtain or an oppressive xenophobia—appear less interested in transcending parochialism and prejudice.

This matter alone—the concerted effort to resolve the anomaly of overlapping jurisdictions in the diaspora, the recognition that nationalism has stealthily, though steadily, encroached on and been accepted as "normal" in Orthodox church life—should be sufficient reason for a council to convene.

The deplorable rise of religious nationalism in the nineteenth and twentieth centuries has rendered the Orthodox churches increasingly independent of and imperious over one another, a practice that ultimately—and paradoxically—differs little from the Orthodox censure and caricature of Roman primacy. How ironic that the First Vatican Council (in 1870) was held almost contemporaneously as the Pan-Orthodox Council of Constantinople (in 1872) that "decried, denounced, and condemned" ethnophyletism (a church being defined by its nationality) while "emphatically declaring its proponents schismatics."

The creation of the Assemblies of Bishops then is itself a test of the willingness and readiness—ultimately the integrity—of the Orthodox churches to be and to work together, to acknowledge and affirm their unity. In this respect, the assemblies are a strikingly radical, even potentially revolutionary, opportunity for such unity to materialize. Otherwise, the Orthodox churches may be avoiding their responsibility and shunning the possibility of a solution to the delicate question of church unity—that is, if they have not become so dysfunctional through division and ambition or if they do not lack the will or the humility to remember and realize the vision of church unity.

An Agenda for the Council

Despite misgivings and resistance, the items on the agenda for the Holy and Great Council were determined by the Synaxis of Primates in 2008 and became public after the Synaxis of Primates in 2014. The topics basically cover the areas of internal relations, pastoral matters, and external relations:

a. Internal relations among the Orthodox churches:
   1. The Orthodox diaspora
   2. Autonomy and how it is proclaimed
   3. Autocephaly and how it is proclaimed
   4. The diptychs

b. Issues of pastoral (or practical) nature:
   5. A common calendar
   6. Impediments to marriage
   7. Regulations for fasting

c. External relations with other churches and the world:
   8. Bilateral and multilateral dialogues
   9. Orthodoxy and the ecumenical movement
   10. The contribution of Orthodoxy to peace, freedom, solidarity, love, and the elimination of discrimination

From March 2014 to October 2015, a special committee and a Pan-Orthodox Conference revised the documents and reduced the items on the agenda to six: the diaspora, autonomy, impediments to marriage, fasting regulations, items 8 (inter-Christian dialogues) and 9 (ecumenical relations) combined into a single issue, and the last item retitled "The mission of the Orthodox Church in the contemporary world."

The Synaxis of Primates in January 2016 issued a formal resolution about what could arguably prove to be the foremost discussion and directive of the Holy and Great Council:

> The assemblies of bishops on the one hand tangibly reveal the unity of the Orthodox Church . . . and on the other hand ascertain the impossibility of immediately transitioning to the strict canonical order of the church. Therefore, the synaxis resolved to propose to the Holy and Great Council the preservation of this institution *until such time as circumstances mature* for the application of canonical precision.

In some ways the question of the diaspora was already resolved with the creation of the Assemblies of Bishops and by being referred to the council. Despite the lack of a formal statement or document for the council, the Assemblies of Bishops remain an agreed-upon methodology and procedure. The real question is not whether the bishops-in-council can formulate a clear resolution to the problem of Orthodox unity in the diaspora, but whether the churches—in each of the regions where Assemblies of Bishops were established—can manage to transcend their narrow nationalistic interests. Someday, when an assembly agrees on a plan for unity in its region, the process of its acceptance and adoption will be determined by a future council, which will be obliged once again to consider and resolve once for all the thorny question of autocephaly.

CONCILIARITY AND COLLEGIALITY

Comprehending Communion

Retrieving the principle and practice of conciliarity, or adherence to a council's authority, involves a process of relearning, perhaps also renouncing preconceptions about hierarchy and primacy; it also involves receptiveness to fresh ways of being and working together. In order to discover or recover the conciliar nature of the church, Bartholomew is convinced that the Orthodox churches must—first of all and above all—assemble and sit together. The Greek word for "council" is *synodos*, which signifies far more than just convocation or cooperation; it literally means "being on the same road with one another."

Moreover, in order to retrieve the lost sense of conciliarity, Orthodox churches must first exercise a reconciliatory spirit among themselves. If they are honest with one another, with their faithful, and with God, they would admit that they have unfortunately misplaced the experience of conciliarity that prevailed in earlier centuries. As a result, it will take a long process of education—a lifetime of cultivating and convening councils—to retrieve and relearn this culture as an intrinsic awareness and gracious etiquette of church life.

That is precisely why conciliarity is a matter of culture and not just a problem of consensus. It is something learned over time. And the truth is that the Orthodox churches have lost the sense and sensitivity—the art and culture—of being and working together. The isolation of centuries has made it appear normal—traditional and natural—for so many of the Orthodox churches to adopt an anti-Western bias. Some of them are literally between past and present.

It is not so much that they are opposed to the West, but they are not adequately exposed to the West. It is not so much that they are allergic to modernity, but they are exceedingly allured by antiquity. It is not so much that they have been resistant to ecumenical openness, but they are asphyxiated by their isolation. Culture matters, but culture matures only with time. It can neither be improvised nor simulated.

Meeting in council then is not a luxury for the Orthodox Church; it is indispensable for its life. Indeed, it is precisely what other churches and communions perceive in and expect from the Orthodox. By rejecting the principle and practice of conciliarity, what the Orthodox Church practices ceases to be what it preaches. There can be no Orthodox Church without conciliarity and collegiality; in the absence of these, the church may well function institutionally, but it is not a church. By ignoring conciliarity and communion, the Orthodox Church may well be able to survive, even demonstrating allure through its sense of antiquity and authority. But it ceases to be what it has been for centuries; it ceases, in fact, to be the Orthodox Church.

In the Acts of the Apostles, at the very first council of Jerusalem, it is only when the disciples were gathered together that "there came a sound from heaven, as of a rushing mighty wind"; and we read that it descended "suddenly" (Acts 2:2)—that is to say, unexpectedly, surprisingly, breathtakingly.

Only time will demonstrate just how much the Orthodox autocephalous churches learn from being together in council; just as time will determine the status of this council for the life of the church. But if they could lay aside their nationalism and antagonism, then the Holy and Great Council promised to be a watershed event in church history, setting in motion a series of regular conciliar gatherings.

Convening the Great Council

In the years prior to the council, there would be further obstacles, but Bartholomew never took his eye off the sacred goal. Those years have been marked by a new leader of the Russian Church, Patriarch Kirill, as well as by an increasingly degenerating situation in Ukraine, in both the political and ecclesiastical spheres. Amid and despite these pressures, Bartholomew convened another Synaxis of Primates, in late January 2016, fewer than five months before the council was scheduled to meet. He expressed his conviction about the importance of the council:

> All of us yearn with the same zeal for the convocation without further delay of the Holy and Great Council of our most holy Church, given that "the time is short" [1 Corinthians 7:29] since over fifty years of deferment and postponement have seriously exposed our church in the eyes of adversaries and friends, not to speak also of God and history. Let us, therefore, advance swiftly with the task that lies before us, "looking unto Jesus, the author and finisher of our faith" [Hebrews 12:2], who through the intercessions of his all-pure mother and all the saints "will not leave [us] orphans" [cf. John 14:18], but rather through the Paraclete will unite us in the same place at the council, just as he unites us in his body and blood. "The things which are impossible with men are possible with God" [Luke 18:27].

In June 2016, during the week surrounding the Feast of Pentecost and the descent of the Holy Spirit on the apostles in the first Christian community, His All-Holiness Bartholomew would convene what so many had said for so many years was impossible—the Holy and Great Council of the Orthodox Christian Church. Some 300 bishops and advisors from every corner of the planet came together on the island of Crete—a semiautonomous church of the Ecumenical Patriarchate—for fraternal dialogue, even if sometimes heated debate, and, ultimately, celebration of their unity in Christ.

Even in announcing the members of his delegation for the Holy and Great Council, Bartholomew would make a formidable and forward-looking statement by including a diverse group of men and women. One-quarter of the delegation of the Ecumenical Patriarchate were non-Greeks (from Finland and Estonia, from Ukrainian and Carpatho-Russian dioceses, as well as from the patriarchal exarchate for Russian parishes in western Europe), more than one-third were from the United States, and two were women.

As the opening of the council approached, the world would marvel. Cynics would be surprised. Critics would be silenced. But one man had seen the harbor long before any shore was in sight.

Note: The manuscript for this book was delivered to the publisher in late March 2016, three months before the Holy and Great Council of the Orthodox Church convened in Crete (June 16–26, 2016). While all fourteen churches had agreed to attend, three churches revoked their commitments within ten days of the opening while the Church of Russia withdrew twenty-four hours after its scheduled arrival. The churches in attendance included the ancient patriarchates of Constantinople, Alexandria, and Jerusalem; and the modern patriarchates of Serbia and Romania; as well as the churches of Cyprus, Greece, Poland, Albania, and the Czech Lands and Slovakia.

AL GORE JR.

Former Vice President of the United States

HIS ALL-HOLINESS ECUMENICAL PATRIARCH BARTHOLOMEW HAS made it his life's work to remove the barriers that separate people from one another, from their Creator and from the creation, of which we are an integral part. His teachings about the sanctity of Earth and the unique passion he brings to his defense of our common home have brought communities together across the lines that too often have divided us, and have contributed significantly to humanity's effort to find common ground in the epic struggle to solve the climate crisis. If, as many have taught, the purpose of life is to glorify God in all that we do, is it not a sin to treat God's creation with such utter contempt?

Throughout history—and even now, when the scale of our despoliation exceeds the grasp of our moral imagination—many have trivialized concern for the environment as an idealistic indulgence. Yet Patriarch Bartholomew has utilized his moral and spiritual authority to stake out a clear path to preserve our natural environment and to ensure the bequest by those now living of a better world to future generations. His eloquent words bridge the gap between the religious and scientific communities, empowering and encouraging them to discover their many shared interests and goals and unite in pursuing them.

The Ecumenical Patriarchate has a long history of concern for our natural environment, but it is Bartholomew's ongoing and relentless drive to ensure that our concerns for human dignity, human rights, and social justice are not separate from our concern for ecological preservation and sustainability that long ago earned him the title "the Green Patriarch." Time and again Patriarch Bartholomew's words and actions have demonstrated to us that concern for the environment is not a political or ideological matter, but is—in its essence—a moral and spiritual imperative.

Since the earliest days following his election, Patriarch Bartholomew has convened symposia on the need for a mindful connection between Creator and creation. He has visited and comforted those most vulnerable to the devastating impacts of global warming, and—perhaps, most importantly—he has forced the pace of religious debate and has helped to convince others in almost every global community of faith that protection of our natural world requires international, interdisciplinary, and inter-religious cooperation. His joint statement with Pope Francis about the environment, issued from Jerusalem after their meeting there, was especially powerful. Patriarch Bartholomew's urgent, prophetic message is that the stewardship of creation is a moral duty required of all humans, regardless of creed or denomination.

CHAPTER 5

The Green Patriarch

Caring about This World as the Next

If human beings were to treat one another's personal property the way that they treat their environment, we would view that behavior as anti-social.
—Ecumenical Patriarch Bartholomew,
Santa Barbara, November 8, 1997

When Pope Francis released his much-anticipated environmental encyclical, *Laudato Si'*, on June 18, 2015, it was hardly surprising that he singled out and highlighted the example of the ecumenical patriarch:

Patriarch Bartholomew has drawn attention to the ethical and spiritual roots of environmental problems, which require that we look for solutions not only in technology but in a change of humanity; otherwise we would be dealing merely with symptoms. He asks us to replace consumption with sacrifice, greed with generosity, wastefulness with a spirit of sharing. (para. 9)

The pope's acknowledgment, both deserved and earned, exemplifies Bartholomew's long-standing leadership in caring for the environment. He has discerned "the signs of the times" and consistently proclaimed the primacy of spiritual values in determining environmental ethics. It is these endeavors that have rightly earned him the title "Green Patriarch"—originally coined and publicized by the media in 1996 but ceremoniously formalized in the White House in 1997 by Al Gore, vice president of the United States. It was precisely for this courageous leadership in "defining environmentalism as a spiritual responsibility" that *Time* magazine named him among the "100 Most Influential People" in the world in 2008.

A Radical Statement of Faith

On November 8, 1997, at an environmental symposium held in Santa Barbara, California, the patriarch presented a daring revision of the Christian perspective of sin by proposing that abusing the natural creation was nothing less than equivalent to sin. Addressing a prestigious gathering on the occasion of his first official visit to the United States as ecumenical patriarch, Bartholomew declared and affirmed his church's long-standing commitment to healing the environment, noting "with alarm the dangerous consequences of humanity's disregard for the survival of God's creation."

It was the first time that a religious leader had ever identified harming the environment with committing sin. His audience included the then US secretary of the interior Bruce Babbitt (representing President Bill Clinton), as well as oceanographic explorer

Jean-Michel Cousteau, and the executive director of the Sierra Club, Carl Pope. The last of these still acknowledges that this event was his first encounter with the intersection of faith and the environment. It was also the first time—though by no means the last—that the patriarch would invite and welcome the presence of an indigenous leader, in this case Paul Nosie Jr., of the San Carlos Apache tribe in Arizona, to an Orthodox environmental symposium.

Patriarch Bartholomew's undiluted criticism of ecological destruction was immediately seized and circulated by the international media:

> *To commit a crime against the natural world is a sin.* For human beings to cause species to become extinct and destroy the biological diversity of God's creation; for human beings to degrade the integrity of the earth by causing climate change, stripping the earth of its natural forests, or destroying its wetlands; for human beings to injure other human beings with disease or contaminate the earth's waters, its land, its air, and its life, with poisonous substances . . . these are sins.

This was a radical, indeed revolutionary, shift in emphasis on a subject that is so fundamental to theology and at the same time so objectionable to some laypeople. The national environmental news journal *Greenwire* (November 10, 1997) highlighted the patriarch's words as the "quote of the day." But, of course, it was much more than this. Bruce Babbitt, who was in the audience at the time of the patriarch's address, declared that "this pronouncement will be seen in the future as one of the great, seminal important religious statements of our time." Larry Stammer, religion writer for the *Los Angeles Times*, called it "an unprecedented religious defense of the environment . . . the first time that a major international religious leader has explicitly linked environmental problems with sinful behavior" (Sunday, November 9, 1997). The watershed event was witnessed by many others, including Paul Gorman, executive director of the National Religious Partnership for the Environment, for whom the patriarch's declaration pointed to "a whole new level of theological inquiry into the cause, depth, and dimension of human responsibility by lifting up that word: sin!" And Carl Pope admitted the profound error and failure of environmentalists, who failed hitherto to recognize the mission of religion to address climate change and preserve creation, confessing that his generation of environmentalists had sinned. As I sat in the audience in 1997, I could not help but smile at the irony of someone by the name of "Pope" repenting!

Even the actual pope, Francis himself, in the *Laudato Si'*, expressed appreciation for this bold assertion:

> Patriarch Bartholomew has spoken in particular of the need for
> each of us to repent of the ways we have harmed the planet. . . .
> He has repeatedly stated this firmly and persuasively, challeng-
> ing us to acknowledge our sins against creation.

There is no doubt that sin has been perceived and diagnosed very narrowly through the centuries, especially during the Middle Ages, which added a legalistic and moralistic dimension to wrongdoing. Instead of defining sin as a breakdown in relationships—whether among people or between people and the planet—it was reduced to a list of transgressions or misdemeanors before a sadist father figure somewhere in the distant heavens. Wouldn't it be amazing if people could begin approaching the sacrament of confession in order to admit their failure to protect God's creation?

Preparing the Soil of the Heart

The ecumenical patriarch's engagement with the environment began years before his enthronement in 1991, starting with his close personal affinity with nature in his youth and assistance with various environmental projects of the Ecumenical Patriarchate as director of the Private Patriarchal Office under Ecumenical Patriarch Demetrios.

During his childhood, the future Bartholomew developed a healthy, organic relationship with nature in his unspoiled home village, Haghioi Theodoroi, still known for its fresh air, clean water, and flowering oleander. He could roam the hillsides, looking for wildflowers for his mother and sister, chase donkeys and long-haired sheep down a craggy hill, and hike to a hilltop chapel. Hens laid eggs each day for breakfast, potatoes were pulled from the earth for roasting, ubiquitous olive trees supplied the family with olive oil, and "free-range" lambs were slaughtered before Pascha. Imvros was a poor island, but rich with nature's gifts and beauty. But it was probably his godmother, Chrysánthē, who first conferred on the patriarch his love for flowers and nature; her garden was filled with chrysanthemums and roses.

As an altar boy, young Bartholomew walked through the hills and valleys with his village priest to assist at the Divine Liturgy in nearby chapels, daily hearing such prayers as: "We give thanks to you, invisible King, who by your boundless power formed all things and by the fullness of your mercy brought everything out of nothingness into being." During Holy Week, just before the Easter Vigil, the hymns included Psalm 104: "O LORD my God, You are very great. . . . [You send] the springs into the valleys: they flow among the hills. They give drink to every beast of the field. . . . By them the birds of the heavens have their home; they sing among the branches. . . . The earth is satisfied with the fruit of Your works" (vv. 1–13). Nature was a refuge and a solace in his youth on Imvros and later on Halki, another unspoiled Turkish island replete with quiet and beauty. These early, intimate connections with the natural world prepared his heart and mind for the extraordinary challenges ahead.

A REVOLUTIONARY MOVEMENT BEGINS

Although the modern environmental movement exploded world-wide in 1962 with the publication of a book decrying the effect of pesticides (*Silent Spring* by Rachel Carson), the Orthodox Church's involvement essentially began with the General Assembly of the World Council of Churches in Vancouver in 1983, which resulted in several inter-Orthodox meetings on "Justice, Peace, and the Integrity of Creation." Three significant Orthodox consultations on the environment inspired by the Ecumenical Patriarchate took place in Sofia, Bulgaria (1987); Patmos, Greece (1988); and Minsk, Russia (1989)—all in the final years of Bartholomew's tenure as assistant to Ecumenical Patriarch Demetrios.

The second of these consultations, held in Patmos (1988), marked the nine-hundredth anniversary of the foundation of the historic Monastery of Saint John the Evangelist, built near the cave where Saint John—the Beloved Disciple of Jesus Christ and author of the fourth gospel, who is also known as the "divine" in the Western tradition and the "theologian" in the East—wrote down his inspired Revelation, the last book of the Christian Scriptures.

On this festive occasion, the Ecumenical Patriarchate and the Greek Ministry of Cultural Affairs jointly organized a conference with the local authorities of the island. Representing Patriarch Demetrios as keynote speaker was Metropolitan John [Zizioulas] of Pergamon, arguably the most influential theologian of our time, the most significant Orthodox spokesman on issues related to ecology and religion, and later chairman of the Academy of Athens. One of the paramount results of the gathering was the proposal that the Ecumenical Patriarchate designate and devote a specific day of the year as a special opportunity for Orthodox believers to pray for the protection and preservation of the natural creation.

Thus, on September 1, 1989—more than twenty-five years before the release of a similar encyclical by Pope Francis—Patriarch Demetrios published the first encyclical letter on the environment. This encyclical, issued on what is also the first day of the ecclesiastical calendar known as the "indiction," formally established the first day of September as a day for all Orthodox Christians (initially within the jurisdiction of the Ecumenical Patriarchate) to offer prayers for the environment. The call to prayer was heeded by all Orthodox churches in the early 1990s, as well as by other Christian confessions, including the World Council of Churches (WCC) and the Conference of European Churches (CEC) at the beginning of the third millennium. In 2015, Pope Francis inaugurated September 1 as a day of prayer for the natural environment for the Roman Catholic Church throughout the world.

A similar patriarchal encyclical has appeared every year on the first day of September. The first two encyclicals were signed by Demetrios; for the last twenty-five years, Bartholomew has signed each of them. As indicated in chapter 3, Demetrios was known for his softness and meekness of character. Therefore, it always seemed fitting that it was during his tenure that the Orthodox Church worldwide first dedicated a day of prayer for the protection of the environment, which human beings have treated so grievously and mercilessly. In 1994, Bartholomew wrote:

On a number of occasions through the ecclesiastical year, the church prays that God may protect humanity from natural catastrophes: from earthquakes, storms, famine, and floods. Yet, today, we observe the reverse. On September 1, the day devoted to God's handiwork, the church implores the Creator to protect nature from calamities of human origin: calamities such as pollution, war, exploitation, waste, and secularism. It may seem strangely paradoxical, but the body of believers, acting vicariously for the natural environment, beseeches God for *protection against itself, against its own actions.*

Bartholomew commissioned the foremost composer of hymns, a monk by the name of Gerasimos (from the hermitage of Little Saint Anne) on Mount Athos, to put together a special prayer service for the environment, an indication of how important creation care was for an otherwise deeply traditional and in many ways inflexible church.

Unfortunately, only two years after Patriarch Demetrios issued the first encyclical and call for prayer, he fell asleep in the Lord in October 1991. Bartholomew, enthroned in November, was well prepared to assume the mantle regarding care of the environment and proceeded to make it a major focus of his ministry. However, what most people may not know is that Bartholomew had already been both formative in guiding Patriarch Demetrios's ecological vision and instrumental in defining the ecological program of the Ecumenical Patriarchate.

EARLY INITIATIVES AND OUTREACH

It was just one month after his election in 1991 when the patriarch would convene an ecological conference on the island of Crete, within his immediate church jurisdiction. The event, titled "Living in the Creation of the Lord," was officially opened by Prince Philip, Duke of Edinburgh and international chairman of the World Wildlife Fund, who was also involved in the 1988 event at Patmos and instrumental in connecting religious communities with secular environmental organizations. The prince's own connections with the Orthodox Church ran deep: his grandfather was King George I of Greece, his grandmother from the Russian Romanov dynasty, and his mother became an Orthodox nun who eventually lived at Buckingham Palace. This was followed, in the summer of 1992, with a visit by the Duke of Edinburgh to Istanbul for another environmental convocation at the Theological School of Halki; and in late 1993, the ecumenical patriarch returned the courtesy, meeting with Prince Philip at Buckingham Palace. The two leaders would seal a friendship of common purpose and active cooperation for the preservation of the environment, including another conference in Patmos in 1995.

In early 1992, again only weeks after his election, Patriarch Bartholomew called an unprecedented meeting of all Orthodox patriarchs and primates at the Phanar, initiating a historical series of such meetings as an expression of unity by inviting all Orthodox leaders to inform their churches about the critical significance of this issue for our times. Never before had such a Synaxis of Primates convened. Care for the environment featured prominently in the sessions, where all of the prelates formally endorsed September 1 as a day of Pan-Orthodox prayer for God's creation.

The patriarch continued to organize seminars and conferences from 1994 through 1998, initially on the island of Halki, addressing a variety of issues integrally related to ecology: education, ethics, communications, justice, and poverty. People were beginning to respond, and Bartholomew received widespread recognition for his direction and influence. Thus, in October 1994, the University of the Aegean in Greece conferred an honorary doctoral degree on Patriarch Bartholomew, the first of numerous awards and a series of degrees. In November 2000, the New York–based organization

Scenic Hudson presented the ecumenical patriarch with the first international Visionary Award for Environmental Achievement. And in 2002, Patriarch Bartholomew was the recipient of the prestigious Sophie Prize in Norway as well as the Binding Environmental Prize in Liechtenstein, each presented to an individual or organization that has pioneered environmental awareness and action.

GLOBAL ENGAGEMENT AND OUTREACH

Religion, Science, and the Environment

As he reached out globally and became immersed in the various issues facing people in different parts of the planet, the patriarch began to realize that his ecological dream was a larger vision, one that involved and compelled other churches and faiths, other disciplines and leaders. Thus convinced that any appreciation of the environmental concerns of our times must inescapably occur in the context of a broader dialogue, in 1993 he established the Religious and Scientific Committee, which spawned an entire movement that came to be known as "Religion, Science, and the Environment" (RSE). The principal concern of RSE was both theological and scientific, while one of the underlying purposes of the movement was to establish common ground on the implications and imperatives of the ecological crisis between representatives of faith communities, professional scientists, and environmental NGOs. Bartholomew was the head of the committee and the heart of the movement.

Members included prominent leaders of the religious and academic worlds. For instance, the founding cochair was a marine ecologist, Dr. Jane Lubchenco, longtime professor of marine biology at Oregon State University and subsequently administrator of the US National Oceanic and Atmospheric Administration (NOAA) as well as undersecretary of commerce for oceans and atmosphere. The religious cochair was Metropolitan John [Zizioulas] of Pergamon, among the most senior bishops of the Ecumenical Patriarchate today and, undoubtedly, the person most responsible for and capable of sustaining a dialogue between religion and science in the Orthodox Church. The facilitator and convener of the committee was a Greek social and political activist with Constantinopolitan roots, Maria Becket (1931–2012), the indefatigable organizer of unparalleled waterborne symposia from 1995 to 2009. There were times when I couldn't help but smile that an ancient patriarchal institution was creating generational waves with an ecological movement, at the very soul of which was a woman.

The Waterborne Symposia (1995–2009)

The committee's mission was to raise awareness of pressing environmental issues in order to create a wider involvement in environmental matters by mobilizing the world's religious leaders, distinguished scientists, and influential environmentalists. The movement operated through symposia conducted as study voyages, with several hundred participants whose aim was to debate the plight of the waters of a specific region, visit sites of special concern, and meet local officials and nongovernmental organizations with a view to discussing issues and proposing solutions for environmental action and education in the area.

It was not coincidental that the patriarch chose water as the focus of his attention. The central role of baptism as a sacrament of initiation for all Christians, the sacred Feast of Epiphany with the blessing of the waters each year on January 6, and the spiritual importance of holy water in the daily lives of Orthodox believers: all of these factors reminded him that the world's water is not ours to use as we please; rather, it is a gift of God's love to us. Moreover, all of these factors demanded the propagation of an ecological ethic related to the serious problem of water in the world. Addressing an intergovernmental and international conference at The Hague, His All-Holiness declared:

> Water can never be regarded or treated as private property or become the means and end of individual interest. . . . Water scarcity will inevitably affect everything from the global food supply to the growth of cities, the location of jobs, the placement of industries, and even prospects for peace in the Middle East. The oil crisis of the late twentieth century will pale in comparison to the emerging water crisis of the twenty-first century.

Underlying the patriarch's vision and RSE's methodology was a core belief that the analytical tools of science and the spiritual messages of religion must work in harmony if the planet's environment is to be safeguarded against further degradation. For Bartholomew, religion cannot resolve the ecological crisis without science; by the same token, however, while science may have the capacity of information required to address the problem, it does not have the capability of transformation demanded to change people's hearts and habits.

The RSE symposia achieved significant outcomes for the regions, financial commitments from international institutions, greater regional cooperation among governments and nongovernmental organizations, as well as environmental training for regional clergy, journalists, educators, and youth.

In all, the Religion, Science, and Environment Committee organized and hosted eight international, interdisciplinary, and interfaith waterborne symposia to impel the pace of religious debate on the natural environment, while reflecting on the fate of seas from the Mediterranean to the Arctic as well as of rivers from the Danube to the Mississippi. The resplendence and reverberation of these symposia left a permanent and indelible mark on presidential figures and policy makers, religious authorities and corporate executives, but especially on civil society and lay believers.

For Bartholomew today, the symposia were crucial in demonstrating that religion was not—and, indeed, could not—remain indifferent before a challenge that affected the entire planet. Moreover, they proved that religion could—and, in fact, should— play a vital and pivotal role in awakening popular conscience to the crisis and consequences of climate change.

Symposium I: The Aegean Sea

The first symposium was entitled "Revelation and the Environment" and convened in September 1995 on the island of Patmos in the Aegean Sea under the joint auspices of Patriarch Bartholomew and Prince Philip on the occasion of the nineteen-hundredth anniversary of Saint John's book of Revelation. In his opening address, Patriarch Bartholomew cautioned: "The earth has been wounded. Conscious of the threat of nuclear destruction and environmental pollution, we shall move toward either one world or none." His sentiments were echoed by American Buddhist author Robert Thurman, who welcomed the patriarch's initiatives, adding that unfortunately religion has hitherto been part of the problem and urging Bartholomew to persist with such symposia. Other speakers included Greek philosopher Christos Yannaras, Vatican Cardinal Roger Etchegaray, and Indian activist Vandana Shiva.

Symposium II: The Black Sea

The patriarch did indeed persist, convinced that his environmental advocacy was an inseparable part of his priestly ministry. In September 1997, under the joint auspices of Ecumenical Patriarch Bartholomew and Jacques Santer, president of the European Commission, a second symposium, entitled "The Black Sea in Crisis" convened at the Black Sea. The patriarch still smiles when he recalls visiting the Livadia Palace near the Crimea, where the controversial Yalta Conference was held in 1945 to establish an agenda for postwar Europe. "There were three chairs," he beamed, "and I sat in the chair of President Franklin Roosevelt."

This symposium engaged in conversation with local religious leaders and environmental activists, as well as regional scientists and politicians, in countries around the Black Sea: Turkey, Georgia, Russia, Ukraine, Romania, and Bulgaria. Speakers included Canadian scientist David Suzuki, international civil servant Prince Sadruddin Aga Khan, and Oxford international law scholar Patricia

Birnie. A direct result of the Black Sea symposium was the "Halki Ecological Institute," organized in June 1999 to promote wider regional collaboration and education among seventy-five clergy and theologians, educators and students, as well as scientists and journalists. The initiative sought to implement the RSE's ecological theory through hands-on application.

Symposium III: The Danube River

The third symposium was launched under the joint auspices of Patriarch Bartholomew and Romano Prodi, president of the European Commission in October 1999, with the title "River of Life—Down the Danube to the Black Sea." Participants traveled the length of the Danube River: from Passau, Germany, through Vienna, Austria; from Bratislava, Slovakia to Budapest, Hungary, and Belgrade, Yugoslavia; through Vidin, Bulgaria, and Bucharest, Romania; reaching as far as the delta of the Danube in Ukraine. The patriarch prayed in silence at the concentration camp of Mauthausen, preached with compassion on ruins of bridges in Novi Sad that were bombed during the military and ethnic conflict in former Yugoslavia, and delivered his keynote address at the parliament or People's Palace in Romania.

Symposium IV: The Adriatic Sea

The fourth symposium journeyed around the Adriatic and explored the theme "The Adriatic Sea—A Sea at Risk, a Unity of Purpose," focusing on the ethical aspects of the environmental crisis. Held in June 2002, under the joint auspices of Ecumenical Patriarch Bartholomew and, again, Romano Prodi of the European

Commission, the symposium commenced in Durrës, Albania, and concluded in Venice, Italy. The patriarch has always insisted that the environment is not merely a field of study or a concern of economics. It is a space where millions of people live and share the responsibility for the planet. Therefore, the need to cultivate a set of ecological values and foster the emergence of an ecological consciousness is becoming increasingly urgent.

Two unique events of the symposium turned much more than a new page in the history books. On June 9, 2002, the ecumenical patriarch celebrated an Orthodox Divine Liturgy in the breathtaking Basilica of Sant'Apollinare in Classe (currently functioning as a Roman Catholic Church), a service that was taking place for the first time in twelve centuries. The unparalleled sixth-century mosaics include a unique image of the transfiguration on Mount Tabor, depicting Christ in the form of a cross (with the face of Jesus in the center), the disciples as lambs surrounding the cross, and the rest of creation as rocks, bushes, and flowers. The overwhelming sense is one of reconciliation between heaven, humanity, and cosmos. In his closing address, titled "Sacrifice: The Missing Dimension," Patriarch Bartholomew observed:

> Such is the model of our ecological endeavors. Such is the foundation of any environmental ethic. . . . The cross *must* be at the center of our vision. Without the cross, without sacrifice, there can be no blessing and no cosmic transfiguration.

The next day, June 10, 2002, delegates attended the closing ceremony in the Palazzo Ducale, where the patriarch communicated via satellite linkup with Pope John Paul II, in order to cosign a historical document on environmental ethics. The Venice Declaration is the first-ever joint text of the two leaders of Eastern and Western Christianity on ecological issues, emphasizing creation care as the moral and spiritual duty of all people.

Symposium V: The Baltic Sea

A fifth symposium in the series was organized in June 2003, under the patronage of Ecumenical Patriarch Bartholomew and the European Commission's Romano Prodi, with the title "The Baltic Sea—A Common Heritage, a Shared Responsibility."

An almost entirely closed and extremely fragile body of water, the Baltic borders on, and receives pollution from, nine countries with widely disparate natural resources, economies, social structures, and values. The symposium assembled more than 250 participants, including some fifty members of the international media. Speakers included German theologian Hans Küng, and European commissioner for the environment and later deputy prime minister of Sweden Margot Wallström.

On the eve of World Oceans Day (June 8, 2003), Patriarch Bartholomew delivered a moving address in the Swedish Parliament to a diverse audience:

> There is one thing that all of us share: We are united by water, which cradles us from our birth, sustains us in life, and heals us in sickness; it delights us in play, enlivens our spirit, purifies our body, and refreshes our mind. Indeed, each of us is a microcosm of the oceans that sustains life. Every person here, every person

in our world, is in essence a miniature ocean. . . . What we do to the oceans, God's vast blue creation, we do also to God's other creations, including ourselves.

Symposium VI: The Amazon River

The sixth symposium was unlike any other, traveling on a convoy of boats down the Amazon in July 2006, with discussion centered on the theme "The Amazon—Source of Life." Organized this time under the patronage of Ecumenical Patriarch Bartholomew and Kofi Annan, secretary-general of the United Nations, this symposium concentrated on the global dimension of problems stemming directly from the Amazon, problems that had perhaps dropped out of view for many decision makers.

Media coverage was prolific, with articles appearing in the *Guardian* and the *Independent*, Vatican Radio, and BBC News. Much interest revolved around the colorful "blessing of the waters," an ancient Orthodox ritual performed by Patriarch Bartholomew. Sunday morning, July 16, found the symposium at the meeting of the waters, the great space where the Rio Negro (Black River) meets the Solimões (White River) and becomes the great Amazon. A dozen or more boats were grouped together in the open water, sterns together roughly in a semicircle, facing a floating platform decked with gazebos, greenery, and loudspeakers. Delegates watched from boats in the bright morning sun as religious leaders—headed by the patriarch, accompanied by cardinals, archbishops, bishops, and others—performed a solemn ceremony.

To the exotic music of pipes, an indigenous religious leader blessed the gathering, recounting traditional stories of the rivers.

On behalf of the Amazonas government, the state secretary Virgilio Viana welcomed the patriarch and designated him "the Patriarch of the Amazon." His All-Holiness spoke about the baptism of Christ in the Jordan River and drew a connection between the indigenous tradition, the Christian experience, and the expectation of the whole world:

> In our unique encounter with the indigenous peoples of this region, we witnessed and felt their profound sense of the sacredness of creation and of the bonds that exist between all living things and people. Thanks to them, we understand more deeply that, as creatures of God, we are all in the same boat: *"estamos no mesmo barco!"*

Symposium VII: The Arctic Ocean

The seventh symposium was held in the fall of 2007, drawing the attention of the world to the melting ice caps of Greenland. I recall a conversation between the patriarch and Maria Becket in his office: "There's no way in the world you're getting me to stand on an ice sheet!" he told her. Mrs. Becket replied: "I'm hoping that you will walk on an ice sheet and also hold a prayer service for the melting ice caps!" In the end, she persuaded him to do at least one of the two.

The title of the symposium, organized under the joint auspices of the ecumenical patriarch, together with José Manuel Barroso (president of the European Commission) and Kofi Annan (former secretary-general of the United Nations), was "The Arctic—Mirror of Life." The symposium considered the plight of indigenous populations, the fragility of the sea ice, and the encroachment of oil exploration in a region considered to be one of the first victims of human-induced climate change. Carl Pope of the Sierra Club reconnected with the patriarch for this event. Other distinguished speakers included Swedish diplomat, and later the head of the International Atomic Energy Agency, Hans Blix, as well as Arctic specialist and American global climate scientist Robert Correll.

Contrasting the colorful exuberance of the Brazilian rain forest with the silent majesty of the Arctic, the journey was planned as a polar pilgrimage conducted in awe and humility. On Friday, September 7, 2007, the patriarch led a moment of silent prayer before the melting icebergs—a symbol of profound repentance for humanity's responsibility for climate change.

Symposium VIII: The Mississippi River

The final symposium was held in October 2009 on the banks of the Mississippi River in New Orleans and titled "Restoring Balance— The Great Mississippi River." As one of the world's greatest rivers, with the third-largest drainage basin on the planet, the Mississippi is among those that have fallen most completely under human domination—a chain of cities along its length discharging domestic and industrial waste for nearly two centuries. The exploitation of the great river produces catastrophic human and natural consequences, as the whole world observed in the aftermath of Hurricane Katrina in 2005. The Mississippi is indeed a challenge, not only to human responsibility for the environment but also for government itself.

Yet as he declared the symposium open, Bartholomew perceived the fate of the Mississippi waters primarily as an ethical crisis:

Let us remember that our responsibility grows alongside our privileges; we are more accountable the higher we stand on the scale of leadership. Our successes or failures, personal and collective, determine the lives of billions. Our decisions, personal and collective, determine the future of the planet.

The patriarch left the symposium to accept an invitation to meet with US President Barack Obama at the White House and attend a formal luncheon at the Capitol arranged by the speaker of the House of Representatives; Vice President Joseph Biden hosted a dinner in his honor. "Climate change was one of the foremost issues that we raised in our conversation with President Obama," he remembers, and the flag that flew over the Capitol during his visit is now proudly treasured in his office at the Phanar.

Two other symposia never came to fruition: One planned for the Caspian Sea in 2005 was postponed indefinitely due to geopolitical challenges. A second, scheduled along the Nile River, or possibly in Lake Victoria, was canceled due to the death of Mrs. Becket.

Undoubtedly, the waterborne symposia elevated and validated the connection between religion and creation care on the world stage, with wide coverage and international publicity in media including—to name but a few English-speaking outlets—the *Guardian* and the *Independent*, the *New York Times* and the *Financial Times*, the *Economist* and the *Wall Street Journal*, *Newsweek*, and the Associated Press. At the conclusion of the symposium on the Adriatic Sea, following the video linkup with the Vatican, where the ecumenical patriarch and the pope signed a joint declaration in the Doge's Palace, an Orthodox choir was featured inside the basilica of St. Mark's Square. "How do you top that?" asked Misha Glenny of the BBC.

The Halki Summits and Beyond

The successful series of waterborne symposia have directed the patriarch's focus to a new method in greening hearts and minds of more people. From large-scale conferences, the Ecumenical Patriarchate is now concentrating on smaller-scale conversations in an effort to address specific subjects and reach out to particular segments of society. In this endeavor, it has partnered with Southern New Hampshire University, the first carbon-neutral campus in its home state of New Hampshire. The result has become established and known as the "Halki Summits," after the island where these consultations are hosted. These gatherings involve focus groups of around forty to fifty leaders in a specific discipline. At the heart of their discussions is the belief that no effort can be successful without a fundamental change in values as manifested in ethics, spirituality, and religion.

The inaugural Halki Summit, held in the summer of 2012, was on the subject of "global responsibility and environmental sustainability," and featured speakers such as primatologist Jane Goodall, Rocky Mountain Institute founder Amory Lovins, Stonyfield Farm president Gary Hirshberg, and American environmentalist Bill McKibben.

One evening over dinner, Jane Goodall recounted to the patriarch how, at the beginning of her time in Africa, it took a long time before the chimpanzees accepted her. "They would run away, disappear into the undergrowth," she explained to him. "But one of them," she added, "lost his fear before the others. I called him David Greybeard, named for his beautiful white beard. Somewhat similar to yours," she said as the patriarch laughed, "except longer and more flowing."

The second Halki Summit focused on literature and the arts with such speakers as prominent and prolific British literary theorist Terry Eagleton, award-winning author and activist Raj Patel, American poet and conservationist Terry Tempest Williams, and *Chasing Ice* photographer James Balog.

More conferences are planned for the future in keeping with Bartholomew's sustained commitment and deeply held belief that creation both sustains and teaches us. Above all, however, the patriarch is currently planning the establishment of an interfaith environment center in order to institutionalize his legacy and love for interreligious dialogue and ecological engagement. Based on the historic and scenic premises of the former orphanage on the island of Prinkipos (Büyükada), just off the shores of Istanbul, the center will highlight the unique role and contribution of religion as a powerful force for global tolerance and ecological sustainability, while also advancing the dialogue between religion and science, as well as society and policy.

ON PLANTS AND ANIMALS

For the patriarch, plants are the wisest teachers and best models for the spiritual life. "They turn toward light," he wrote in 2010 for a

Roman Catholic journal, *Seminarium*, "and their roots run deep."
Moreover, they yearn for clean water and cherish clean air:

> They are satisfied and sustained with so little. They transform
> and multiply everything that they draw from nature, including
> some things that appear wasteful or useless. They adapt sponta-
> neously and produce abundantly, whether for the nourishment
> or admiration of others. They enjoy a microcosm of their own,
> while at the same time equally contributing to the macrocosm
> around them.

The same may be said of animals. On the final days of creation,
God is said to have made the variety of animals, as well as created
man and woman in the divine "image" and "likeness" (Genesis 1:26).
What most people seem to overlook is that the sixth day of creation
is not exclusively dedicated to the creation of Adam; it was, in fact,
shared with the creation of every "living creature according to its
kind: cattle and creeping thing and beast of the earth, each according to its kind" (Genesis 1:24).

Knowing the patriarch's love for animals, in 2008 (a leap year),
Mrs. Becket organized with friends for a donkey to be delivered to
the Theological School of Halki as a gift for the patriarch's birthday during a meeting of the Religion, Science, and the Environment
Committee at the Phanar while committee members were organizing the Mississippi symposium. The patriarch broke out in laughter
as he opened his birthday card containing a photo of his new pet,
which continues to graze on the school grounds today. With animals as prominent in sacred Scripture as in the natural world, what

does this mean for the way we live? For the patriarch, the answers lie in the tradition of the saints:

> This is a continual theme in the witness of the saints. Saint Gerasimos of the Jordan healed a wounded lion near the river; Saint Hubertus of Liège received a vision of Christ while hunting deer; Saint Columbanus of Ireland befriended wolves, bears, birds, and rabbits; Saint Sergius of Radonezh tamed a wild bear; Saint Seraphim of Sarov fed the wild animals; Saint Innocent of Alaska healed a wounded eagle; even contemporary saints, such as Elder Paisios of the Holy Mountain, lived in harmony with snakes.

The saints of the early church understood the close connection between human beings and the animal kingdom. The mystics knew that a person with a pure heart was able to sense the connection with the rest of creation. The connection is not merely emotional; it is profoundly spiritual. Perhaps this is why seventh-century mystic Abba Isaac the Syrian wrote in his *Ascetic Treatises*: "A merciful heart burns with love for all creation: for human beings, birds, and beasts—for all God's creatures."

CONTROVERSY AND COURAGE

Although the patriarch's focus is primarily on the excessive limits reached by human beings in their dominion over nature, and while his statements on human responsibility for the dilemmas we face were unequivocal, I admit my amazement and pride at the courage and clarity with which he has from time to time touched on a variety of controversial issues related to creation care. Since the beginning of the modern movement in the 1960s, the political, economic, scientific, and religious reactions to environmental issues have been complex and contentious, dealing with subjects such as sin, evolution, controversial technology, Scriptural misinterpretations, and greed versus grace.

The patriarch had already defined and condemned pollution as a sin as early as 1997. However, during the eighth symposium in New Orleans in 2009, speaking in a politically and religiously conservative state on a thorny and divisive issue such as evolution, he remarked:

> As the Mississippi links the prairies to the sea, we ourselves form the link between the past and the future. Science has developed a theory to explain the beginning of the universe almost fourteen billion years ago, the beginning of simple life forms some four billion years ago and the birth of human beings a mere 160,000 years ago. Although the time we have been on the planet is insignificant in the context of the life of the planet itself, we have reached a defining moment in our story.

Bartholomew does not hesitate to accept the age of the universe and the date of the appearance of man on earth derived from the theory of evolution agreed upon by the established scientific community. Yet evolution continues to generate controversy within certain political and religious communities that also tend to deny man's contribution to climate change and global warming. Bartholomew, a leader in countering such denial of evolution, would on another occasion address a group of scientists at the European Organization for Nuclear Research (CERN) in December 2014:

> In the experience of the early church tradition and in our own humble opinion, the Orthodox Christian approach to creation is not irreconcilable with scientific theories about the origin of the universe. No science or knowledge can ever detract from our surprise at the beauty of God's creation. On the contrary, we are always called to perpetual wonder. In the words of St. Basil the Great: "Our amazement is never diminished simply because we discover the reason for the paradoxical." After all, knowledge is not about obtaining information, but rather about creating relationships; it never leads to division, but always issues in communion. Above and beyond our vocation to stand as scientists before a telescope or a microscope, we are called to serve as priests at the altar of the universe.

The Green Patriarch is fearless in his proposal of technological solutions. In March 2011, in the wake of the nuclear explosion at Fukushima, he immediately communicated with the metropolitan bishop of Korea and Japan to convey his condolences for the victims and his support for the survivors of the disaster in the Land of the Rising Sun. "Every corner of the planet," he wrote, "is offering prayers both for the repose of the departed souls and for the support of those who continue to be grieved and imperiled by the ensuing seismic tremors and ferocious tsunami." Yet in an official press release issued by the Ecumenical Patriarchate on March 13, 2011, he did not refrain from criticizing the implications and consequences of the tragedy:

> Our Creator granted us the gifts of the sun, wind, water, and ocean, all of which may safely and sufficiently provide energy. Ecologically-friendly science and technology has discovered ways and means of producing sustainable forms of energy for our ecosystem. Therefore, we ask: "Why do we persist in adopting dangerous sources of energy? Are we so arrogant as to compete with and exploit nature? Yet we know that nature invariably seeks revenge."

Bartholomew is also undaunted in his criticism of misinterpretations—including narrow interpretations—of fundamental texts from Scripture. Thus, even "catchy" phrases describing the vocation and obligation of Christians with regard to the natural environment—commonly adopted and conventionally propagated in various religious circles—are not taken for granted by the patriarch. In the Norwegian magazine *Strek*, he broke down the associations implied with the phrase "stewards of creation":

> We wish to draw attention to the limitations of the phrase "stewards of the earth." Not because it is wrong as such. But because it conveys a sense of human management and control, which is precisely the attitude we are trying to correct as being too controlling and abusive. For we are called to offer creation back to God as priests, just as the priest in the Eucharist offers the bread

and wine to God, who in turn transforms them into his body and blood for the life of the whole world. So, rather than speaking of becoming "stewards of creation," it may be more helpful to speak of becoming "priests of creation" in accordance with our donation and vocation to be part of the "royal priesthood."

Creation care has been a central and vital part of Bartholomew's ministry over the last twenty-five years as ecumenical patriarch, though his appreciation of the beauty of God's creation, the conviction that "the heavens declare the glory of God," began well before 1991. It could not be otherwise for a man who recognizes how profoundly we are shaped by relationships and dialogue.

In his Santa Barbara speech of 1997, Bartholomew reminded the audience:

At the heart of the relationship between man and environment is the relationship between human beings. As individuals, we live not only in vertical relationships to God, and horizontal relationships to one another, but also in a complex web of relationships that extend throughout our lives, our cultures, and the material world. Human beings and the environment form a seamless garment of existence; a complex fabric that we believe is fashioned by God. . . .

How we treat the earth and all of creation defines the relationship that each of us has with God. It is also a barometer of how we view one another. . . .

By reducing our consumption, we come to ensure that resources are also left for others in the world.

What makes the patriarch's effort especially difficult and delicate is the presumption that the core beliefs of libertarian ideology and the gospel message are somehow fundamentally compatible (if not identical), when, in fact, they are profoundly contradictory (if not irreconcilable). Libertarian ideology is the engine behind the market economy; it is the backbone of free trade based on supply but above all on demand—often the result of unbridled desire and greed. Ultimately, Bartholomew's arguments are based on the gospel message of sacrifice and sharing.

GLOBAL PROGRESS AND GREEN PRIESTS

Have all the symposia and summits, all the pleading statements and groundbreaking initiatives—including common declarations with popes John Paul II, Benedict XVI, and Francis I—made a difference? After all, since the Orthodox Church became involved in environmental issues in 1983, the temperature continues to climb despite countless secular and religious conferences and alarm bells.

However, at long last in December 2015 a worldwide agreement to reduce rising temperature was reached at the international United Nations Climate Change Conference (COP 21) in Paris. Faith communities have been helping to prepare the public for years, especially in the year leading up to COP 21.

On February 26–27, 2015, Ecumenical Patriarch Bartholomew was invited to accompany French president François Hollande on his official state visit to the Philippines in preparation for COP 21, which would be held in Paris later that year. What the patriarch remembers most vividly from his visit to the Philippines is the time spent at Guiuan, on the island of Samar, where Typhoon Yolanda left its searing mark on soil and souls alike. He stood in shock and silence as he gazed at the havoc wreaked on the island, from which its inhabitants had still not recovered. "This is precisely why global warming is a moral crisis and a moral challenge," he remarked, visibly disturbed.

Four months later, on June 18, 2015, Pope Francis released his environmental encyclical, *Laudato Si'*, also bringing worldwide attention to creation care. And a day after the papal appeal, the *International New York Times* featured an article by Patriarch Bartholomew and Archbishop Justin Welby of Canterbury on "climate change, human health, and moral responsibility":

> We are now—like never before—in a position to choose charity over greed, and frugality over wastefulness in order to affirm our moral commitment to our neighbour and our respect toward the earth. Basic human rights—such as access to safe water, clean air, and sufficient food—should be available to everyone without distinction or discrimination.

So did religious leaders make a difference? I think it would be safe to presume so. Bartholomew's principal delight rests in spreading the message of "green" as a spiritual and sustainable alternative to the message of "greed" in local communities. He aspires to the formation of "green parishes" and "green priests." On a personal, day-to-day level, however, it is difficult for people to accept a message that demands sacrifice. Unfortunately, people normally perceive sacrifice as loss or surrender. Yet the English word *sacrifice* derives from the Latin root noun "*sacer*" (sacred) and the Latin verb "*facio*" (I make). Sacrifice has less to do with "going without" and more to do with "making sacred." Just as pollution has profound spiritual connotations related to the destruction of creation when disconnected from its Creator, so, too, sacrifice is the necessary corrective for reducing the world to a commodity to be exploited by our selfish appetites.

"Our faithful," he told me, "are beginning to realize that the environment is not simply one among many other issues to which the church must respond. In many ways, it is the most critical issue; it is *the* issue that defines all other aspects of our faith. The environment is not a secular or fashionable issue. It is at the very heart of what matters for the God who created our world and who assumed flesh to dwell among us."

Jane Goodall, PhD, DBE

UN Messenger of Peace

IT WAS A VERY SPECIAL DAY FOR ME WHEN I FINALLY MET THE "Green Patriarch." I was invited to a small gathering of scientists and theologians for a discussion about the dire environmental problems we face today. I was able to hear him speaking in person and spend time in private conversation. This centered on the importance of developing a different mind-set that puts consideration of the needs of future generations ahead of immediate gratification.

My grandfather was a congregational minister who, sadly, died before I was born, but I heard many stories of his love for nature. I grew up loving animals, but when I went to church, there was never mention of the natural world or the need to protect it. So I was immensely heartened by the strong commitment of His All-Holiness to the protection of the environment.

His vision is holistic: he links scientific facts about our destruction of natural resources with the religious ethic: God surely did not mean for us to destroy, for short-term profit, the rich biodiversity of his creation. And as Christians we surely have a duty to respect and protect animals. For someone of the patriarch's stature to have such a strong voice for God's creatures makes my heart sing, for my years studying animals have taught me that we are not the only beings with personalities, minds, and above all, feelings. And I am only too aware that our greedy materialism is resulting in the extinction of many species of animals and plants—as well as great suffering for the millions of humans living in poverty.

Patriarch Bartholomew emphasizes that we continue to destroy the planet at our own peril; that nature provides services, such as clean water and air, that we cannot do without; that our insistence on continued economic growth on a planet of finite natural resources is absurd; and that if we carry on with business as usual, the future for our children is grim—indeed, Earth may become uninhabitable for life as we know it.

His All-Holiness has brought greater understanding of the environmental disasters that threaten us to the attention of millions. His environmental teachings resonate with young people, so many of whom, as I know only too well, are desperately seeking hope. And if our young people lose hope, there is, indeed, no hope. For without hope we give up and do nothing, for we do not know what to do.

My hours in the presence of the Green Patriarch enriched me, providing me with renewed energy to pursue our joint fight to change minds and convert hearts, to make this a better world for people, animals, and the environment, and, above all, to strive for a meaningful future for our children.

CHAPTER 6

PROFILE OF A PATRIARCH

Personal and Pastoral Dimensions

I promise to preserve the peace of the church.
—FROM THE SERVICE OF A BISHOP'S ORDINATION

PERSONAL DIMENSIONS: A LIFE OF SERVICE AND LOVE

"Axios!"

The general public became aware of the ecumenical patriarch, Bartholomew I of Constantinople, when *Time* named him one of the world's "100 Most Influential People." Named along with him in 2008 were other "leaders, thinkers, heroes, artists, and scientists," such as Barack Obama, Oprah Winfrey, Steve Jobs, and the Dalai Lama. The description of His All-Holiness Bartholomew by Rowan Williams, archbishop of Canterbury of the Church of England, emphasized that "more than any other religious leader from any faith [he] . . . has kept open [the] spiritual dimension of environmentalism." While it is a fact that the patriarch received this honor for his extensive work in connecting religion and the environment, the archbishop's kind words do not begin to explain who the patriarch is and his contribution not only to his Orthodox Church but to the world. His All-Holiness is often seen on television and the Internet in his flowing vestments, but the man beneath the vestments is little known.

The *Time* magazine website also featured a section entitled "Are They Worthy?" where the pros and cons of the one hundred influential awards are presented. It is doubtful that the *Time* team had any idea of the significance of the word "worthy" in the Orthodox community, yet the word is both relevant and crucial to the story of the ecumenical patriarch. At the end of every ordination of an Orthodox deacon, priest, and bishop, as well as the elevation of every metropolitan, archbishop, and patriarch, the entire congregation shouts, *"Axios!"* ("Worthy!") Of course, only time will tell if the newly ordained is worthy. Only time will tell whether he has successfully gone through the necessary spiritual growth and personal sacrifice, the religious rigor, and the professional challenge to merit the accolade. However, throughout his life, Bartholomew has shown himself worthy.

Whether celebrating a Divine Liturgy in the ruins of a bombed church dedicated to the Christian soldier and martyr Saint George in post-civil war Lebanon; or whether serving at a small Transylvanian monastery in post-Ceauşescu Romania; or whether again holding an open-air service in post-Milošević Serbia . . .

Whether welcoming President Clinton at the Phanar in 1999

or being received by President Obama in the White House in 2009; whether meeting with Yasser Arafat in Palestine in 1995 or Fidel Castro in Cuba in 2004; or whether addressing the European Parliament at Brussels in 1994, the World Economic Forum at Davos in 1999, or the World Heritage Center of UNESCO (the United Nations Educational, Scientific, and Cultural Organization) at Paris in 2011 . . .

Whether visiting the poorest of Orthodox countries and most ancient of pre-Chalcedonian churches in Ethiopia in 1993 for a pastoral and ecumenical pilgrimage or one of the wealthiest Arab nations, the Kingdom of Bahrain, in 2000 for an interfaith forum on religious freedom and peace; whether standing in silence at the Holocaust museums in Jerusalem and Washington, DC, or witnessing the pledge of an Australian prime minister to support a Greek Orthodox school for special-needs children in Sydney . . .

Whether presiding over celebrations for the one-thousandth anniversary of Xenophontos Monastery on Mount Athos in 1995, the five-hundredth anniversary of Neamţ Monastery in Moldavia in 1997, or the two-thousandth anniversary since the dawn of Christianity in Jerusalem; whether attending the five-hundredth anniversary since the establishment of the Greek Orthodox community in Venice in 1998, or the one-hundredth anniversary of the Greek Orthodox community in Tarpon Springs, Florida, in 2006 . . .

Now, fifty years after Bartholomew first heard the word *"Axios!"* at his ordination to the diaconate, he has proven himself worthy indeed.

Enthronement of a New Patriarch

On November 2, 1991, Bartholomew was enthroned Archbishop of Constantinople—New Rome and Ecumenical Patriarch. Just ten days earlier, on October 22, he was unanimously elected to be the successor of Patriarch Demetrios.

But the previous weeks, ever since Patriarch Demetrios had died on October 2, there was a great deal of quiet tension. Archbishop Iakovos of North and South America was regarded as one of the contenders to the vacant patriarchal throne. Some speculated that there was tension between Bartholomew and Iakovos, but the reports that circulated were more like tabloid rumors. Iakovos's name was a red flag for authorities in Ankara; he had been outspoken against the Turkish invasion of Cyprus. But there was also never any doubt about Bartholomew's election so long as his name was not deleted from the list of candidates by the Turkish government—as his mentor's name had been almost twenty years before.

For his part, Bartholomew remained inexplicably calm—for no other reason than he believed that whoever was elected would be the right person for the throne, just as Patriarch Demetrios surprised everyone when he proved to be a popular, irreproachable leader of the church. After performing the funeral service of Patriarch Demetrios, Bartholomew continued to manage the daily affairs of the patriarchal office without interruption.

Three weeks after Demetrios had died and the names of potential candidates had been submitted to the authorities, Bartholomew was presiding as usual over a regular session of the Holy and Sacred Synod when the chancellor knocked on the door to inform him that the prefecture had called: "The envelope is ready to be picked up."

Bartholomew asked the chancellor to bring it to the synod, where it was opened. No names had been deleted. The members of the synod requested that the election take place immediately; one of the senior bishops insisted: "Most reverend president, this is Turkey; anything can happen. A simple phone call could request that the envelope be returned." Bartholomew replied: "If no names have been deleted in three weeks, then they have already decided not to interfere." It is not so much that Bartholomew was apprehensive about being elected; as he explained:

> Demetrios certainly didn't want the position. He was begging not to be elected. But I was calm. I was certain that whatever ensued would be fine. Just as yéro-Meliton was calm when his name was deleted; and he never appealed the decision, although no explanation was ever proffered.

The election of Bartholomew came as no real surprise; in fact, it came with warm acclamation.

His brother Andonios remembers how proud the patriarch's father was, introducing himself to everyone as the father of the new patriarch; his mother took it more in stride, though she clearly beamed as she stood beside her son. His father passed away just over two years later, in early 1994; his mother followed in late 1995. His mother never really grasped that her husband had died; she believed that he was still working hard, as he had done throughout his life, in their coffee shop at Haghioi Theodoroi. But she left this world with the indelible memory of seeing her son on the patriarchal throne of an ancient—the most prominent—see. The patriarch's parents are buried in Chalcedon (Kadiköy) on the Asian side of Istanbul, where he served before his election; from time to time, he visits their graves in the cemetery where his mentor Metropolitan Meliton and his beloved childhood priest, Father Spyridon, are also buried.

Bartholomew remembers his father and mother very affectionately; he commemorates them at every Divine Liturgy. He clearly inherited his indomitable, hardworking nature from his father, and he certainly acquired his mother's social skills. Andonios remembers their mother staying with him in Divonne, France, just minutes by car from Geneva; Meropi would go on her daily afternoon walk to the town square and sit with the local seniors, returning each evening with endless stories. The funny thing is that she didn't understand a word of French, while her company didn't understand a word of Greek or Turkish.

Bartholomew likewise never ceases to commemorate his predecessor, Patriarch Demetrios. His grandfather was also Demetrios, the name Bartholomew received at baptism. And his godfather, Iakovos, was also named Demetrios before his ordination. "I remember them all together, all the time," he says.

A Vessel of Tradition

Above all, Bartholomew remembers how yéro-Meliton would describe—in fact, define—the patriarchate:

> The Phanar is . . . a concept. It is a symbol of life's potential to transcend destruction, of the possibility for survival in coexistence. The Phanar is the art of deriving the highest excellence from the worst circumstances. The Phanar is the bearer of supreme

values. It is patience; it is silence; it is nobility, the dignity of the past. . . . It is the guardian of the treasure of our blameless faith and the sacred tradition of the East, vested with the other sacred traditions of our race; but it is an active and dynamic guardian. . . . The Phanar is a school.

In fact, this concept of the Phanar plays an important part in the patriarch's ministry. Bartholomew regards himself as a fragile vessel holding an undiminishing flame before the memory of the past. The Greek word for "memory"—*mnémē*, from which we derive the term "mnemonic"—was the name of one of three mythological sisters or classical muses, together with *aoidē* (modesty) and *melétē* (contemplation). Remembrance of the past, self-effacement before the past, and reflection on the past comprise the "stuff" of the ecumenical patriarch's perception of tradition—a tradition that he contains, carries, and conveys.

Winston Churchill was right when he observed that the farther back one looks, the farther forward one can see. However, memory is not merely or solely a rational, intellectual abstraction; it is primarily or essentially a spiritual conception. The word *mnémē* has the same etymological root as the Greek term for "lover" (*mnēstér*), signifying that one's disposition toward tradition and the past is an attitude of admiration and affection for history and those who have gone before.

So Bartholomew remembers. He remembers details. He remembers names and places and dates—of his own time but especially of previous generations. He remembers historical facts—the pain and suffering, the fires and massacres over the last hundred years.

He remembers institutional details—names of bishops, priests, and deacons over many decades and centuries. He remembers personal features—dates of people's ordinations, the provenance of their islands, and even local festivals of their native villages. I recall a few years ago introducing someone to him from Chicago; my friend was taken aback when the patriarch asked about his brother, who was ill and whom he had met briefly many years earlier during one of his visits to the United States.

He is the patriarch of memory. He is still moved to tears as he shares with his small congregations in the "remnant" Orthodox community of Turkey the events of 1923, with the forced exchange of populations between Turkey and neighboring Greece but especially with the destruction of Orthodox communities and slaughter of Greek residents in Turkey.

In Smyrna, as he reminds his congregation in a sermon, there are no street names today; only street numbers. "But we remember the names," he adds with the conviction of an eyewitness and the record of a palimpsest. "We can never forget." In 2016, when the cross was cast into the waters of the Smyrna harbor as part of the Orthodox celebration of Epiphany on January 6, marking the baptism of Christ, "the waters that were once red with the blood of martyrs" were blessed to their everlasting memory. "If only these waters could speak," declared Bartholomew to the crowd of faithful.

It is this element of recollection that marked the agenda of his ministry, already outlined from the day of his enthronement on November 2, 1991, as archbishop of Constantinople in the Patriarchal Church of St. George, when he literally took measure of his history and destiny:

We assume from the hands of the blessed Patriarch Demetrios, our great predecessor, the cross of Andrew the First-called Apostle in order to continue the ascent to Golgotha, to be co-crucified with our Lord and his church, to perpetuate the light of the resurrection.

A Bearer of the Cross

The sense of the cross echoes his own intuition from his childhood journal but especially resonates with his resolute sense of sacrifice and service.

How then does the profile of this remarkable patriarch emerge from twenty-five years of governance and guidance of the Christian East? Despite unrivaled achievements, there is surely no room for triumphalism. He anticipated as a child that his life would be one of renunciation and tribulation. And when he was elected patriarch, he knew that he would be bearing a cross—a personal cross, a pastoral cross, an institutional cross. On the occasion of his twentieth anniversary on the patriarchal throne, he wrote:

In looking back at our patriarchal ministry, we behold days of joy, but also days of sorrow; days of light, but also days of darkness; days of glory, but also days of bitterness; days of excitement and optimism, but also days of anxiety and disappointment. . . . With the grace of God, we neither lost our footing as a result of pride nor were crushed by pressure . . . but we simply labored, as much as humanly possible, [and he goes on to quote Saint Paul] "in all things commending ourselves as ministers of God: in much patience, in tribulations, in needs, in distresses . . . in sleeplessness . . . by the armor of righteousness on the right hand and on the left." (2 Corinthians 6:4–7)

It is the cross that he acknowledged in his interview with Bob Simon of CBS's *60 Minutes* about the relationship with the Turkish government in December 2009.

Indeed, like any honest and genuine leader, he is conscious of and confesses his weaknesses. So the cross that Bartholomew bears also reflects personal shortcomings that he is charitably prepared to embrace as growing pains and learning curves from which to offer only more prudent leadership. Thus, when the patriarch's appointment of a replacement for Archbishop Iakovos proved short-lived after creating almost irreparable conflict within the institutions of the Greek Orthodox Archdiocese of America (with painful consequences on the families of all involved), Bartholomew was contrite and humble enough to rescind his decision and request the resignation of Archbishop Spyridon [Papageorge] in the late 1990s. In so doing, Bartholomew was certainly far humbler than many of his detractors, who had vehemently resisted any change whatsoever. As a result, he appointed Archbishop Demetrios [Trakatellis], a discerning spiritual leader—one both familiar with the context of Orthodox Christianity in America and held in high regard by clergy and laity alike—as a harbinger of peace to generate stability and consolidation in a divided community.

In many ways, however, the cross that Bartholomew bears transcends his own vulnerability or deficiency. The patriarch's tenure mirrors the story of the Ecumenical Patriarchate through the centuries. British scholar Sir Steven Runciman liked to emphasize that the great achievement of the patriarchate was that, despite humiliation and disdain, the Orthodox Church endured and continues to endure as an immense and important spiritual force in the world.

God Grant You Many Years

Just as *"Axios!"* is the cry used to acknowledge the worthiness of an ordinand, the expression "God grant you many years!" is the conventional wish addressed to an Orthodox bishop. But "many years" is not something always associated with an ecumenical patriarch.

The very history of the tenures of ecumenical patriarchs keeps Bartholomew grounded. In fact, in two thousand years, only three patriarchs have served more than twenty-five years: Titus in the third century, Sergius in the seventh, and Nicholas in the twelfth. In the twentieth century, only Ecumenical Patriarch Athenagoras— "from America," as he was called—served for twenty-four years (1948–1972); Ecumenical Patriarch Demetrios served for nineteen (1972–1991). In fact, over seventeen centuries, only ten patriarchs completed twenty years of continuous ministry on the ecumenical throne. Indeed, Athenagoras and Bartholomew are the only ones to serve for at least twenty years since the mid-sixteenth century.

In fact, the history of the Church of Constantinople is replete with examples of patriarchs serving for very few years. In 1397 and 1466, there were actually three patriarchs enthroned in the same year. From the sixteenth to the early-twentieth centuries, some 159 patriarchs were in office, 105 of which were forced to renounce their throne and several of which were assassinated by official decree. In the same century, there were fifty-two separate enthronements (for twenty-eight patriarchs).

While historians normally regard Ecumenical Patriarch Gregory V, who died a martyr on April 10, 1821—a few weeks after Greece declared its independence from the Ottoman Empire—as an exception, inasmuch as he was one of the most prominent hierarchs of the Orthodox East, he is actually more of an example. And as such, he is also a symbol: the main entrance to the Phanar has been closed since he was hanged there with his patriarchal vestments on Easter Sunday 1821; today, all visitors enter the Ecumenical Patriarchate by the side door. The patriarch holds a memorial service and lights a candle on that spot every Easter.

However, both before and after Gregory, there were numerous patriarchs who were tortured, exiled, or executed through the centuries. For example, Joasaph I (1464–1466) was dethroned, his beard shorn publicly. Raphael I (1475–1476) was unable to submit the mandated "tax" for reenthronement and was imprisoned and died. Raphael II (1603–1607) was dethroned, exiled, and submitted to horrible death. Kyrillos I [Loukaris] was enthroned and dethroned on six different occasions, finally being strangled by janissaries. Kyrillos II (1633–1639) was dethroned and tortured to embrace Islam, then sentenced to hanging for his refusal. Parthenios II (1644–1646, 1648–1651) and Parthenios III (1656–1657) were drowned at sea. Gabriel II (April 23–May 5, 1657) only remained on the throne of Constantinople for twelve days after being falsely accused of baptizing a Muslim; he was executed by hanging. Evgenios II (1821–1822), the immediate successor to Gregory V, was tortured by being dragged through the streets by his hair and beard, ultimately dying from his wounds.

So it was quite an achievement that Athenagoras served for

twenty years. He is known to have remarked: "Twenty years in this ministry are neither many nor few. They are few before eternity; but they are many when one has conscientiously labored to achieve something." As for Ecumenical Patriarch Bartholomew, what he has achieved in twenty-five years is nothing less than—to paraphrase the twelfth-century patriarch and canon lawyer Theodore Balsamon—"sensational and symbolical."

Pastoral Dimensions: A Life of Unifying and Sanctifying

Promoting Unity

As Metropolitan of Philadelphia, Bartholomew once delivered an address to the Archaeological Society of Athens on the ecumenical nature of the church; the lecture was entitled "The Ecumenical Conscience of the Church of Constantinople and Its Concern for All Churches." That "ecumenical conscience" and "ecumenical concern" were early instilled in him and deeply informed his vision. In his understanding, the principal task and vocation of an ecumenical patriarch is to express and manifest, across historical limits and cultural borders, the unity and universality of the church beginning with early church history: Canon 28 of the Fourth Ecumenical Council held in Chalcedon (451) offered Constantinople equal ranking to Rome and special responsibilities throughout the rest of the world, even expanding its jurisdiction to territories hitherto unclaimed. The phrases "ecumenical patriarch" and "Ecumenical Patriarchate" date from the sixth century and belong exclusively to the archbishop of Constantinople. Originally they signified universal jurisdiction—in theory, over the inhabited earth but, in practice, over the Roman Empire. They were first adopted by Patriarch John IV (582–595), also known as Saint John the Faster, who embraced the wider pastoral responsibility of the Church of Constantinople and envisioned its supranational character.

Unfortunately, in many parts of the Orthodox world, national interests and loyalties have often obscured the universality of the church. People consider themselves as Greek, or Russian, or Serbian, or Romanian, before thinking of themselves as Orthodox. Bartholomew, however, is motivated by unity, rather than by raw ethnic tensions, which are often reduced to what the media likes to sensationalize as rivalry among the various churches. The same unity has been his primary concern whenever there were problems with Greek-speaking autocephalous churches, such as the Patriarchate of Jerusalem (in the 1990s, resulting in penalties imposed against that ancient patriarchate by a Supreme Synod in July 1993, for ecclesiastical infringements) and even the Church of Greece (in 2003–2004, over territorial claims of jurisdiction by then Archbishop Christodoulos of Athens).

Through the centuries the church has often flirted with the power of the state, sometimes resorting to collusion but most times creating confusion. This arrogance was, in fact, the downfall of the Byzantine Church, and it is the unspoken temptation for many of the national Orthodox churches to this day. Confronting nationalism head-on, Bartholomew warned his peers in a keynote address to the Fourth Synaxis of Primates on October 8, 2008:

We have received and preserve the true faith, as the holy fathers have transmitted it to us through the ecumenical councils of the one undivided church. We commune of the same body and blood of our Lord in the Divine Eucharist, and we participate in the same sacred mysteries. We basically keep the same liturgical typikon and are governed by the same sacred canons. All these safeguard our unity, granting us fundamental presuppositions for witness in the modern world. Despite this, we must admit in all honesty that sometimes we present an image of incomplete unity, as if we were not one church, but rather a confederation or a federation of churches . . . frequently attributing priority to national interests in their relationship with one another.

As I listened to his words, I could patently discern the echo of the great Athenagoras, who once remarked in an interview to French theologian Olivier Clément, "Are we Orthodox even worthy of our faith? Up until efforts that we have made in recent years, we have been united in creed and chalice, but have become strangers and even rivals."

Such then are the contours of the patriarch's ecumenical breadth and ecclesiastical vision as they have been revealed and realized over the last twenty-five years, sketched out with farsightedness and resolve on the day of his enthronement when he spoke of cross and resurrection. His ministry would oscillate somewhere between Golgotha and Tabor, embracing history and destiny. The two pillars of this intuition were—and would always remain—a sense of tradition and a concern for unity. However, it is a tradition without formalism and a unity distinct from uniformity manifested in the tradition of Orthodox conciliarity.

Building Conciliarity
At the Phanar

Bartholomew deeply adores and sensitively administers the conciliar dimension of the church, a characteristic feature of the Orthodox Church, fundamentally distinguishing it from structures in Roman Catholicism and Protestantism. However, this culture of conciliarity and communion is not merely intended for the global level. He once wrote:

> At the Phanar, all hierarchs work with their patriarch as one heart and one mind, together bearing the cross of Christ, together witnessing to the gospel of Christ, and together advocating for the rights of God, humanity, and creation.

It came as no surprise then that he was the first-ever patriarch to convene gatherings of around seventy-five bishops called the Synaxis of Hierarchs within his own immediate jurisdiction of the Ecumenical Patriarchate throughout the world. While not formal decision-making bodies, these gatherings have taken place more or less biennially in Istanbul, beginning in 1992.

Moreover, the administrative or decision-making council at the Phanar—called the Holy and Sacred Synod (historically known as the "permanent" or "endemousa" synod)—has functioned since as early as the late-fourth century, although it is clearly attested by the mid-fifth century. This synod, composed of bishops either permanently dwelling in (perhaps near) or else passing through Constantinople, was traditionally the most powerful organ of the church in Byzantium. In recent centuries, it was essentially—and since 1923, it was exclusively—reduced to bishops living at the Phanar.

Thus, in March 2004, in a bold move that was received with skepticism even by the innermost circles at the Phanar, Bartholomew introduced six (out of a total of twelve) new members from outside of Turkey to this Holy and Sacred Synod, the highest decision-making body of the Church of Constantinople. In September 2013, he further expanded this to include eleven out of twelve from abroad. This means that, by rotation, at any given time, there are bishops from every region of the world under his jurisdiction seated on the synod: from the United States, Canada, Latin and Central America; from Great Britain and Western Europe; from Australia and Southeast Asia; as well as from the Greek islands of Crete and the Dodecanese.

In the Orthodox World

Once again then, it came as no surprise that within weeks of his election, Bartholomew became the first patriarch to convoke a Synaxis of Primates, namely, the heads of the autocephalous Orthodox churches. Six of these synaxes have convened since 1992—assembling the fourteen churches that comprise the world-wide Orthodox family of churches that would be invited to the Holy and Great Council. The Fifth Synaxis of Primates, held in Istanbul in March 2014, unanimously decided that the Holy and Great Council should be held in 2016, while the most recent, convened in Chambésy, Geneva, in January 2016, unanimously decided that the Holy and Great Council should commence on the Feast of Pentecost on the island of Crete.

The role of the ecumenical patriarch is highly significant and sensitive, and by no means merely symbolical or ceremonial, yet the ecumenical patriarch neither commands nor compels. The notion of interdependence or conciliarity is vital in Orthodox ecclesiology. The aim of Bartholomew is constantly to walk a tightrope, achieving what Leo the Great in a fifth-century letter called "a confirmation by the incontestable agreement of the entire college of brothers." Yet there is no doubt that, while the Orthodox Church is allergic to any sense of universal primacy as this has developed and is perceived in the West, it recognizes the need for a universal leadership, coordination, and spokesmanship by its "first among equals," without which conciliarity is impossible.

Bartholomew has certainly labored to provide authoritative and objective leadership in synods with patience and respect for the past twenty-five years, all the while knowing that change in the Orthodox Church is normally subdued, even imperceptible. It is always a natural and organic process, never a reform from above or a revolution from below.

Demystifying Primacy

Despite the indisputable fact of Canon 28 and Canon 3 of the Second Ecumenical Council held in Constantinople (381) conferring upon the bishop of the city second rank after the bishop of Rome, Bartholomew's primacy does not lie in power but actually in sacrifice and service. That is because primacy is not merely an honor,

nor is it an Eastern form of the papacy. In fact, Constantinople's weakness in human and material resources, its suffocation and suffering under historical circumstances, are precisely what perennially ensure its impartiality and paradoxically increase its prestige. The ecumenical patriarch has no pretensions to being a "universal bishop." He claims no dogmatic infallibility, no direct jurisdiction over all. This is why the Church of Constantinople has been called "the church of Christ's poor"—a phrase possibly coined by Gennadios Scholarios, the first patriarch to serve after the fall of Constantinople in 1453. It describes the humility of the Ecumenical Patriarchate—paradoxically also known as "the great church of Christ"—for its resilience and service through the centuries, including centuries-old traditions and practices, such as the consecration of sacred myron (oil of chrismation) and the canonization of holy men and women.

Consecrating the Oil of Chrismation

Every ten years or so, it is the hallowed honor of the ecumenical patriarch to consecrate the holy myron—the sacred oil used in the sacrament of chrismation to initiate the newly baptized through anointing as well as to dedicate new places of worship through sanctification.

Blessed by the ecumenical patriarch with a special service that extends from Palm Sunday through Holy Thursday during Holy Week, this oil is distributed in vials to dioceses throughout the world. A practice with roots dating back to Hebrew times (first mentioned in the book of Exodus, chapter 30), it is made up of more than fifty fragrances. The same oil is used to receive non-Orthodox

Christians into the Orthodox Church through chrismation and to bless objects and utensils for ceremonial use. In former times, it was also used to anoint the Orthodox kings and emperors during their coronation.

This means that Orthodox Christians throughout the world share something very unique; they are united in a very tangible way. An Orthodox Christian baptized in Melbourne, Australia, is chrismated with the very same consecrated oil as an Orthodox Christian baptized in Chicago, Illinois; an Orthodox Christian in Seoul, Korea; an Orthodox Christian on the island of Crete or Rhodes in Greece; an Orthodox Christian in Toronto, Canada; or an Orthodox Christian in Thessaloniki, northern Greece.

In the early Christian centuries, only bishops could consecrate the holy myron. Gradually, however, this common right of all bishops was transferred to bishops of churches with greater jurisdiction, namely, to the patriarchs and finally to the ecumenical patriarch. Historically and traditionally, there were three reasons that restricted the right to consecrate the holy myron to the ecumenical patriarch: (a) the scarcity of the materials and the difficulty for bishops to prepare the sacred compound; (b) the steady increase of dependence on larger, metropolitan churches; and (c) the special position of the Ecumenical Patriarchate through the centuries in relation to the other Eastern patriarchates as well as the spiritual bond between the Church of Constantinople and the local missionary churches.

This right of the Ecumenical Patriarchate to consecrate the holy myron does not mean that local churches are dependent on or subordinate to Constantinople. Rather, it is a tangible sign of the unity that bonds all local churches—patriarchates and autocephalous churches—with the Ecumenical Patriarchate. It is not a sign of superiority or authority of the Ecumenical Patriarchate, but a visible sign of sacramental communion within the family of local Orthodox churches. The contemporary Patriarchates of Moscow, Belgrade, and Bucharest also consecrate holy myron.

Bartholomew is the only patriarch ever to consecrate holy myron on three occasions during his ministry: in 1992, 2002, and 2012.

Canonizing Saintly Men and Women

Bartholomew also works for unity among Orthodox Christians through prayer and spirituality with the canonization of saints. This process has been a silent, albeit compelling, way of reaching out to the faithful. Most people are unaware of just how many saints—both men and women—have been canonized during the patriarch's tenure. A mere glance at the official record of the Ecumenical Patriarchate, *Orthodoxia*—a journal that first appeared in 1926, whose publication was interrupted in 1963 when the printing press at the Phanar was forcibly closed by the Turkish government, and which Bartholomew himself revived in 1994—will reveal a startling number of new saints over the last twenty-five years.

Bartholomew's formal acts recognizing new saints in the church are integrally related to his consecration of the holy myron. After all, the English word *saint* has its etymological root in the Latin term *sanctus*, which in turn is the derivation of the noun *consecration*. This is because acts of "canonization" are the festive evidence of the vitality of a church, not simply a commemoration of the death of some holy person. They are signs that the vision of God has been notably and noticeably revealed in the eyes of at least one human in our world and in our own generation. For if this has occurred, then it is clear that the face of God can also be reflected in the face of all human beings, despite any distortion or suppression of the divine image wrought by human frailty or failure.

Thus, Orthodox saints are "recognized," "proclaimed," or "classified" into the book of saints. The understanding is that no one is "made" a saint, but that saintliness is perceived by the community of believers and proclaimed by the official church. For the Orthodox, saints are neither superhuman nor subdivine. Saints are neither victors of a military sort (which is how we normally imagine many of the early saints) nor heroes of a mythical force (which is how we traditionally imagine most of the medieval saints). Indeed, saints are truly and fully—in fact, *only*—human; perhaps this is the deeper reason why they are said to compel the divine in the first place.

Since Bartholomew assumed office, there have been more than twenty formal "acts of recognition" for a total of 225-plus new saints from Greece, Russia, Asia Minor, and western Europe, including 150 martyrs at Daou Penteli (d. 1690) and an "unknown number" of martyrs at Naoussa (d. 1822).

The formal process of recognition and reception of saints in the Church of Constantinople is based on a synodal decision dating to 1931. This pronouncement cites three elements for the recognition of saints: blameless Orthodox faith; acquisition of all virtues, which might include the sacrifice of one's life for one's faith; and the divine manifestation of supernatural signs.

In practice, however, miracles are neither mandatory conditions nor quintessential attributes of saintliness. Instead, miraculous boldness before God is the distinctive characteristic of saintly men and women. Saints are those who lead a good life, in good faith, even if they perform no supernatural miracles. John the Baptist, according to Jesus himself the greatest prophet ever born, is nowhere described as performing miracles. And Jesus Christ emphasized that people will recognize his disciples not by their miracles, but "if [they] have love for one another" (John 13:35).

Even the formal act of proclamation is of secondary importance in the Orthodox Church. There are many saints for whom Orthodox are not certain there was ever an official decree of canonization. Nonetheless, since 1931, and especially since 1988, the recognition of saints has been incorporated formally and instituted liturgically in the Patriarchal Church of St. George, where the act is solemnly read.

A new period of "recognition" or "reception" of saints began in 1955 with the tenure of Ecumenical Patriarch Athenagoras, under whom nine new saints were added to the "list of saints" (*haghiológion*) or "list of feasts" (*eortológion*) in the church, sparking what was widely recognized at the time as a renewal of Orthodox spirituality. The revival coincided with the blighting and looting of scores of churches in Istanbul, provoked by political problems in Cyprus, which demoralized the dwindling Orthodox community in the city and resulted in further voluntary emigration.

Some of the names among the new saints recognized by Athenagoras included Nikodemus of the Holy Mountain (editor of the classic anthology on prayer entitled *The Philokalia*), Kosmas of Aetolia (the itinerant monk and preacher), Nektarios of Pentapolis (the beloved miracle worker of the twentieth century), and the

Mytilenian saints Raphael, Nikolaos, and twelve-year-old Irene (fifteenth-century martyrs at the hands of the Turks).

As Metropolitan of Philadelphia, Bartholomew published an article about the importance of this development. During his own patriarchal tenure, some of the proclaimed saints include: the icon-painting monk Savvas the New of Kalymnos (d. 1947); the simple parish priest Nikolaos Planas (d. 1932); Rostislav, the illuminator and duke of Moravia (ninth century); Stephen of Hungary (d. 1038); the Estonian martyrs Platon, Michael, and Nicholas (twentieth century); the twentieth-century martyrs of western Europe: Fr. Alexis Medvedkov, Fr. Dimitri Klepinine, Mother Maria Skobtsova and her son, Iuri Skobtsov, the little-known female ascetic Sophia Chotokouridou (d. 1974), the sensitive clairvoyant elder Porphyrios of Kafsokalyvia (d. 1991), and most recently the soft-spoken spiritual elder Paisios of Mount Athos (d. 1994).

The experience of the saints is, in the end, the experience of the whole world. It serves to illumine the entire world in the light of Christ. And the official church acts of recognition or proclamation ultimately aspire to revive in everyone what the Letter to the Romans would describe as being "called to be saints" (Romans 1:7).

Addressing Injustice

However, what do these ancient saints have to say to a modern world and its contemporary demands? How does a patriarchal church respond to a global crisis, where millions are persecuted and billions are marginalized? In what meaningful manner can a spiritual community address the ever-expanding culture of possession and profit?

The patriarch feels that the church—indeed, he—can never be silent on issues related to injustice or inequality, and gluttony or greed, as well as prejudice or violence. He strives for an encounter and exchange of civilizations, rather than surrendering to a confrontation or clash of civilizations. He defends the rights of the Phanar, just as he champions the rights of every minority in every part of the world. The only thing he cannot tolerate is lack of tolerance.

Clearly, the church cannot ignore the immense financial and social challenges of our time. However, its response emerges from the Christian gospel. Bartholomew was part of the delegation from the Ecumenical Patriarchate that chaired the third Pan-Orthodox Pre-Conciliar Conference in Chambésy, Geneva (October 28 through November 6, 1986). The text of that consultation also addressed world hunger and poverty:

> Hunger not only threatens the sacred gift of life for entire peoples in the developing world, but also totally crushes the dignity and sacredness of the human person. Economically developed nations—with their unjust and frequently even criminal distribution and management of material resources—insult not only the image of God in every human being, but also God, who clearly identifies himself with the hungry and needy, saying: "Inasmuch as you did it to one of the least of these My brethren, you did it to Me" (Matthew 25:40).

Therefore, any insensitivity or indifference on the part of the church before people's suffering is tantamount to betrayal of the gospel and absence of faith. The patriarch remembers ever so vividly the slogan of the ecumenical movement in the 1970s, which was, in fact, borrowed from an Orthodox philosopher, Nikolai Berdyaev: "Bread for me is a material question; but bread for my neighbor is a spiritual matter."

Bartholomew is painfully aware that the unjust and unjustifiable inequality between rich and poor condemns our world both in its own eyes as well as in the eyes of God. Without being dismissive or aggressive against Western civilization and values, which have clearly offered freedom and prosperity to the world, the ecumenical patriarch assumes a dialectic and critical stance in order to expose the consequences of limitless individualism and exploitation.

In his Christmas encyclical of 2012, Bartholomew declared 2013 as "the Year of Global Solidarity" in an effort to raise awareness about the "great inequalities," as well as the "extensive and expansive poverty" in the world. It was not the first time the patriarch had spoken a prophetic word of compassion and solidarity. In Strasbourg, addressing the plenary of the European Parliament on April 19, 1994, he referred to a basis of values or "common principles of coexistence" that lead to a civilization beyond economy and politics, above nationalism and racism:

A united Europe cannot simply be some plan for a uniform financial development, some program for a uniform defense policy. From its very nature, the vision also demands a uniform social and political strategy of peaceful and productive cooperation among all European peoples. The vocation is cultural.

In this regard, the ecumenical patriarch knows very well that he is the continuation and bearer of a great tradition of philanthropy and charity:

> Our city of Constantinople takes great pride in the exemplary social contribution of our fourth-century predecessor, St. John Chrysostom, that great prophet of philanthropy and preacher of charity. It is in the name of that philanthropy and charity that Chrysostom clashed with the imperial palace and secular powers of his time.

Responding with Dialogue, Respect, and Love

Bartholomew's answer is simple, issuing from a long and deep tradition of dialogue. The Ecumenical Patriarchate has never desisted or obstructed openness and communication with the world: with society, science, and even skepticism—or with faith, spirituality, and even atheism. His church does not simply present the fundamentals of a creed; it provides the foundation for a community. The beauty, justice, and peace that are integral to its theology must also be integrated into its worldview. "The kingdom of heaven is at hand" (Matthew 10:7)—that is the inspiration of liturgy, the motivation for dialogue, and the justification for ecology in action. Otherwise, this world is disengaged from heaven and becomes a realm of division and domination. Otherwise, the world becomes the domain of consumption and competition, rather than of community and communion.

For him, dialogue is precisely transcending lack of respect and lack of trust. Religions can contribute to the creation of a society and culture of solidarity. This is why he says,

Human beings are not fulfilled as individuals. They discover their true selves only as persons capable of communicating with other persons—whether neighbor or God.

Bartholomew goes so far as to profess that the Orthodox spiritual worldview can prove both a challenge and an inspiration for contemporary life. The church can provide a legacy of life for future generations:

> In an age when "values are overturned"—where significant matters are undermined and insignificant matters are rendered absolute—the church promotes a hierarchy of values beginning with the sacredness of the human person created in the image and likeness of God as well as the integrity of the world created "very good" by God. The church proposes an alternative way of life for a world that idolizes "having" instead of "being."

Through the eyes of the church, the patriarch can see further; he measures success otherwise. He knows that truth and dialogue render one more vulnerable, less tyrannical, truly democratic. Loving others means "bear[ing] one another's burdens" (Galatians 6:2). As she gave her life in place of a Jewish mother condemned to the gas chamber in Ravensbrück in 1945, Mother Maria Skobtsova—recognized as a saint in 2004, in a session of the Holy and Sacred Synod chaired by Patriarch Bartholomew at the Phanar—affirmed, "The way to God lies through other people; there is no other way."

Shaping the Future

There is a powerful image employed by the controversial Greek writer Nikos Kazantzakis in his novel *Christ Recrucified,* where he depicts a young Jesus sitting quietly in the carpentry workshop of Joseph in Nazareth, carving small crosses out of the remnant cuttings of wood. With humility and dedication, from his childhood years and seminary formation as well as from his ordination as deacon, priest, and bishop at the Phanar—Bartholomew has been carving and shaping the many personal and pastoral dimensions of his profile, ministry, and events that the Orthodox Church and the world have witnessed over the last twenty-five years and are anticipating today.

GEORGE STEPHANOPOULOS

Chief Anchor, ABC News

AS THE SON AND GRANDSON OF A PRIEST WHO STILL SERVES IN the Greek Orthodox Church, I have followed closely and with deep personal interest the ministry of His All-Holiness Bartholomew. In the twenty-five years since his election as ecumenical patriarch, Bartholomew has propelled the ancient Church of the East into the modern world. Building on the foundation of his predecessors, Athenagoras and Demetrios, His All-Holiness has tackled the thorniest issues of our age: confronting intolerance and religious violence, preaching stewardship of our planet's fragile ecology, engaging in prayerful dialogue across the borders of Christendom and Islam. He has patiently transformed the "Dialogue of Love" with the Catholic Church into a "Dialogue of Truth" that aims to truly heal the schism that has divided Christendom for nearly a thousand years. And as so many Orthodox Christians emerge from the shards of the Iron Curtain, Bartholomew has remained a steady helmsman at the ark of the church, bringing together the

Eastern Church into its first worldwide Council of Bishops since the eighth century.

The power of the patriarch's personality is profound. His humility, dignity, empathy, and energy have put him at the center of a worldwide network of religious and political leaders. Inspired by the example of Archbishop Iakovos—who strikingly marched with Martin Luther King Jr.—Bartholomew has been a champion of civil rights and human rights. Leading from the tiny Christian enclave of a Muslim country—the Phanar ("lighthouse") district of Istanbul, once ancient Constantinople—Bartholomew has shined a light of reason and responsibility far beyond the humble walls of the Patriarchate, revealing the living heart of Orthodoxy.

As a member of the Orthodox Christian family, I am grateful for his vision and leadership. As a member of the human family, I join with countless others who value deeply his clarion voice for the health of our shared world, and for that, we all can be grateful.

CONCLUSION

The Phanar does not rest on its laurels or titles. With its
acquired experience and accumulated wisdom, it seeks to give
content to its authority and responsibility as "ecumenical."
—Ecumenical Patriarch Bartholomew,
public lecture, Athens, 1986

SO HOW DOES ONE DESCRIBE BARTHOLOMEW IN A WORD OR phrase? Having watched him from a distance for decades and worked with him more intimately for many years now, I have heard any number of qualities and qualifications singled out. People immediately recognize his charisma, his accessibility. Some speak of his empathy or sensibility. Others indicate his openness, even perceptiveness. There's his mnemonic adeptness, his capacity to remember names and faces over many years, though he complains this has somewhat diminished recently; I certainly haven't noticed. There are even those who integrate, perhaps obfuscate, the historical institution of the Ecumenical Patriarchate with the personal identity of the ecumenical patriarch, referring to Bartholomew as "holy" or "godly"—expressions that he will outwardly credit to people's piety, but inwardly resist with centrifugal conviction.

In researching his life story, I was amazed that for twenty-five years he had discouraged the composition of any biography whatsoever. It is impossible to find anything more than a brief summary by way of a prelude to a collection of articles in his honor. In 1968, on the twentieth anniversary of the patriarchal tenure of Athenagoras, Metropolitan Meliton of Chalcedon—Bartholomew's ecclesiastical advisor—observed:

> I respect Your All-Holiness's desire for no celebration of this occasion. But above and beyond your own desire stands history, the history of the church. And in the name of history . . . we have been eyewitnesses to the apostolic experience of your patriarchal tenure.

A Transformative Tenure

Much the same could be said of Bartholomew's tenure, despite his aversion to biographical tributes.

He has traveled more widely than any other Orthodox patriarch in history; he has also conducted liturgical services in historically significant places in Asia Minor, such as Cappadocia and Pergamon, Pontus, and Smyrna, where acts of worship would have been inconceivable just twenty-five years ago. He has received sympathetic, albeit sometimes controversial, attention in the Turkish media and been invited to offer public lectures in Turkish on Christian-Muslim relations, while receiving accolades and doctorates from local universities.

I have watched him transform the popular image and respect for the Ecumenical Patriarchate over the twenty-five years of his tenure. In 1991, when invited to formal events and ceremonies, one could almost sense the indifferent, even inhospitable manner with which he was received. One could literally carve through the tense, often frigid atmosphere with a knife as the elite of the political, social, and academic worlds wondered about his motives: What did he want? What was he trying to prove? Was he perhaps there out of retaliation or revenge? By contrast, today one can actually sense the entire room turning, even visibly gravitating toward the patriarch as soon as he enters a room, officials and guests vying for his attention and conversation.

His tenure has been characterized by inter-Orthodox cooperation and inter-Christian and interreligious dialogue, as well as by formal trips to other Orthodox countries seldom visited previously. He has exchanged official visitations and accepted numerous invitations with church and state dignitaries.

But Bartholomew has also transformed his home city of Constantinople and the neighboring metropolitan regions of Fener, Beyoğlu, Kurtuluş, Boğaziçi, Kocamustafapaşa, as well as Kadiköy, Terkoz, his own island of Gökçeada and Bozcaada, and the Princes' Islands (Adalar), and farther beyond, where he has restored all of the existing structures that survive within his spiritual jurisdiction, including churches, monasteries, pilgrimage sites, and charitable centers that were formerly either abandoned or dilapidated—well over 150 historical edifices and lesser-known properties. Indeed, there are the buildings of the patriarchal residence and the priceless patriarchal library, but also unknown and unnoticed chapels.

And while he may proudly display the revivals, restorations, and reclamations, he humbly declares that none of this would be possible without the generosity and solidarity of many—from the respective government entities in Greece to countless Orthodox pilgrims, and from the Archons of the Ecumenical Patriarchate to the eparchies of the Mother Church throughout the world.

NOT THE LAST PATRIARCH

Humility and simplicity would be appropriately descriptive of his person and ministry. After all, if he can see further, it is because the once-diminutive Demetrios now stands as the Ecumenical Patriarch Bartholomew on the tall shoulders of untold forebears of a long apostolic succession, 269 revered predecessors on a historical throne. Even as Americans prepare for the transition into office of their forty-fifth president—or, depending on the tallying of royal houses, even as Prince George of Cambridge will be the sixty-fifth British monarch since Alfred the Great, with Queen Elizabeth enjoying a reign of more than sixty-five years—it would behoove us to remember that Bartholomew is the 270th archbishop of the see that came to be known as Constantinople or "New Rome."

A 2010 story by television network CNN was entitled "The Last Orthodox Patriarch in Turkey?"—sensationalizing a phrase borrowed from a novel. Actually, Bartholomew has always insisted that he would never move his church's central see to any other part of the world. Some have naively suggested Greece's northern city of Thessalonika (an ancient Byzantine bastion) or Mount Athos (the male-only monastic republic), and even Geneva (as the site of international organizations) or Washington, DC (as the site of political diplomacy). After all, even under the worst of conditions under Ottoman rule and the direst of negotiations under Turkish authorities, the Treaty of Lausanne in 1923 guaranteed that the patriarchate bore an international status and could not be removed from Constantinople. In addition, the increased worldwide awareness of His All-Holiness and the constant stream of guests at the Phanar have brought a new level of informal protectiveness of him and the institution in the historic city. This is precisely why Bartholomew has publicly stated from the day of his election, just as he has confided to friends,

> By what authority? With what right? How can I even consider moving this historical institution? It has been here for seventeen centuries. Haghia Sophia and Haghia Irene were here one thousand years before the presence of any mosque.

He is *not* "the last Orthodox patriarch in Turkey." In fact, he is the patriarch that has ensured he *won't be* the last patriarch in Turkey.

An Enduring Presence

History and Humility

While the Phanar complex today contrasts sharply with the magnificent cathedral, now-museum, Haghia Sophia (a fact first-time visitors never fail to note), Bartholomew maintains and balances the Phanar's humility with the spiritual beauty of the Orthodox faith.

Still, nothing quite spoke to me about the noble humility and arresting simplicity of the history and present headquarters of the Ecumenical Patriarchate as when I attended the funeral of the late Demetrios in 1991. There were of course numerous religious and political heads, and the grieving congregation spilled over onto the neighboring streets. However, what I was not prepared to witness was the plainness and unpretentiousness of the solemn occasion, which was remarkable, if not refreshing. Indeed, were it not for the obvious presence of some recognizable heads of state and religious leaders, there was absolutely nothing that indicated the status or stature of the man lying in repose. There was nothing extravagant, nothing exceptional. What was extraordinary about this funerary ceremony was that it was so very ordinary. The funeral might have been for a simple monk or, at the very least, for a simple bishop— just the way that Demetrios had lived most of his life before being plucked by history to lead the Orthodox Church.

This is the atmosphere within which daily services take place at the Phanar. Whether attended by just the court clergy—a priest at the altar and a few deacons chanting—or whether the surrounding area is filled with enthusiastic pilgrims, the tones and the notes remain the same; it is only the colors and flavors that vary. At Easter, the darkness will be overcome by the brilliance of candlelight; at Christmas, snowfall accentuates the soft-lit trees of the enclosure; in the August summer, grapes are blessed and distributed to the faithful; and—since 2003—in the winter of January at Theophany (Epiphany), the patriarch casts a large cross into the Bosphorus for a lucky diver to retrieve. In recent years, even local Turkish youth have joined this January feast.

Charm and Charisma

The words *grace* and *gift* are closely linked—etymologically and theologically, but also literally and pragmatically. How much of Bartholomew's character reveals extraordinary God-given gifts reflecting an inner spiritual strength of ordinary influence? There is no doubt that the gifts of charm and charisma were already obvious in his early childhood years and apparent also in his early high school essays. From as early as his time in Haghioi Theodoroi, he both acknowledged and asserted the importance of working hard and respecting others, of being observant and responsive, of studying and praying, and of opening up to and being in dialogue with others. Moreover, his mentor-bishop yéro-Meliton discerned early on an astuteness and perceptiveness in the young Demetrios. But what word would eventually most fittingly describe Bartholomew's refinement of these extraordinary gifts?

Beyond Bartholomew's simplicity and solemnity in the liturgical world, there's also his comfort level in a broad range of conditions and contexts. Bartholomew is as confident preaching about the church and its spiritual legacy as he is considerate in validating the personal convictions and religious principles of others; he can simultaneously promote respect for all religions, including Islam, even as he staunchly advocates religious rights and freedom of worship in his own country and abroad; and he is as constructive in encounters with political leaders of antithetical ideologies as he is attentive to a chance group of visitors in the courtyard of the patriarchate.

I have seen him on numerous occasions leaving the patriarchal offices and stopping—seemingly without being rushed, though his time is always so precious—to greet Orthodox pilgrims, taking out gifts from his pockets: a prayer rope, a small cross, or even a chocolate. I have witnessed young Muslim children approaching him in an airport lounge to gaze at his beard or robes; again, he will always have something to offer them: worry beads or a talisman.

He "gets" theology—he studied with some of the greatest Roman Catholic and Orthodox thinkers of the twentieth century—but I'm not sure that even this is what uniquely distinguishes him from others in the past or from among his peers. He has a profound respect for members of monastic communities and takes his own monastic commitment very seriously—his vow to celibacy, his discipline of prayer—but he will be the first to admit that he isn't first and foremost called to be or serve as a monk.

He also understands people and loves working closely with them; in that respect, he is always ready to recognize and reward talents in others. In fact, he quite simply loves being with people; even when he retires somewhere for much-needed retreat and recreation, he will unfailingly take friends with him.

And, like no other person before him or in his time, he has unquestionably brought the Orthodox Church to the forefront of global attention. He has addressed diverse media outlets like America's Public Broadcasting Service and Vatican Radio, as well as dozens of political think tanks, such as the Brookings Institution in Washington, DC, and Prague's Forum 2000. He has spoken at celebrated cultural venues, such as the British Museum in London and the Guggenheim Museum in New York as well as prestigious settings ranging from Buckingham Palace to Lambeth Palace. And among his recurrent visits to the Vatican—as a senior metropolitan and as the ecumenical patriarch—in 2008, at the personal invitation of Pope Benedict XVI, he addressed the Roman Catholic Synod of Bishops in the Sistine Chapel.

But I am convinced that—above and beyond all else—he has a God-given gift for administration, for leadership. In his rare moments of self-disclosure, he has even admitted this in private conversation. That's precisely where he excels. I think he honestly believes that his vocation is not primarily to be a preacher or pastor but to offer direction and guidance. He is (for all intents and purposes, and in the most profoundly spiritual way) a "good shepherd"—the word or phrase that combines his extraordinary gifts with his ordinary virtues.

Conscience and Conviction

Leadership requires not only listening, compromising, and directing, but a moral compass at a time of crisis. Bartholomew had learned from the late Patriarch Athenagoras that scrupulous advocacy and integrity were the noblest qualities of a leader.

In September 1954, when Bartholomew was ready to commence studies at Halki (initially to complete secondary school), Metropolitan Meliton gave him an envelope with a card introducing him to the deputy secretary of the Holy and Sacred Synod at the time and asking him to present the fourteen-year-old

Demetrios to Patriarch Athenagoras for his blessing in order to enroll at Halki seminary. Athenagoras told him, "I've heard good things about you. Now that you are starting at Halki, be sure to maintain your good grades and retain your good character so that you don't offend—"

The tall prelate stopped abruptly, turned to the young Demetrios, and asked, "Whom?"

Bartholomew replied, "The church and my bishop."

Athenagoras continued: "Of course, but whom else?"

Bartholomew replied, "My parents."

Athenagoras repeated, "Yes, but whom else? Who is even above them?"

Bartholomew replied, "God."

Athenagoras insisted, "Yes, but whom else? Whom perhaps above everyone and everything in this world should you never offend?"

The teenage Bartholomew was baffled; who else could there be? "I had no idea what to say," he admits.

Athenagoras gazed into the young Bartholomew's eyes and said, "Yourself!"

Bartholomew learned very early on never to surrender or sacrifice the least in the face of conscience and conviction. It may account for his fearlessness before personal intimidation and political harassment.

For more than five decades after this interaction in the office of Patriarch Athenagoras, when it came to addressing his peers and brothers on theological principles and canonical regulations of the church, Bartholomew has always been more than prepared.

A Pastoral Council

It is in this perspective and context that we should see the patriarch's noble struggle to convene the Holy and Great Council.

This is a bold move for an Orthodox bishop. Most Orthodox churches have resisted—and will doubtless long continue to desist from—embracing modernity and "democracy," that is, conciliarity in its fullness. Their historical and cultural experience has proved so debilitating that they are seemingly being dragged screaming into the twenty-first century. Several Orthodox churches are torn by the Christian identity and vocation to be "in the world" but not "of the world" (John 17:13–16).

It seems so much easier and indeed tempting for the Orthodox churches to assert their primary role or prime contribution as somehow transcending this world. In this regard, they like to emphasize their liturgy and spirituality (or theology), their mysticism and mysteries (or sacraments). They concentrate on how antique their heritage is, how mystical their iconography is, how exotic their nationalism is, how superior their theology is, how definitive their canon law is. Indeed, they brandish these with triumphalism as both unique and exclusive.

This is where the patriarch's emphasis on the council is of paramount importance. Already in 1997, in an interview with the *National Catholic Reporter* on January 21, Bartholomew, then the thirty-six-year-old metropolitan of Philadelphia, declared:

> Our aims are to update the church and promote Christian unity. . . . Our faithful want more accessible ways to live their

faith. . . . The council will mark the end of twelve centuries of isolation of the Orthodox Church.

His words echoed the sentiments of his mentor, Metropolitan Meliton of Chalcedon:

The council must articulate in contemporary language—and in terms and norms that are intelligible to today's people—the doctrine of the Council of Chalcedon [that Jesus Christ is both human and divine].

It may appear that little has resulted—albeit at sometimes frustratingly glacial speed—from more than fifty years in preparation for and anticipation of the Holy and Great Council. But, in fact, a lot happened even in the preparatory process itself, where the rediscovery of the universal and ecumenical nature of the church, together with the celebration of its sacramental or doctrinal culture has little by little at least exposed, if not chipped away at, the stifling boundaries of "autocephalism." The truth is that the Orthodox churches would not have gathered at all, were it not in response to the patriarch's persistent invitation and prophetic call to prepare for such a council.

Truthfully, with so many clarion calls, with so much history coalescing at the right time, with such a well-equipped and well-prepared shepherd to call for the convening of the Holy and Great Council, it is important to remember that Bartholomew's legacy is solid and striking even without the council; his legacy would not be diminished if he had not risked convening the council. It is actually the Orthodox Church's future and legacy that would be at stake with the Holy and Great Council.

Nonetheless, something has profoundly and permanently changed for the Orthodox Church; things will not be the same moving forward. Through the work of the patriarch, the spotlight is now focused on the Orthodox Church, and people will be able to clearly recognize the motivations and intentions of this apostolic and historic part of Christianity. Whether it is witnessing developments in the Orthodox churches in Palestine and the Middle East, as well as in Northern Africa—in the fate of the ancient Patriarchates of Constantinople, Jerusalem, Antioch, and Alexandria—or whether it is watching the trends in the Church of Russia with its posturing in Ukraine or Syria, Bartholomew has brought the focus of the public and the attention of the media to bear on an ancient church with not only widespread roots in established ethnic centers but also a global presence in new regions of the world.

It is in the light of the Holy and Great Council that the Orthodox churches of the Middle East would contend over the last grain of desert sand in their effort to survive. It is in the light of the Holy and Great Council that Balkan and former Soviet Orthodox churches would strive to stake their place in the modern world by defending their conservative roots. And it is in the light of the Holy and Great Council that the Russian Orthodox Church would struggle nervously to maintain a balance between church and state in Putin's "Russkiy mir," between war and peace in Crimea and Ukraine, as well as between isolation and dialogue—as it recently demonstrated on the world scene with Patriarch Kirill's meeting with Pope Francis in Havana in February 2016.

A Witness and Model of Unity

The question is: how will the Orthodox Church learn to "sing the LORD's song in foreign land[s]?" (Psalm 137:4) There is no doubt that the Orthodox Church can play a major role in our world; it can serve as the critical and prophetic conscience of the peoples entrusted to it. However, to do so, it must first disabuse itself of the idolatry of parochialism and nationalism in order to embrace a more open, ecumenical Orthodoxy. Moreover, it must learn to speak with one voice for it to be heard and for it to matter.

And here is where the importance of the Ecumenical Patriarchate comes into play; this is where the leadership of the ecumenical patriarch—with the Pan-Orthodox Conferences, the Synaxes of Primates, the Assemblies of Bishops, and the Holy and Great Council—is critical. Because with the guidance of the Phanar, the Orthodox Church can cease to be an institution turned toward the past and, instead, prove to be an institution charged with evangelizing—with bearing witness to the life and hope of the resurrection—in the present for the life of the whole world.

A seventh-century Syrian mystic, Isaac of Nineveh, once said that the only unpardonable sin is insensibility to the possibility of resurrection. If Orthodox Christianity can discern the joy of the resurrection in "whatever things are true, whatever things are noble, whatever things are just, whatever things are pure, whatever things are lovely, whatever things are of good report, [wherever] there is any virtue and [wherever] there is anything praiseworthy" (Philippians 4:8), then it will rise above materialism and consumerism, as well as modernism and fundamentalism. What a refreshing—in fact, what a revolutionary—example of resurrection this would prove for a church that claims to be "in the world" but not "of the world"!

ACKNOWLEDGMENTS

TO **HIS ALL-HOLINESS ECUMENICAL PATRIARCH BARTHOLOMEW** for the extraordinary privilege of being associated with him through-out my ministry—in Australia as protodeacon and in America as the archdeacon of the Ecumenical Throne, an honor personally bestowed by him. I am profoundly grateful for his unconditional benevolence and confidence. This book is dedicated to him on behalf of all those who have watched and witnessed his apostolic and visionary ministry over the last twenty-five years.

To HIS EMINENCE ELDER ARCHBISHOP DEMETRIOS for the exceptional blessing of generously authorizing me to serve the Greek Orthodox Archdiocese of America at the exclusive dis-position of the ecumenical patriarch.

To the VERY REVEREND ALEXANDER KARLOUTSOS for imagin-ing and realizing this publication as well as for knocking on the right doors to make this biography possible; to TINA ANDREADIS of Harper Collins for opening those doors in order to make this possibility a reality; and to MATTHEW BAUGHER for welcoming us inside the chambers of Thomas Nelson and bringing this proposal to fruition with personal, perhaps providential devotion. Paula Major, senior editor at Thomas Nelson, added the final touch.

To Rev. Federico Lombardi, SJ, at the Vatican, Archbishop Georg Gänswein, and Rev. Andrea Palmieri at the Pontifical Council for Christian Unity for their gracious guidance and assistance.

To my colleagues Mark Arey, Dr. Anton Vrame, and Rev. Mark Sietsema for their extensive research and invaluable drafts under dire deadlines. To friends and family—without whom I could not conclude this monumental task in a timely manner: Roberta Powers (photo selection) and Marissa P. Costidis (photo rights), as well as Nikos Tzoitis and Julian Chryssavgis.

To all offices and officers at the Phanar for their support and assistance, especially Archimandrite Bartholomew Samaras (chief secretary of the Holy Synod) and Archimandrite Agathangelos Siskos (director of the Patriarchal Library); Metropolitan Gennadios of Sassima and Rev. Dr. Theodore Meimaris; and to my fellow workers in the English Office (Rev. Nephon Tsimalis, George Sarraf, and Stephen Salzman).

To Themistoklis Karanikolas for sharing with me his passion for Imvros. To Niko Manginas for the nights we burn the midnight oil. And to Archon Peter Vlitas for his invaluable friendship and kindness.

Finally, to my editor and associate, MARILYN ROUVELAS, for her unwavering diligence and priceless dedication. This book would still be random reflections without her vital contribution and convivial collaboration.

BIBLIOGRAPHY

THE AUTHOR IS DEEPLY GRATEFUL TO FORDHAM UNIVERSITY PRESS for the generous permission to use the following publications, which contain formal documents or personal texts of Ecumenical Patriarch Bartholomew. This trilogy comprises the official selection of statements and addresses by His All-Holiness in the English language:

Chryssavgis, John, ed. *In the World, Yet Not of the World: Social and Global Initiatives of Ecumenical Patriarch Bartholomew.* Bronx, NY: Fordham University Press, 2010.

———. *On Earth as in Heaven: Ecological Vision and Initiatives of Ecumenical Patriarch Bartholomew.* Bronx, NY: Fordham University Press, 2012.

———. *Speaking the Truth in Love: Theological and Spiritual Exhortations of Ecumenical Patriarch Bartholomew.* Bronx, NY: Fordham University Press, 2011.

Bartholomew, Ecumenical Patriarch, *Encountering the Mystery: Understanding Orthodox Christianity Today*. New York: Doubleday, 2008.

Bartholomew of Constantinople, *When I Was a Child, School Essays*. Athens: Kastanioti Editions, 2003 [in Greek].

Chryssavgis, John. *The Ecumenical Patriarchate Today: Sacred Greek Orthodox Sites of Istanbul*. Istanbul: London Editions, 2014.

———. "Turkey: Byzantine Reflections." Originally published in longer form in *World Policy Journal* 28, no. 4 (2011). *World Policy Journal* is currently published by Duke University Press.

Clément, Olivier, *Dialogues avec le Patriarche Athénagoras*. Paris: Fayard, 1969.

Obama, Barack, "Remarks by President Obama to the Turkish Parliament," press release, April 6, 2009, White House, Office of the Press Secretary.

Pope Francis, *Laudato Si': On Care for Our Common Home*. Vatican City: Vatican Press, 2015.

Rusch, William G., ed. *The Witness of Bartholomew I, Ecumenical Patriarch*. Grand Rapids, MI: Eerdmans, 2013.

INDEX

INDEX

ABOUT THE AUTHOR

JOHN CHRYSSAVGIS, THE ARCHDEACON OF THE ECUMENICAL Patriarchate, was born in Australia, studied theology in Athens and New York, and holds a doctorate from the University of Oxford. He cofounded St. Andrew's Theological College in Australia, where he taught religious studies at the University of Sydney before moving to Boston as professor of theology.

A clergyman of the Greek Orthodox Archdiocese of America, Chryssavgis currently serves as theological advisor to the ecumenical patriarch on environmental issues. He is also the author of more than thirty books and numerous articles in several languages on theology and spirituality. His publications include the award-winning *In the Heart of the Desert* and three volumes of collected works by Ecumenical Patriarch Bartholomew. He lives in Harpswell, Maine.